Global Macrotrends and Their Impact on Supply Chain Management

Global Macrotrends and Their Impact on Supply Chain Management

Strategies for Gaining Competitive Advantage

Chad W. Autry
Thomas J. Goldsby
John E. Bell

Vice President, Publisher: Tim Moore
Associate Publisher and Director of Marketing: Amy Neidlinger
Executive Editor: Jeanne Glasser
Editorial Assistant: Pamela Boland
Operations Specialist: Jodi Kemper
Marketing Manager: Megan Graue
Cover Designer: Chuti Prasertsith
Managing Editor: Kristy Hart
Project Editor: Anne Goebel
Copy Editor: Gayle Johnson
Proofreader: Leslie Joseph
Indexer: Erika Millen
Compositor: Nonie Ratcliff
Manufacturing Buyer: Dan Uhrig

© 2013 by Chad W. Autry, Thomas J. Goldsby, and John E. Bell
Publishing as FT Press
Upper Saddle River, New Jersey 07458

FT Press offers excellent discounts on this book when ordered in quantity for bulk
purchases or special sales. For more information, please contact U.S. Corporate
and Government Sales, 1-800-382-3419, corpsales@pearsontechgroup.com.
For sales outside the U.S., please contact International Sales at
international@pearsoned.com.

Company and product names mentioned herein are the trademarks or registered
trademarks of their respective owners.

Printed in the United States of America
First Printing December 2012

ISBN-10: 0-13-294418-9
ISBN-13: 978-0-13-294418-2

Pearson Education LTD.
Pearson Education Australia PTY, Limited
Pearson Education Singapore, Pte. Ltd.
Pearson Education Asia, Ltd.
Pearson Education Canada, Ltd.
Pearson Educación de Mexico, S.A. de C.V.
Pearson Education—Japan
Pearson Education Malaysia, Pte. Ltd.

Library of Congress Cataloging-in-Publication Data

Autry, Chad Wheeler, 1970-
  Global macro trends and their impact on supply chain management : strategies for
gaining competitive advantage / Chad W. Autry, Thomas J. Goldsby, John E. Bell.
-- 1st Edition.
    pages cm
  ISBN 978-0-13-294418-2 (hbk. : alk. paper) -- ISBN 0-13-294418-9 (alk. paper) 1.
Business logistics. 2. Strategic planning. 3. Economic development--Social aspects.
I. Goldsby, Thomas J. II. Bell, John Edward, 1968- III. Title.
  HD38.5.A9398 2012
  658.5--dc23
                              2012034562

Chad:
To Bill, Jennifer, and Todd Autry, who gave me my start; to Anna Kate, Drew, and Alex, who lift me to greater heights every single day; and to my life's love, Kari, who makes everything I do worthwhile.

Tom:
To my dear wife, Kathie; my kids, Emma and Aiden Goldsby; my parents, Joe and Sujane Goldsby; my brother, Mike Goldsby; and my in-laws, Doug and Carole Boyd; all of whom make life one splendid, joyful, and transformative journey.

John:
To my parents, Lonnie and Marty Bell, who continue to be my greatest role models, and to my children, Molli, Marti, and Julia, who inspire me daily and whose future depends on how we manage this transforming world.

Contents

Acknowledgments

No book is written without the help, assistance, and vision provided by many persons other than its authors, and this one is no exception. The editorial team at Pearson/FT Press, spearheaded by Jeanne Glasser and her outstanding development group, played an integral role in our manuscript's genesis, development, and eventual publication. For his phenomenal feedback and guidance, we are also deeply indebted to our editorial intern Ryan Croy of the University of Tennessee, who took on this project as though it were his own. His insights and assistance with revisions were invaluable, and we never could have completed the project without him. We additionally drew much inspiration for many of the key ideas herein from our academic and professional colleagues. At the great risk of forgetting someone important, it seems necessary to single out at least the following short list of key contributors: Fazleena Badurdeen, David Ecklund, Stan Griffis, I.S. Jawahir, Douglas Lambert, Robert Martichenko, Diane Mollenkopf, Fred Moody, Mark Moon, Ken Petersen, Shay Scott, Ted Stank, Hannah Stolze, and LaDonna Thornton. We also thank the members of the University of Tennessee Supply Chain Forum, who provided a key venue to test-drive our ideas and predictions. The Global Supply Chain Forum at The Ohio State University provided the critical foundational framework upon which we could explore the transformational forces. Two additional research centers, the Center for Operational Excellence at The Ohio State University and the Institute for Sustainable Manufacturing at the University of Kentucky, provided expertise, research funding, and company access that were essential to the book's completion. Our departmental colleagues at the University of Tennessee and The Ohio State University, respectively, foster dynamic learning environments that nurtured the development of ideas presented in this book. We can only hope the others we've undoubtedly omitted will forgive us until we regain the energy to write another book, and in the meantime know they were, indeed, appreciated.

About the Authors

Chad W. Autry, Ph.D. is an associate professor of supply chain management in the College of Business Administration at the University of Tennessee. He holds a doctorate in business administration/supply chain management from the University of Oklahoma. He has worked with and for numerous professional and civic organizations related to supply chain process improvement. He is a committed contributor to the Council of Supply Chain Management Professionals and the Warehouse Education and Research Council. He has assumed active leadership roles at the state and national level for the Production and Operations Management Society and the Institute for Supply Management, among other organizations. Dr. Autry's research has primarily addressed supply chain relationships and networks, resulting in over 50 articles published in academic and professional outlets. He has won numerous awards for research and was named a Rainmaker in the supply chain field by *DC Velocity* magazine in 2005. He also has served as an editor for three leading academic journals addressing supply chain management topics.

Thomas J. Goldsby, Ph.D. is a professor of logistics at The Ohio State University. Dr. Goldsby holds a BS in business administration from the University of Evansville, an MBA from the University of Kentucky, and a PhD in marketing and logistics from Michigan State University. He has received recognitions for excellence in research and teaching at Iowa State University, The Ohio State University, and the University of Kentucky. Dr. Goldsby serves on the advisory boards of several professional organizations and academic journals. He is an associate director of the Center for Operational Excellence and a research associate of the Global Supply Chain Forum, both of The Ohio State University. He also serves on selection committees for many industry awards, including CSCMP's Supply Chain Innovation Award, Gartner's Top 25 Supply Chains, *Logistics Quarterly's*

Sustainability Study and Awards program, and the University of Kentucky's Corporate Sustainability Awards. Dr. Goldsby is coauthor of *Lean Six Sigma Logistics: Strategic Development to Operational Success.* He has supervised more than 100 Lean/Six Sigma supply chain projects with industry partners and has conducted federally funded research projects on the subjects of supply chain risk management and sustainable supply chains.

John E. Bell, Ph.D. is an assistant professor of supply chain management in the College of Business Administration at the University of Tennessee. He earned his doctorate in management from Auburn University and taught on the faculties at the Air Force Institute of Technology and Georgia College and State University prior to joining the University of Tennessee faculty in August 2010. Before that, Dr. Bell spent more than 20 years in the U.S. Air Force as a logistics and maintenance officer. He has published more than 20 articles in academic and professional outlets related to vehicle routing, facility location selection, supply chain strategy, and other related topics. Dr. Bell is a frequent contributor at national and international meetings of the Decision Sciences Institute, Council of Supply Chain Management Professionals, and other professional organizations. He is currently a board member of the Western Decision Sciences Institute. He also serves on the editorial review boards for two of the leading academic journals in the field of supply chain management.

Preface

"To India!" With over a billion people consuming goods and services, India has represented a potential bonanza for many global companies since the end of the 20th century. The former British colony, independent since 1947, has vast natural resources and a large English-speaking population and is currently the world's fourth-largest economy. However, for many potential market entrants, India remains an uncharted and mysterious opportunity. Though ripe with potential, it brings a vast array of unfamiliar challenges for outsiders. With 28 state governments, over 1,500 native languages, and a primarily Hindu population, India's cultural and demographic differences yield a unique and somewhat incomprehensible frontier for foreign business to penetrate. Western companies often admit that they know they "need to be there" but are unsure exactly how to enter the market and how their offerings would be received there. Above all, they struggle to understand who the Indian customer really is, given the heterogeneity of India's multiple and diverse subcultures.

Most companies seeking to enter the Indian marketplace are also poorly prepared to do business there from a logistical standpoint. The Indian transportation system is quite challenged in many respects, primarily due to the relative lack of infrastructure and ensuing traffic congestion. The country's road network is primitive by modern standards, with many underdeveloped roads, and less than 3% of the road network consisting of passable highways. Indian seaports serve as logistical chokepoints, where as many as 30 container ships can be backed up at any given time, waiting to offload their cargo. It is not uncommon for delivery lead times from U.S. producers to Indian consumers to range from 20 to 30 days.[1] In addition, the country

---

[1] Jeffress, Conrad. Head, Automotive-North America, Panelpina Inc. "Logistics Challenges in India" Online interview, November 2008, Globalindustry.com.

suffers from serious basic commodity shortages and imbalances that inhibit economic development, the most pressing of which is the lack of freshwater delivery systems and wastewater treatment facilities. As an illustration, the city of Delhi has the capacity to treat only 40% of its own wastewater supply, and it is in constant conflict with neighboring regions that refuse to supply it with more fresh supply. The local groundwater is unfit for consumption due to metals pollution, and a local river in the Delhi area has essentially been turned into an above-ground sewage system.[2] As these issues illustrate, India is a forum of extremes for doing business. The massive marketplace is most certainly enticing for outsiders, but securing and transporting supplies, manufacturing products, and executing final delivery can present enormous challenges.

In spite of India's logistical complexities, the Coca-Cola Company has a long history of doing business there. From 1970 to 2000, Coke established itself as a leading Indian brand. In attempting to secure a permanent foothold, by 2005 it had established over 70 India-based bottling plants, and the country had been designated its largest growth market.[3] Often recognized as the most valuable brand in the world, Coke is no newcomer to global expansion. It has long displayed great expertise at entering foreign markets. (It has often been remarked that Coke contains more nations in its portfolio than the United Nations.)[4] However, in 1998, a Coke subsidiary opened a new soft drink plant in the village of Plachimada that remains a monumental headache for the company almost 15 years later.[5] Plachimada is in the state of Kerala, in southwestern India. Though the region receives a

---

[2] Sahni, Diksha. (21 June 2012). "Why Is Delhi Running Out of Water?" *Wall Street Journal India*.

[3] Stecklow, Steve. (7 June 2005). "Virtual Battle: How a Global Web of Activists Gives Coke Problems in India." *Wall Street Journal*.

[4] "Coke in the Cross Hairs: Water, India, and the University of Michigan." Case 1-429-098, 25 July 2010, the ERB Institute and William Davidson Institute at the University of Michigan.

[5] "Call for presidential assent to Plachimada Bill."(5 June 2012). *The Hindu*.

large amount of monsoon rain each year, it has been suffering from freshwater scarcity since at least the 1980s due to deforestation, high population density, fast runoff of rains to the ocean, and water mismanagement issues.[6] Water scarcity thus has emerged as an existential threat to the Indian economy and public health, given that nearly 90% of new water extraction goes to agricultural purposes.[7] For Coke, access to potable water for its bottling production plants is a critical market success factor. By some estimates, it uses over 294.5 billion liters of water annually, with 2.26 liters required to produce 1 liter of cola.[8] In some locations, this would prove to be a great challenge in the Indian marketplace.

When making network design decisions and determining where to locate plants, warehouses, and other facilities, a company may not always consider factors such as water scarcity. Since transporting water from wells and streams to factories has never been considered economically viable, bottling facilities are often located near large populations. Or bottled products are first delivered as concentrates to demand locations, where water is added as a final processing step before sale (as with orange juice). The extent to which Coke considered the potential for water scarcity in its Kerala market analysis prior to building the Plachimada plant remains unknown. Regardless, the company decided to locate the bottler where the stability of the water supply needed to make its products represented a significant supply chain risk.

The outcomes were unfortunate, but predictable. Within two years of the Plachimada plant's establishment, local farmers and villagers were accusing the Coke plant of lowering the local water table and polluting both surface and groundwater near and around the

---

[6] Venugopal, P.N. (31 March 2006). "Kerala: rain-blessed and short of water." www.indiatogether.org.

[7] "For Want of a Drink." (20 May 2010). *The Economist*.

[8] "Water Stewardship." 2010/2011 GRI Report, the Coca-Cola Company, www.thecoca-colacompany.com/sustainabilityreport.

plant site. Farmers complained of decreased crop yields as a result of the shortages, and many nearby wells ran dry or were contaminated, plausibly due to Coke's overuse and alleged misuse of the local water supply.[9] Local protestors began picketing the plant in April 2002 and continued throughout 2003. Finally, following a Kerala court ruling in March 2004, the $16 million Plachimada Coca-Cola plant was shut down.[10] Throughout the protests and hearings, Coke continually denied that it was in any way contaminating or polluting the Kerala water system. It claimed that many of the tests conducted in the area were unscientific and that officials could not substantiate that the plant was the cause of the water issues. In fact, Kerala's courts later rejected similar claims against Coke when, in April 2005, the wells continued to dry up after the Coke plant in Plachimada had stopped operating. The judges believed that the more significant inhibitor of water quality and supply was lack of rainfall in the area.[11] Nonetheless, the damage was done, and the company was forced to permanently close the Plachimada plant due to political and legal pressure. In fairness to Coke, its chief rival, Pepsi, has also suffered from allegations of water misuse in India,[12-13] while Coke has made great strides in the last several years to more wisely manage water use and resource scarcity in its supply chains.[14]

What can managers of other enterprises, large and small, global and domestic, take from this story? Why did Coke's new plant in southern India fail? Was this just a simple mistake made during a plant location decision, for just one of Coke's 70 Indian plants? On its

---

[9] "Indians force Coca-Cola Bottling Facility in Plachimada to shut down 2001-2006." Global Nonviolent Action Database, Swarthmore College, http://nvdatabase.swarthmore.edu.

[10] Stecklow, Steve. (7 June 2005). "Virtual Battle: How a Global Web of Activists Gives Coke Problems in India." *Wall Street Journal*, A1.

[11] Ibid.

[12] Rai, Saritha. (21 May, 2003). "Protests in India Deplore Soda Makers' Water Use. *The New York Times*.

[13] "Kerala assembly panel moots curbs on Pepsi plant." (17 March 2010). *The Hindu*.

[14] "2010/2011 GRI Report." The Coca-Cola Company, 16 December 2011.

face, it could simply appear that Coke, in India, has found itself seeking growth while a critical input (water) was unavailable, and thereby created risk to its brand, reputation, and profits. But taking a broader perspective, the example also shows that the world we live in is changing, and is doing so in some ways that undermine the basic assumptions many of us have long held about business. Global companies can no longer afford to assume that they will have unlimited access to a natural resource, either when establishing new market ventures or perpetuating old successes. Social and physical scientists alike point to numerous exogenous factors that are intertwined and rapidly evolving and that have great potential for disrupting business conducted in the old familiar ways. In this book we call these global phenomena *macrotrends*. Based on our research, we believe they have the potential to substantially impact—and disrupt—modern business practices, leading to great frustration for modern supply chains and the managers who administer them. These new and disruptive macroeconomic factors include the following:

- **Continued population growth and migration.** Although some countries in the world are seeing declining population growth rates, other areas such as many in Africa and Southeast Asia continue to see population growth. World population levels of 9 to 10 billion people are expected in the decades ahead.
- **Rising economies and buying power.** The economies in nations such as Brazil, Russia, India, and China are continuing to escalate. Their populations are gaining increasing levels of buying power and associated quality of life and consumption desires.
- **Global connectivity.** Communications and computer system advances, as implemented through the pervasiveness of the Internet around the world, make it easy for global markets to find and demand modern products and services from global companies.

- **Increased geopolitical activity.** The governments around the world seek to ensure access to scarce natural resources. In addition, they intervene in the marketplace activities of global businesses when the safety or security of their nation's interests seems threatened.

- **Environmental and climate change.** The Earth's climatological environment is in flux. Issues such as changing ocean temperatures, global warming, and the movement of the jet stream have resulted in climate changes around the planet.

The question we attempt to provoke in our readers is, "What is your company doing to identify and manage the impacts of a transforming world on your supply chain?" In other words, are you looking to adapt and make changes to your supply chains today that will ensure a sustainable future for your company? It is in supply chain execution that business strategy becomes a reality. Supply chain management involves far-reaching implications for your organization's success, such as determining the following:

- Which goods and services to offer the market
- How to design product and service bundles that meet the market's needs and the company's financial expectations
- Which customers and suppliers to work with closely
- When to walk away from business and when to proceed
- How to structure activity within the company and with supply chain members for concerted action

We believe that the challenges presented to future supply chains and supply chain managers will continue to increase in frequency and severity over the next three decades (and longer). We also believe these will have serious implications for business and operations. Managers must prepare. As Coca-Cola discovered, the macrotrends that characterize our transforming world will require proactive solution seeking. Therefore, we not only explore the threats brought about by change to the global commercial environment, but also provide general directions for how to prepare for these challenges and turn them into opportunities that can be exploited compared to competitors' efforts. The sustainable long-term success of your company may depend on it, just as the strength of the future global economy will depend on the thought leadership and innovation of today's supply chain leaders.

Part I
Global Macrotrends Impacting the Supply Chain Environment

1

Supply Chain Management in the 21st Century

The world is changing and growing at rates and in ways unrivaled throughout history. These changes will test how far humans can push the Earth's limits. Businesses and their supply chains will similarly struggle under the strain of skyrocketing demand and erratic supply. This book illustrates that the companies most poised to handle these pressures in the future will be the ones best positioned to service customers—and turn a profit in the process.

In early 1983, 30 short years ago, China became the first nation on Earth to surpass one billion inhabitants. However, the Chinese automobile market at the time was disproportionately tiny in terms of both production and sales. Less than 1% of Chinese citizens owned a car, and most of those owned were old and dilapidated. Very few were purchased new, and the nation's domestic auto-manufacturing sector was essentially inconsequential in the scope of the global industry. At the time, owning an automobile was considered a status symbol for Chinese consumers, and the average citizen had little hope of ever having one of his or her own.

Halfway through the 1980s, though, China's new-vehicle demand exploded. Sales increased by over 600% in just 24 months as both the Chinese population and its rate of participation in world commerce grew exponentially. With dollar signs in their eyes, automakers scrambled to meet the nascent market's needs, but their attempts to supply the massive—and suddenly very enthusiastic—market were unexpectedly frustrating. In reacting to their own demand forecasts, which had always indicated little need to invest in Chinese distribution infrastructure, foreign automakers found themselves trapped in a relative state of helplessness. The makers' demand planners and decision makers had long since decided that there was little market viability to be had within the foreseeable future. Their apathy, combined with an inadequate understanding of the Chinese market's financial and physical complexities, left the automakers totally unprepared.

Fast-forward to today: One in ten Chinese citizens owns a personal-use vehicle. Though low by world standards, this ownership rate represents a huge unitary increase in demand over the past three decades for manufacturers—and the growth continues to accelerate. China's auto demand has more than doubled since 2009. Manufacturers like Ford Motor Company are realizing that they must do business in China just to remain internationally competitive. Ford has found that its 400 Chinese dealerships aren't enough to even approach the current market potential. While the company's current strategic decision is to attempt to open two dealerships a week, the company struggles to fulfill consumer needs in the car-hungry Chinese market. The Chinese middle class is growing at never before anticipated rates, and demand for products like automobiles remains problematic due to difficulties in matching demand with supply. Such complexities can prevent foreign automakers like Ford from capturing Chinese demand while sustaining a profit.[1]

Half a world away, for a 53-hour period in 2011, the most populous county in the United States—Los Angeles—closed the world's most heavily traveled highway—the I-405—to add another lane. The move was part of a civil engineering initiative intended to dramatically alleviate highly congested and rapidly deteriorating road conditions in southern California. The construction project's forecasted impact on local life led to the dubious moniker "Carmageddon," reflecting a time when enormous traffic volumes would, if expectations were accurate, come to a grinding halt. Experts predicted the event would greatly impact both individual and commercial life. The 48-foot trucks carrying important supplies to California businesses, as well as the cars that were to carry customers to those businesses to shop, were expected to be delayed for up to a week or more, depending on how the construction project progressed.

---

[1] Priddle, Alisa. (6 May 2012). "Middle class eager to buy cars in congested China; automakers try to keep up with demand." *Detroit Free Press.*

In this instance, though, some companies were ready for the anticipated chaos, and a few actually thrived during the period of expected gridlock. Forward-thinking restaurants like Spumoni,[2] an Italian-style pizzeria in Newbury Park, anticipated that more residents would dine locally and overstocked its key inventories ahead of time. Showing similar farsightedness and heeding the California Trucking Association's advice, carrier Liberty Linehaul West ordered its truckers to leave 5 hours earlier than normal to make deliveries.[3] Though the expected nightmarish traffic conditions never really materialized, these companies' innovative and insightful leaders were able to adjust on the fly for the I-405 closure due to supply chain awareness. In this instance, by thoughtfully considering possible supply infrastructure failure and executing deliberately devised contingency plans, forward-thinking companies were ready for the commotion if it had occurred.

With proper precaution, most companies can survive an occasional, short-term disruption within their business ecosystem. But what happens if the cost and service implications of disruptions are more frequent or long-lasting? As booming populations continue to strain commercial infrastructures globally, Los Angeles may not be the only city forced to routinely address "Carmageddon"-like disturbances. In fact, many civil planners envision a day when road congestion and deteriorated conditions become the norm in even the wealthiest nations. Skyrocketing populations in countries like India and on continents like Africa mean that intricate demand fulfillment won't be limited to products like automobiles in countries like China. What Ford, Spumoni, Liberty Linehaul West, and even Coca-Cola illustrate is the importance of managing well-planned and effective supply chains in a rapidly transforming world. Due to abnormally accelerated, macro-level social and economic changes (macrotrends), many companies are struggling to align supply with demand. They cannot provide consumers with the necessary goods and services for affordable living.

---

[2] Khouri, Andrew. (28 June 2011). "Westside and Valley businesses are preparing for Carmageddon." *Los Angeles Times.*

[3] "Truckers cope with I-405 shutdown - Overdrive Magazine." (15 July 2011). *Supply Chain Review.*

We wrote this book for anyone interested in understanding how a collection of such macrotrends will impact industry over the next two decades and how modern supply chains will help stymie their side effects. We want to provoke future business leaders to think about critical supply chain issues beyond just the immediate opportunities and problems. Supply chain leaders need to consider future modifications to the global business environment that will affect their ability to provide end users with goods and services. Our collective experiences lead us to believe that far too often, modern companies' productivity measures force managers to obsess over issues that are imminently important but distract them from the type of visionary, futuristic thinking that leads to long-term, sustained marketplace advantages. A periodic approach is of course necessary to achieve the immediate objectives that propagate organizational survivability. But companies and managers who have greater prescience—whether their vision is of the next week, year, or decade—will be those best positioned to prosper *ad infinitum*.

Though we devised this book to be a thought-provoking primer for anyone concerned with how global trends will impact businesses and their supply chains, it has three primary audiences. The first consists of senior managers and executives who, through their visions and strategies, will set the course for how their businesses prepare for the challenges and opportunities the macrotrends will offer. A second audience consists of early-to-mid-career professionals who execute an organization's financial and strategic missions. These are the managers best positioned to keep our advice in mind within their natural career life cycles. The final audience is policy makers, because supply chain issues do and will influence cities', states', and even nations' competitiveness in the changing global marketplace. A wide range of readers interested in studying these macrotrends, and how they will impact society in unprecedented ways, should enjoy this book.

Our value proposition is simple: We compile and discuss cutting-edge research and reasons related to some hyper-accelerated transformations currently acting on our planet and its citizens. Most of this content draws on the most modern scholarship in fields such as economics, sociology, ecology, engineering, and hard sciences. We then integrate these viewpoints and connect their implications to what we believe will be the most pressing issues businesses will face over the coming years. Particular emphasis is placed on how business processes that operationally balance supply with demand will be affected. Finally, we offer some concrete strategies that help companies mitigate the hindrances, if they are willing and ready to adopt a supply-chain-oriented perspective to the opportunities and challenges to be faced.

Our efforts concentrate most prominently on the global economic consequences of societal changes that will directly impact organizations as they strive to serve customers with optimal efficiency and effectiveness. The strategies presented here are drawn from many real-world examples, experienced firsthand or otherwise, to illustrate key points. We hope our shared experiences will stimulate actionable thoughts for professionals to act on as their careers progress. We also hope that a general awareness of these issues will motivate business leaders and citizens alike to rally around common solutions.

A Note on Futurism

Before proceeding, we want to provide an advisory note related to our subject matter's forward-looking perspective. While conducting our research, we became well acquainted with the emerging collection of event-forecasting quasi-sciences that can be colloquially called "futurism." Futurism can best be described as the use of science-based processes to predict future occurrences, usually by extrapolating past and present data and/or trends into the future. This led us to examine various progressive social and physical scientists' works within peer-reviewed journals. These works span many fields of interest and often are disseminated by prediction-focused organizations such as the World Future Society. Published critical evaluations of futurism have concluded that extrapolating past/current trends into the future, when done thoughtfully, yields generally reliable results. However, this is true only in proportion to the likelihood that the trends themselves are unlikely to deviate radically from established patterns.

By way of analogy, consider two props used in a popular science fiction TV show and movie decades ago. On the 1966 program *Star Trek*, producer Gene Roddenberry's depiction of a portable 21st century interstellar communication device is hauntingly similar to the Motorola cellular flip phone of the mid-1990s. Similarly, the holographic technology used to project Princess Leia's three-dimensional warning message in George Lucas's *Star Wars* must have seemed farfetched to contemporary viewers. Yet such communicative imagery has been demonstrated in lab settings in recent years. The original props were developed based on contemporary futurists' technological projections. The actualized objects, which appeared in the last two decades, emerged in slightly different configurations and were intended for somewhat different uses than the futurists had imagined, but they have in fact appeared. In fact, based on their most recent exhibitions, it would seem that the key distinguishing factors separating the movie and TV producers' projections of the future, and the eventual reality, were the specific form and time.

Our observations lead us to believe that many futurists are very good at what they do, and their predictions are often closer to "right" than "wrong" if enough time is allowed to elapse. Nevertheless, the science is somewhat inexact, and in concluding the analogy, our predictions made here indicate as much. Whenever possible, the calculations made herein to produce forecasts of the future were made based on simple "straight-line" extensions of current trend data. As a result of this technique, many of our predictions may seem to have nonsensical or perhaps even somewhat shocking implications. Our point is, you should understand that we did not assume that any of the relevant phenomena would accelerate, slow, shrink, or grow at a rate different from the current trend, unless there was a compelling and identifiable reason to believe otherwise. As is true for all forecasting models, such as those used to make meteorological and stock market predictions, some errors are expected. This problem has the potential to compromise or even someday invalidate our own estimations.

However, we also believe that our systematic analyses lead to some compelling conclusions that are both valid when approached in the right context and worthy of managerial consideration. By grounding our future business predictions in current scientific reality, we seek to minimize conjecture and try to focus on broad issues taking place over more extended time frames. This keeps us from becoming mired in specific details related to when, where, and how while maintaining significant managerial relevance.

The Underpinnings of Supply Chain Management

If we were to ask a pool of business managers to define the term supply chain management (SCM), we would likely receive many different definitions. All too often SCM is confused with the notion of logistics, or mistakenly juxtaposed with an organization's procurement function.[4] In some companies, the supply chain is visualized and operated as a "chain" of companies that extends from the receiving dock's door back to the sources of raw materials. They think of it as an upstream pipeline through which the internal production process's necessary supplies flow. To such companies, SCM is simply a collection of company initiatives designed to influence these inbound material flows. Unfortunately, this definition proves to be overly limiting, for it fails to accurately describe the end-to-end, source-to-customer processes that lead to shareholder value and customer satisfaction. To remedy this issue, the Council of Supply Chain Management Professionals (CSCMP) has derived a "consensus" definition of SCM:

> Supply Chain Management encompasses the planning and management of all activities involved in sourcing and procurement, conversion, and all logistics management activities. Importantly, it also includes coordination and collaboration with channel partners, which can be suppliers, intermediaries, third-party service providers, and customers. In essence, SCM integrates supply and demand management within and across companies.

As can be deduced from this definition, supply chain management spans a broader domain than simply a single business's procurement

---

[4] For a clear distinction between "logistics" and "supply chain management," see Cooper, Martha C., Douglas M. Lambert, and Janus D. Pagh (1997). "Supply Chain Management: More Than a New Name for Logistics," *International Journal of Logistics Management*, Vol. 8, No. 1, 1–14.

or logistics functions, or the physical path from a firm's raw-materials providers to its inbound loading dock. In fact, limiting the organization's view of SCM to these functions and physical spaces has become a dangerous impediment to firm value maximization. Because of the confusion, many companies have failed to give SCM the attention in the boardroom that it often deserves. Considering the importance of supply chain management to solving tomorrow's problems, companies cannot continue to view it as a low-priority business function or simply a cost of doing business. Supply chain management offers a broader, more impactful means for navigating the major challenges and creating advantage for businesses that learn to leverage their muscle and influence.

In the lagging companies' defense, cutting-edge SCM thinkers understand that handling the supply chain is a complex endeavor that requires both cross-functional processes as well as managing relationships within and across the organizations that make up the source-to-consumer network. In top-flight companies, supply chain management simultaneously incorporates all the organization's business functions with the functions within partner organizations. The ability to maximize shareholder returns hinges on the focal organization's ability to put forward a comprehensive and integrated offering to customers dependent on fully coordinated, interfunctional activity. As the supply chain leaders of best-in-class companies such as Apple, Nike, Procter & Gamble, and Walmart often publicly attest, it is likely that no other business discipline will play as critical a role in the success or failure of companies throughout the remainder of this century.

In other words, we are entering an *"age of supply chain management,"* where seamlessly integrated groups of organizations are uniting multiple functional efforts around a singular goal of delivering optimum value at the entire system's lowest landed costs. This proposition begs two questions. Why do such well-established companies view SCM as being so critical for future successes? Equally important, where the rubber meets the road, how are firms and functions integrated throughout the supply chain for SCM initiatives to deliver value?

To answer these questions, we rely on two conceptual frameworks that provide the foundation for our SCM views. The University of Tennessee's Demand-Supply Integration (DSI) framework, shown in Figure 1.1, addresses the "why." It proposes that the best supply chain companies, both now and in the future, are those whose driving mission is to perfectly balance customer demand with product and service supply. They do so through internal planning, external planning, and integrated processes. Anything less is viewed as either ineffective, creating customer dissatisfaction, or inefficient, creating waste. Adopting a DSI philosophy implies that businesses recognize that they must address what management guru Peter Drucker called the "great operational divide." This is the philosophical and operational chasm that often exists between the business enterprise's demand-fulfilling and supply-provisioning functions. Each of these traditionally has operated autonomously and with limited regard for the planning, goals, and structures of the other.

As shown in Figure 1.1, by uniting supply and demand planning efforts within and across organizations, relevant business function groups can share an aligned view of the necessary steps of creating shareholder value. On the supply side, DSI implies that companies must do a better job of identifying supply sources, with a focus on meeting customer requirements at an acceptable cost. On the demand side, the philosophy requires that demand must be "shaped," wherever possible, to coincide with supply market realities and opportunities. Furthermore, identifying a subset of customers—"customers of choice"—who can best be served profitably becomes paramount.

One electronics company executive indicated the following during a DSI interview session: "We make 110% of our profits on the first 40% of our customers." Thus, he is implying that the remaining 60% of the firm's customer base was actually served at a loss. Taking this statistic into account, it may have been better for the company not to serve them at all. Another electronics company found that it derived 90% of its profits from just 15% of its customers, indicating a more persuasive argument for selective engagement than even the 80/20 Pareto Rule. This rule suggests that 80% of revenues come from 20% of customers or products.

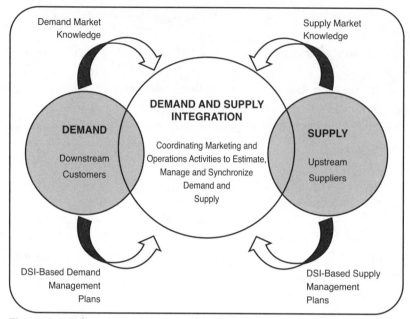

Figure 1.1 Demand-supply integration framework

What the DSI framework tells us, then, is that balancing demand with supply is the most critical philosophical direction a company can take when intertwining the goals of maximizing shareholder value and optimizing customer outcomes. This can happen only through fully integrated supply chain management that considers both sets of functional elements within and across formal organizations. It is reasonable to conclude, then, that the future of supply chain management hinges on demand and supply integration.

To address *how* firms integrate supply chain processes to attain maximum value, we rely on the Global Supply Chain Forum (GSCF) framework developed by researchers at The Ohio State University (see Figure 1.2). By collaborating with executives from leading global companies, the GSCF devised the architecture for managing supply chains. The GSCF framework breaks supply chain management into eight critical business processes that span an organization's functions. A multifirm, cross-functional team manages each of the processes, with input from all business functions, including procurement, production, finance, logistics, marketing, and research and development (R&D). As such, SCM is not a function, but rather an orientation for managing the business and its relationships with external customers and suppliers. The eight business processes are as follows:[5]

- **Customer relationship management** (CRM) provides structure for how the relationships with customers are developed and maintained.

- **Supplier relationship management** (SRM) provides structure for how relationships with suppliers are developed and maintained.

- **Customer service management** (CSM) is the firm's face to the customer. It seeks to proactively address potential disruptions and service failures.

- **Demand management** (DM) balances demand and supply through planning and flexible accommodation.

- **Order fulfillment** (OF) includes all activities to design a supply chain network, plan for the delivery of orders, and execute logistics activities.

- **Manufacturing flow management** (MFM) includes all activities necessary to obtain, implement, and manage manufacturing flexibility and move products through the plants.

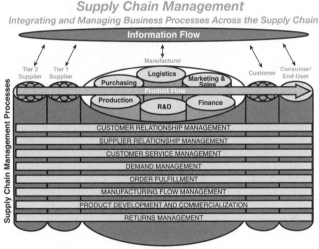

Figure 1.2 Global Supply Chain Forum framework

---

[5] Adapted from *Supply Chain Management: Processes, Partnerships, Performance*, 3rd Edition. D.M. Lambert (Ed.). (2008). Sarasota, FL. Supply Chain Management Institute.

- **Product development and commercialization** (PD&C) facilitates developing and bringing products to market jointly with customers and suppliers.
- **Returns management** (RM) facilitates the activities associated with returns, reverse logistics, gatekeeping, and avoidance such that customer complaints are reduced as problems with products and services are identified and remedied.

By integrating these processes across functional areas and organizational boundaries, firms optimize their ability to integrate supply and demand. For example, one major pet products manufacturer had been making and distributing a certain dog care product through a prominent retail chain when new circumstances forced the manufacturer to recall the product. Because the supply chain's manufacturing flow management and returns management processes were integrated across both the retailer's and manufacturer's business interface, the recalled goods were replaced almost immediately by the same manufacturer's secondary brand, which was deemed safe for animal consumption. Though the particular product was rightfully removed from store shelves, the incident resulted in nominal consumer impact and only minor losses in sales for the manufacturer and retailer. Such examples of cooperation and value creation across company lines underscore the value of a supply chain orientation, where companies effectively team up to address major opportunities and challenges.

The processes defined in the GSCF framework represent the methodology and processes that leading supply chain companies use to generate heightened value for the involved companies and the end customers they collectively serve. The driving theory of supply chain management is that working effectively as a team maximizes the profits and market capitalizations of the participating companies.[6] In essence, supply chain management is a "team sport." The macrotrends identified in this book are simply too big and complex for any single company to address on its own. The upcoming chapters

---

[6] Lambert, Douglas M. in *Supply Chain Management: Processes, Partnerships, Performance*, 3rd Edition. D.M. Lambert (Ed.). (2008). Sarasota, FL. Supply Chain Management Institute.

illustrate how the macrotrends will differentially impact the eight key business processes, as well as the supply chain as a whole.

What You Will Learn from This Book

The remainder of this chapter sketches the mission, methods, and roles of supply chain management in the modern business organization. Then it explains how the supply chain should react to leverage opportunities and countermeasure risks. We do so by integrating the DSI and GSCF concepts to achieve the best outcomes for companies seeking to compete in the transforming world. We juxtapose the two theoretical bases with our research predictions addressing the future of the business environment. The result takes the form of an organizing framework, as shown in Figure 1.3.

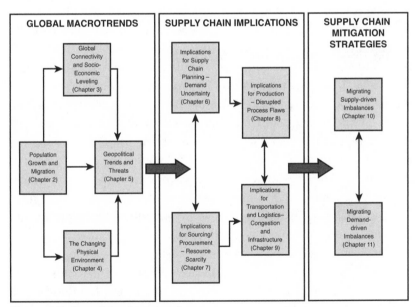

Figure 1.3 Organizing framework

Part I outlines four sets of intertwined macrotrends that are shaping supply chain management theory and practice. These forces are currently challenging business leaders' commonly held assumptions related to both consumer demand patterns and companies' and industries' supply capabilities. Thus, our macrotrends framework emanates from the rapid and somewhat unpredictable sociological and economic changes presently occurring. These changes influence the demand for products and services that supply chains are designed to fulfill and, in addition, inhibit supply-side systems capabilities. We believe that ignorance of these factors will lead to great risk of failure in the future if the forecasted changes reach fruition and are not proactively addressed. We begin our analysis in Chapter 2, which focuses on how some identifiable changes in population growth and human migration are rapidly affecting global demand. There are more people on Earth than ever before, and they are relocating at an unprecedented pace, creating potential chaos for mostly static supply chain processes. This chapter unpacks the reasons for our current population dynamics and illustrates several common problems companies will face if they fail to proactively design their supply chains to accommodate such changes.

The immediate outcomes of population change are, of course, a primary concern for future business leaders and policy makers. Each of three subsequent forces represents a unique macrotrend in its own right, although it emanates from population change itself. Chapter 3 looks at the global population's increased interconnectedness and the economic leveling it will soon stimulate across world regions. The Information Age has spurred many great innovations and benefits for society, but the changes it has brought are also undermining the assumptions firms have traditionally made about demand market— the same assumptions that enable cost control in the supply chain. Likewise, Chapter 4 addresses the environmental, climatological, and sustainability-related issues that are already beginning to impact global demand and supply as more humans consume more resources. The environment has been damaged during the harvesting and collection of these resources. Not only are new consumer tastes swiftly beginning to reflect environmental conscientiousness, but these issues also are impacting the supply. Weather, climate, and their human reactions have already started to affect worldwide logistics practices. Chapter 5 concludes Part I by approaching a handful of political and governmental issues that may adversely impact demand and supply in the coming years. Here we focus on the potential regulations, market controls, conflicts, and interregional disputes that are projected to impact global market competition. Such issues have the potential to create great supply chain inefficiencies for companies that fail to account for them in planning and supply chain operations.

Part II turns to the implications of the aforementioned forces on four selected, critical areas of supply chain functionality. Chapter 6 examines the effect of the macrotrends on the supply chain planning function. The four forces of interest can greatly disrupt supply chain planning by obscuring important information related to supply and demand quantities and assortments. They also can increase variation both geographically and in terms of rote quantity. Chapter 7 addresses the potential disruptions presented to firms' sourcing and procurement functions as a result of the combined macrotrends. Summarily, we anticipate that sourcing will become more complex as populations with different but homogenizing product expectations increase. This also will happen as the world's supplies of many key commodities become strained due to overuse and/or suboptimal location versus established supply networks. Chapter 8 considers the macrotrends' collective implications for production of goods and services. The diversity and migratory nature of populations, combined with geopolitical strains and leveling of purchasing power, could yield a confusing, complex, and disaggregated production process, such that ubiquitously favored lean strategies may not suffice. Alternative strategies are presented that should allow for more effective matching of customer needs to production outputs. Finally, Chapter 9 is concerned with the impacts on firms' transportation and logistics functions. A key focus is managing more complex networks with scarce assets and addressing the implications of issues such as fuel shortages and congestion on supply chain logistics costs and customer-facing metrics.

Part III describes strategies for mitigating the aforementioned problems' effects. Chapters 10 and 11 present two unique and compelling frameworks for analyzing and mitigating the resultant issues that will influence supply chains in the 2020s and beyond. Included within these chapters are strategies for allaying the risks of both supply- and demand-driven imbalances. We also discuss how failing to address these macrotrends holistically and proactively will influence the company's services, customers, financials, and, ultimately, vitality. We conclude with actionable initiatives for each set of imbalances so that managers may begin to enact our recommendations immediately and be ready for the more distant issues on the horizon. The proposed initiatives should allow firms to develop a set of interconnected resource utilization and supply chain sustainability strategies that specifically address the problems we all will soon face.

Our message should resonate with managers and executives alike. When considered together, the identified macrotrends imperil world commerce, but it isn't too late to prevent such chaos; today's supply chains need to be adapted to take into account and prepare for tomorrow's issues. Our book aims to assist forward-thinking managers seeking to do just that.

Managing the Supply Chain to Mitigate Macrotrend Risks

Our primary mission is to illustrate how future supply chain managers need to address the growing risks associated with complex environmental factors that will impact future business. The good news? Modern managers are already getting better at dealing with supply chain risk as it occurs. What the Spumoni and Liberty Linehaul West stories tell us is that proactive companies can turn a potentially disastrous situation into a market opportunity with proper forethought and action. The story of Nokia offers another classic example. Nokia's supply chain managers were able to quickly bounce back in late 2000 after a fire damaged wafer inventory at their supplier's factory—which just so happened to fulfill rival Ericsson's demand as well. Nokia's fast action relative to Ericsson positioned it to grow at Ericsson's expense. Similarly, Toyota was able to recover relatively quickly in the aftermath of the 2011 Japanese tsunami and continue producing with only moderate hiccups. Nearly a decade ago, one major study found that a supply chain disruption could drop share prices by as much as 15%.[7]

---

[7] Hendricks, Kevin B. and Vinod R. Singhal. (2005). "An Empirical Analysis of the Effect of Supply Chain Disruptions on Long-Run Stock Price Performance and Equity Risk of the Firm," *Production and Operations Management*, Vol. 14, No. 1, 35–52.

With today's supply chains more visible than ever before to investors, it's hard to see how a company can afford to ignore potential disruptions we foresee on the horizon.

The differences between these examples and future outcomes are couched in orders of magnitude and event expectancies. The risks that supply chain managers face today pose only temporary threats that are relatively minor in magnitude (with a few exceptions). However, the future's "new norm" appears to encompass the permanent and systemic occurrence of what we would today classify as major threats. "Carmageddon" may soon spread through cities like the plague, and China won't be the only country that automakers struggle to service. These incidents are isolated today. Tomorrow, they will not be.

We believe that only firms that have painstakingly prepared for the macrotrends' long-term impacts will be sustainable. Effective supply chain management can save companies from the megatrends heating up in the global landscape, facing challenges with the help of models like DSI and GSCF as ways to separate from the pack of competitors. This will require attentive management of the eight GSCF processes, with consideration given to the shifts in the business environment we describe. Even those who have been successful in the past must realize that the rules are constantly changing. New threats will call for shifts in supply chain strategies and practices. The remainder of this book outlines the future of supply chain management as we see it. It also provides details on how to develop the necessary strategies for your organization to flourish in light of unprecedented global business transformation.

2

Global Population Growth and Migration

For centuries, scholars have studied the stories of the past to predict what will happen in the future. Our story begins in the *very* distant past—400 million years ago, to be exact. In a sparsely populated area that would later encompass the United States' upper Great Plains region and Canada's southernmost provinces, a massive petroleum deposit formed within and beneath a 15,000-square-mile shale bed.

Advancing to the 1950s, the most significant petroleum deposit ever unearthed in North America was discovered on the property of North Dakota grain farmer Henry Bakken. Back then, Williston, North Dakota, was fairly unknown outside the plains and was not the center of any major industrial activity. In 1953 Stanolind Oil and Gas first drilled into what is now called the Bakken Formation. Modern-day geologists believe its reserves contain over 4 *billion* barrels of oil and natural gas—enough to meet current worldwide demand for over a decade. Despite half a century's worth of drilling, though, many ignored the region's significance because of preconceived notions about domestic petroleum development.

Typically, wealthy nations satisfy their large-scale demands for petroleum by importing it from the resource-rich (albeit underdeveloped) states surrounding the Persian Gulf, Niger Delta, and Caspian Sea rather than establishing or increasing domestic production. Importing is rooted in simple economics. It's just cheaper to extract petroleum resources from soft, sandy ground in distant regions and pay transportation fees than to extract from the concrete-like rock layers dominating local areas like the Bakken region. For the longest time, scientists, engineers, and oil companies were uncertain that drilling in shale fields would even yield quantities large enough to justify local production. The extensive damage that would occur to pricy drilling equipment was a virtual certainty.

But out of necessity arises innovation, and in the late 2000s, America saw just that from its petroleum industry. At the time, crude oil prices were skyrocketing across the world due to depleted supply and the Middle East's political tensions. At approximately the same time, new technological advances for hydraulically fracturing, or "fracking," rock formations were being devised, along with other techniques that enabled diagonal and horizontal drilling. This perfect storm of technology finally provided viable access to hardened shale formations, and though expensive, it rendered equipment costs bearable.

Only then did social, technological, and economic forces converge to make the Bakken region attractive to producers—and ripe for development. Seemingly overnight, the Bakken Formation became a de facto source for U.S. producers, representing a surprisingly lower-risk substitute for the politically unstable OPEC nations' crude. All of a sudden, petroleum-rich geological sites like Williston were no longer blips on the radar. Between late 2007 and early 2008, producers rushed people, equipment, trucks, and technology to towns in North Dakota, Montana, and even the Canadian province of Saskatchewan to take advantage of the first true oil and gas boom since the west Texas wildcatter days a century before. Local populations exploded, and overnight the quaint little northern towns isolated by hundreds of miles of plains became bustling hubs of activity for drilling personnel and their families.

Humans have a habit of moving around to pursue resources, and local populations can rapidly grow or shrink as they do so. The Roman Empire expanded outward from modern Northern Italy to acquire more food grain, just as 19th century U.S. explorers went west of the Rockies to search for gold. Searching for new employment and better lives, immigrants from Spain and France, and later the Netherlands, Britain, and Mexico, have come to the United States to pursue the American Dream. Though earlier historical migrations were often natural responses to slavery, oppression, or religious persecution, humans in modern times tend to move en masse to acquire new resources. The key difference between the past and present, however, is that large-scale migrations used to take place over many years or decades. This allowed local infrastructure changes to evolve naturally and methodically, according to the exodus or influx of people. For instance, accompanying the Gold Rush's westward expansion was the transcontinental railroad, which workers in Utah finished only a few years following peak gold extraction.

Mass population movement creates a temporary, but meaningful, imbalance between the local demand for goods and their local supply. With forty-niners arriving in California faster than its settlements were prepared to accommodate, shelter, cattle, equipment, and service shortages were problematic early on. To alleviate the maladies and inconveniences that such imbalances create, systems that balance supply with newly derived demand must be extended to the new location of interest, or invented wholesale. When large-scale migrations occurred in the past, people found a way to develop the infrastructure for providing supplies, whether they did so by bringing the groundwork with them or creating it along the way. As the Romans slowly moved northward into what now are Switzerland and Germany, they assembled complex supply lines along self-built roads to provide food, water, horses, and weapons to their newly conquered territories. When the native Germanic tribes learned their military technology was no match for the advancing Roman forces, they resorted to attacking their enemies' supply lines to level the playing field. The plan worked. The Romans were starved, and their headway slowed. Such is the importance of supply infrastructure in a new or booming population center.

Though ancient, the Roman example holds truth today by illustrating how important a seamless supply chain is to organizational success. Modern and future populations depend on local supply chain ecosystems that are carefully designed to address forecasted supply and demand ranges for citizens to thrive or survive. The designed systems need to be flexible and agile to support the dynamic demand patterns that are characteristic of migratory locations. If they aren't, profits and businesses may face the same fate as the early Roman conquerors.

Additionally, though its supply chain implications are substantial, large-scale migration is not the only source of population growth concern that future supply chain practitioners need to prepare for. In technologically modernizing places like China, Brazil, India, and Africa, the consumer population is simply growing organically—and rapidly, at that. Medical care, food and water quality, and lifestyle advances are causing developing nations' populations to flourish at both ends of the human life cycle. Whereas one in three infants in a nation like Nigeria was historically unlikely to reach his or her tenth birthday, infant mortality in traditionally underdeveloped areas is rapidly ebbing. At the age continuum's opposite pole, people in both underdeveloped and developed nations alike are living longer. They are surviving cancer, eating healthier, and extending their lives through vitamin intake, education, exercise, and better eldercare. The result of these forces in combination is the large, serious population growth—either organic or via migration—that the world has witnessed over the past several decades.

Although lengthened human lifespans are in many ways encouraging, because they indicate social progress, the leveling of health indices across major world regions comes at a consequential economic cost. Population growth is straining various economic systems. Workers must produce more to support an increasingly large number of nonworkers (the young and old). Relatively equal production volumes must be more efficiently allocated across geographies. Finally, when combined with underdeveloped nations' recent per-capita wealth increases, population growth is creating new markets that are increasing goods and services that supply chain managers are charged with making available.

This chapter looks at how both organic and migration-induced population growth will affect future supply chains. The basic premise is simple: Demand can shift much more rapidly than supply chain managers can adjust to the changes that are occurring, and the imbalances caused will yield severe cost and service considerations for businesses. Additionally, population changes lead to other social phenomena that will exacerbate these imbalances, such as resource scarcity, deterioration of the physical environment, demand decentralization, and the natural geopolitical strains that are linked to each of these issues. This chapter explores population change, with an eye on these potential opportunities and threats. We provide some initial directions for supply chain managers to consider when taking future action in response.

Impacts of Population Change on Demand and Supply

Much of the Bakken extraction activity since 2007 has taken place within a highly concentrated 300-mile-wide circle with Cartwright, North Dakota, at its center. The hamlet is only a few miles from Montana and a couple hours' drive from the Canadian border. The 2000 U.S. Census cataloged the entire region's population at about 50,000 people. Supply and demand were relatively balanced, and the local economy was stable, based primarily on grain agriculture. But we're confident that no one could have predicted what would happen next.

When populations grow and move, some economists have noted that these changes present socially tenuous challenges for global and local societies. The Bakken Formation's newfound importance yielded an influx of workers and their families to the area, swelling the population by an estimated 200%, which unleashed migration-related chaos. While the Great Recession of 2008–2011 brought about severe worldwide unemployment challenges, Bakken officials describe an inversely dire situation. Currently there are roughly nine jobs per applicant, and employers are inviting people to move to the area by promising lucrative paychecks and lifestyles. Though the region may have vast stores of natural resources, it doesn't do the world any good if there isn't enough manual labor available to develop and commercialize them.

In Richland County, Montana, mounting traffic clogs the few existing roads connecting fire stations, schools, and grocery stores around the clock. Vacant hotel rooms are long gone, leased on annual contracts rather than nightly ones. Tent cities are popping up in farm fields that are no longer harvested because their farmers make a better living driving supply trucks and selling silo space to be filled with fracking sand. The high-paying oil field jobs have also depleted the local labor pool. Finding new schoolteachers—the supply of which elsewhere often exceeds 150% of classroom need—has become nearly impossible. Fast-food restaurants such as Taco Barn offer signing and retention bonuses for *hourly* workers. Crime in Sidney, a neighboring town, has exploded. Because the government cannot allocate additional resources to its police force, and because there are no people to fill these jobs anyway, the residents carry guns, much like in the Old

West. County officials have expressed a need for new cellular towers and electricity substations, but other, more critical issues supersede them. Interviews with transient workers reveal even more pressing issues involving the availability of fresh drinking water, proper washrooms, adequate food supply, and shelter suitable for harsh northern winters.

The problems caused by population shifts are both very real and difficult to predict. Yet most businesses and governments fail to plan for such scenarios, instead burying themselves in periodic issues that reflect their stakeholders' more immediate needs. Had Richland County been better prepared, would workers be sleeping in tents on the prairie? Perhaps. Or would innovative companies and governments already be profiting from the newfound opportunities that have presented themselves? This question is worth asking: How could contingency planning principles borrowed from other scenarios have impacted the area and business as a whole in a more positive way? For instance, a public-private partnership between local or federal government and industry could be formed that would temporarily facilitate the transportation of goods and equipment to rapidly industrializing areas. This would be much like how the Federal Emergency Management Agency transports food and temporary housing to locations hit by natural disaster. Not all disruptions to the supply chain are negative. One form of supply chain risk is that something positive will occur to an area or institution, but the key stakeholders are unprepared to take advantage of it. Unleashing the power of forecasting, demand planning, and inventory management—all key supply chain functions—on a rapidly growing area may yield greatly positive impacts on both industry and the area as a whole. This is but one key example of how better coordination of goods and material flows might not only bolster the citizens living in an area afflicted by risk, but also would provide great opportunity for the profit-seeking organizations working within it.

When areas grow in population, scarcity of commodities like fossil fuels and drinking water, as well as scarcity of services such as farm labor, may present serious supply chain dilemmas for the foreseeable future. We address this problem later in the book. To better comprehend what causes scarcity, it is important to understand first how and why populations change and why such changes are confusing. The following section presents two competing population growth perspectives that are diffusing through modern political and media systems. The ultimate goal is to define guidelines for future supply chain managers to follow when situations like those facing North Dakota and Montana arise. But first we must explain our logic for why population growth presents both threat and opportunity for the supply chains of the future.

Population Growth Perspectives

The Earth's population has been exploding for the better part of the past century. The planet currently is home to just over 7 billion people, a massive number that stands in stark contrast to the 2 billion Earthlings at the end of the Great Depression. This is still far more than the 3.5 billion people who were around when man first landed on the moon. Not only are we all mingling with the largest number of people ever to occupy the planet, but the annual population growth rate is also increasing faster than ever before. Figure 2.1 illustrates how the world population has grown (and may continue to grow), and Figure 2.2 identifies the places where it has been growing the fastest. Based on data compiled by the U.S. Census Bureau and the United Nations, Figure 2.1 charts world population by decade beginning in 1928. It took many millennia for the Earth to reach the baseline of 2 billion people, but if the current population growth trends continue, *it will take only another century to more than quadruple that number*. By 2050, less than 40 years from now, the world could be home to an astonishing 9.5 billion people if growth rates don't change.

Future population growth predictions such as these tend to be where the disputes manifest, and two general schools of thought are prevalent. The first traces its roots to Thomas Malthus, an 18th century English philosopher and religious figure. In 1798, Malthus wrote his famous *Essay on the Principle of Population*, a work that was among the first to publicize potential negative impacts that a growing populace could have on global resources and citizens. Adherents to the classical Malthusian school believe that the Earth is endowed with a finite and definable supply of natural resources. They also believe that the human population's plausibly infinite growth will eventually deplete these resources unless we take active measures to either slow birthrates or increase death rates. This view holds that populations should increase over the long term because any emerging human innovations will increase the population, thus satisfying a basic need for survival of the species. This view also holds that innovations won't advance the standard of living of the few via greater human productivity (satisfying an advanced social need for the few). Classic Malthusians generally agree that in pursuit of familial self-interests, the population will continue to grow until the Earth's resources are insufficient to sustain life.

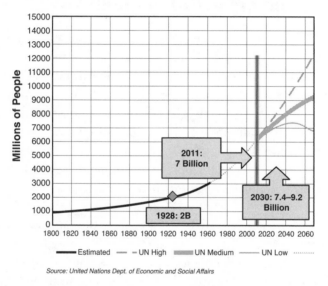

Source: United Nations Dept. of Economic and Social Affairs

Figure 2.1   World population growth and projections[1]

The historical situation on Easter Island is a classic illustration of Malthusian theory. Several hundred years ago, Polynesians settled the formerly unpopulated island and immediately set about cutting down trees to make boats and tools. When European explorers found Easter Island some time later, they noted the island's large population. Roughly 200 years after that discovery, returning explorers were stunned to find that the natives had deforested the island, effectively depriving themselves of their primary food and shelter sources and

[1] Historical and projected world populations (1950–2050) drawn from U.S.Census Bureau estimations. www.census.gov/population/international/data/idb/worldpopgraph. php. Populations from 1930–1940 provided by a 2006 United Nations report. www.un.org/esa/population/publications/sixbillion/sixbilpart1.pdf.

forcing them to abandon their homeland. They estimated that the population had decreased by nearly 80%. Malthus's central argument—that populations will eventually outpace and devour their available resources—has been demonstrated across multiple historical scenarios, not just Easter Island. However, adherents are not entirely pessimistic, because they also agree that it is indeed possible to break out of the "Malthusian trap" via radical innovation. They believe the human race will continue to grow until a critical resource, such as oxygen, potable water, or food, is catastrophically exhausted. At that point the human race should be capable of innovating a solution that will ensure their survival by reducing the absent resource's harmful effects.

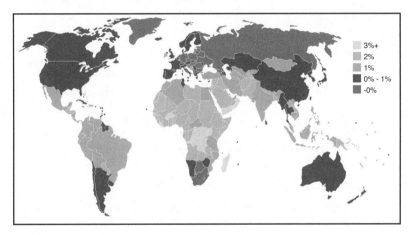

Figure 2.2 Population growth rate by country

Stanford University biology professors Paul and Anne Ehrlich might be classical Malthusianism's contemporary high priest and priestess. In 1968, the Ehrlichs wrote *The Population Bomb*, a book intended to spark worldwide dialog related to the problems they believed would result from Earth's overpopulation. According to the Ehrlichs' research, the Earth has a "finite carrying capacity" for inhabitants. Based on their contemporary data, they predicted a large, nonlinear increase in human population would overload the planet's biological and geological ecosystems before the turn of the 21st century. To avoid the forthcoming Malthusian trap, they proposed a basic, albeit controversial, solution: Earth's population must be quickly stabilized or reduced, preferably by decreasing birthrates through contraceptive education. (The Ehrlichs admitted that increased death rates, based on disease, war, and famine, would lead to an equally effective outcome.) Furthermore, if we failed to alter our birth and/or death rates, the Ehrlichs argued, the alteration would eventually happen involuntarily. This is because massive food and water shortages, severe ozone depletion, and political conflicts over increasingly scarce resources would occur. These factors would combine to form an uninhabitable planet by the late 20th century.

Though the "population bomb" didn't explode at its expected magnitude, its predictions were not entirely without merit. In a recently published revision, the authors reconciled their initial predictions with modern history. They noted that, as they had predicted, humans did innovate: Birthrates have indeed slowed due to contraception innovation, but only in the world's more industrialized nations. In agreement with the Ehrlichs' primary thesis, national populations' age distributions have widened as medical innovations have prolonged human lives. Oceans are overfished, metal and mineral stores are being diminished, alternative food sources aren't developing fast enough, and many world regions have dangerously low food and freshwater availability.

In underdeveloped nations, things have proceeded much as the Ehrlichs originally predicted, because these are the last areas to gain access to technological advances usually required to stave off self-destruction. Of the top ten population growth rates, all are occurring in nations below the median world gross domestic product (GDP). The rapid population expansion of the Third World has stemmed from the availability of neonatal medicine, malaria-controlling mosquito nets, HIV and AIDS treatments in sub-Saharan Africa, and greater access to emergency medicine. Yet hunger and starvation plague nearly half the world's nations. Nearly a third of the global population, which resides almost entirely in poorer nations, has insufficient drinking water, and this number is expected to rise.

Even in wealthier nations like the United States, where food and water are plentiful, people can feel the effects. Demand for products designed for senior citizens, such as eldercare and golf courses, is surging and reflects overall growth at the upper end of the age spectrum. More effective cancer treatments and greater knowledge of the cardio system are extending their lives. But cities are getting more crowded and traffic more congested, creating longer commutes, polluted urban vistas, and more aggregate crime. Bordering U.S. states like California and Arizona, as well as Georgia and Tennessee, have clashed over freshwater rights or are expected to. Another foreboding sign is prophetic commodity speculators such as T. Boone Pickens anticipating future price spikes by buying up water rights in rural and suburban areas. What does this mean for the developed world? In short, there are more of us, we are living longer, and although population growth is tempering, we are all demanding goods and services at an unprecedented rate.

The Ehrlichs do admit in their recent rejoinder that their original theory was incorrect or shortsighted in many ways. Currently we can state with certainty that there remains enough supply of most goods and services to sustain the world population for a while longer, and overcrowding has not had the disastrous effects on the planet that were predicted. The discrepancies from the Ehrlichs' original projections are twofold. Population growth shows signs of slowing worldwide. And although the current demand-satisfying supplies are distributed very inefficiently around the globe, they do tend to eventually become available when a true resource crisis emerges.[2]

---

[2] This has ensured that the classical Malthusian philosophy remains a tenet of "politically moderate" environmentalists. In some cases, however, the original Malthusian theory has been twisted to serve political purposes that are disingenuous to the original theory's postulates. A modern-day offshoot known as Neo-Malthusianism purports that negative environmental impact is a result of population size, affluence level, and technological efficiency. According to the Neo-Malthusians, population growth is bad for society simply because they increase negative environmental impacts with a multiplier effect. Similarly, affluence is seen as bad because it proportionally increases consumption, and technological efficiency is bad because it enables mass consumption more than it diminishes birthrates. Because people seek both affluence and technology progress, Neo-Malthusians see each additional person in the populace as a threat to the environment, a disease spreader, a resource exhauster, and a potential war starter. Limited empirical evidence supports their key premises; thus, Neo-Malthusians have actually damaged the Classical Malthusians' cause. Population impact skeptics can point to them as radical reformers detached from the "realities" of growth. Unfortunately, by taking a similar position a bit too far, the Neo-Malthusians have made it convenient for casual observers and detractors to lump the two together.

Because empirical evidence supporting these weaknesses is available, an alternative school of thought, known as the Cornucopian philosophy, has developed. Cornucopian ecologists believe that the Earth possesses infinite resources for human purposes. In the rare occasions when we truly run out of something, we immediately innovate to find more supply or create a viable substitute. To Cornucopians, innovation will increase exponentially forever, such that population growth's disadvantages will never overtake innovation's benefits. The Cornucopian logic adheres to the following sequence:

- As nations progress through developmental life cycles, they initially consume as many resources as needed to survive, disregarding consequences.

- As they consume resources beyond a critical point, their civilizations modernize and become highly productive.

- At a certain point, highly productive societies become innovative and self-actualized, eventually becoming efficient.

- As efficient societies use fewer resources to meet end goals, they encourage others to do the same, thus creating an endless cycle of innovation and resource protection.

Chief Cornucopian economist Julian Simon argued the following in *The Ultimate Resource*, a more modernized response to *The Population Bomb*:

Because we can expect future generations to be richer than we are, no matter what we do about resources, asking us to refrain from using resources now so that future generations can have them later is like asking the poor to make gifts to the rich.

Obviously, this implies a view diametrically opposed to that of the Malthusians, suggesting that innovation is expanding exponentially and infinitely. Agreeing with the Cornucopian philosophy means believing that each successive innovation will be better than its predecessor, and that we humans will find infinite numbers of ways to use the Earth's resources to meet our needs.

We wrote this book about future supply chains. Nobody really knows if humanity will develop (and retain) the innovative capabilities required to solve the multitudinous problems we will create for ourselves. Therefore, we believe it best to adopt a moderate position on the Neo-Malthusian/Cornucopian continuum for the purposes of this book. From a pragmatic standpoint, it makes little sense for us to embrace either end of the spectrum. Doing so would imply that the next 25 years' innovations are unknowable or that we'll all be dead by then anyway, rendering our position (and this book) irrelevant. But empirical reasons also support our adopted perspective. The Neo-Malthusian view becomes untenable when hard data indicates that innovation does take place in response to population growth problems, such as the birth control pill and the current experimental successes with seawater desalination. Similarly, the Cornucopian view wilts when we consider that hunger and disease are indeed major world problems and that many critical commodities (oil, zinc, copper) are increasing in price far beyond and much earlier than the expectations of years past. Factual evidence supports the notion that population growth is slowing into a classical Malthusian equilibrium, with some innovations supplanting demand, and others lagging behind. Adopting one extreme view or the other in this ideological debate would distract us from the more pressing issues we are advocating. Thus, the neutral, classical Malthusian position we take in this book ensures that we remove as much bias as possible from our advice to tomorrow's managers and allows us to play the percentages as well.

Organic Population Growth Issues for Supply Chain Managers

Seven billion people can consume an enormous amount of resources, but modern managers can reengineer their supply chains to balance disparity among us. More people put pressure on global supply chains because supply and demand shifts introduce imbalance into the networks in place. Take China as an example of impending supply chain instability. Whereas China has long been a net exporter, the country's increasing population growth and developing production economy have shaken the world economy since the late 2000s. This confluence of forces is generating a sizable Chinese consumer class as factory managers, accountants, teachers, and the like have started consuming much like their Western counterparts.

As shown in Figure 2.3, rapid changes in demand location based on population shifts have great potential to disrupt even the most well-thought-out supply chains. In the figure, a Western company has established a supply chain network designed to serve customers in North America and Europe, based on supply bases constructed there and in Brazil. If, as predicted, demand shifts to the locations indicated by the ovals (where organic growth is occurring most rapidly), the company faces difficulty in adjusting in the short term. Even small consumption increases in highly populated nations like China and India can create enormous strains on global supply chain processes. The population growth projections for Western Europe, Canada, and the United States for consumers ages 15 to 60 allow us to calculate that slightly less than 600 million people there will be primed for goods and services consumption in 2010–2015. This same consumer category is estimated at over 2.5 billion people in Southeast and Eastern Asia by 2015.[3] Even if we assume that only half the new citizens there would have Westernesque buying power, that would mean that the Asian markets would have *more than twice* the market potential of Western markets. As an example of the potential impact, you can imagine the impact that this sort of growth would have on goods manufactured in Asia intended for insertion into Western companies' supply chains. When transportation costs and higher fuel prices are factored into the equation, will it be more economical for manufacturers like Acer and Sony to divert supply to Asian consumers rather than ship overseas to smaller but wealthier markets? Managers can only speculate, but the playing field is changing in ways that Westerners could hardly have imagined 20 years ago. These types of changes will wreak havoc on contemporary demand management functions and make supply chain network design a nightmare for many companies in the coming decades.

Additionally, a number of underdeveloped nations sustaining significant growth are also home to untapped deposits of natural resources. The United States Central Intelligence Agency has long known of the vast resource stores—and political strife—that exist in the Central African Republic. As is typical during disputed

---

[3] Voeller, John C. (June 2010). "The Era of Insufficient Plenty," *Mechanical Engineering Magazine*.

government transitions, the country has seen a number of conflicts resulting in lawlessness and violence throughout its regions.[4] Such political instability makes it difficult for global organizations to take advantage of the Central African Republic's vast natural resources pool. The U.S. Department of State reports that untapped resources include gold, uranium, and possibly even oil,[5] yet diamonds are the only mineral the country is truly exploiting. And the Central African Republic isn't the only country with yet-to-be-tapped natural resources. Nearby Zimbabwe, which mines both metallic and non-metallic ores, is still recovering from hyperinflation and government instability,[6] but it also possesses enormous resource stores. Niger, too, has only recently started exploiting its natural resources, and it may see future industrial significance—if it can manage to develop vast coal and oil deposits.[7]

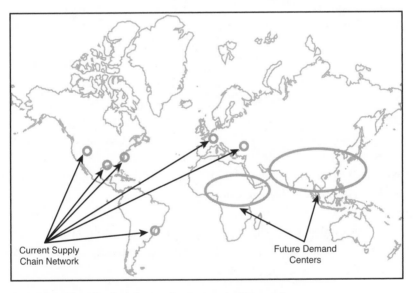

Figure 2.3 Hypothetical demand-supply misalignment

4 *The World Factbook: Central African Republic.* (2011). Central Intelligence Agency.

5 Bureau of African Affairs. "US Relations with Central African Republic," U.S. Department of State, 24 July 2012.

6 *The World Factbook: Zimbabwe.* (2011). Central Intelligence Agency.

7 *The World Factbook: Niger.* (2011). Central Intelligence Agency.

Present-focused companies and their managers will need to develop more robust supply chain networks that can support these emerging, value-generating consumer and supply markets. Several different areas of supply chain thought will be affected. In terms of supply chain strategy, the question of whether to be agile and customer-focused or lean and efficiency-focused will become more difficult to answer. Given perpetually adjusting supply-and-demand centers, you can easily envision a scenario in which a trend toward supply chain agility will begin to trump the current "efficiency" mantra. Any additional costs will be passed along to customers or redacted from supplier accounts and contracts. Managing physical demand uncertainty comes at a cost, and many (but not all) customers will be willing to pay it. An outgrowth of this strategic decision process may be the innovation of supply chain "flexworks." These are rapidly morphing networks that consist of publicly or privately shared manufacturing facilities, warehouses, and carriers whose purposes change in real time in response to shifts in demand patterns. Flexworks are similar to the information networks used by modern cellular communications companies to distribute data packets. When a call is placed, then and only then does the intelligent network decide how best to route it. Similarly, when a customer order for grapes, tree mulch, or power tools is placed in the future, will each shipment be picked, packed, and routed based on the assets available for use in real time? If so, two consecutive, identical orders placed by the same customer might be filled via two wholly different supply chain systems, each maximizing profit for the entire system on an order-by-order basis. These are but a few of the ideas that future managers should consider when optimizing the supply chain of the near future based on population trends.

Supply Chain Problems Created by Migration-Based Growth

Though organic population growth is problematic for companies and supply chain managers, rote increases in numbers of people tend to be predictable in the short-to-medium term and often can be addressed with careful demand planning, as described at the end of this chapter. On the other hand, we believe that migration issues will present even greater challenges.

For thousands of years, people have trekked across the Earth to meet various objectives. The planet's earliest inhabitants engaged in nomadic behavior as the most natural way to satisfy their basic needs, searching for food and lands having a habitable climate. As societies evolved and organized, migration became a way to avoid war, persecution, natural disaster, social displacement, or even slavery. Yet modern migration patterns don't truly reflect the globalization hype we often hear of in news reports related to immigration, internationalization of trade, and cross-border commerce. In his *World 3.0* treatise, Pankaj Ghemawat sifted through hard industrial data from many sources. He found that only less than 3% of persons migrate annually, a relatively miniscule amount considering the business media hype surrounding globalization. Still, a fraction of 7 billion people is still a lot of migrators. This means that in 2011–2012, nearly 210 million people packed their bags and moved to another country. By mid-century, experts predict this number will be closer to 500 million.

Why are Earth's citizens so interested in moving around? Population ecologists agree that in modern times, most people migrate to pursue economic opportunity. Labor is now the primary motivator, because modern society views remittance as more important than permanent residency. As a simple example, busloads of people leave Seattle each week to work a 14-day shift in the Bakken region before returning home to spend their paychecks and then return later. As another example, each year thousands of Mexican nationals cross the border (legally or illegally) to earn U.S. dollars to send back to their homeland.

As supply chain management professionals, we should be concerned with how migration will upset local supply-and-demand balance and increase companies' costs, especially as global supply chains meet broader, faster migration. Whereas in the past people developed social identities with strong ties to their homeland, many children of today were born—or have become—"global citizens," ready to move almost anywhere if the opportunity is right. Naturally, this means we take our demand for coffee, toffee, swimwear, and software with us.

It isn't that unusual to hear of a child born in India, raised in England, educated in the U.S., and employed in China before being transferred to Canada, where he or she starts a family. Present and future companies will have to react decisively to massive numbers of people moving from city to city and nation to nation to remain sustainable. This issue will be challenging, given modern supply chain networks' semipermanent structures built around medium-to-long-term agreements involving multiple companies, and relatively fixed assets such as warehouse buildings, roads, mines, fields, and production plants.

Two particular manifestations of modern migration could create significant mayhem for future supply chains and their managers. First, when populations migrate, their demographic subgroups often do not migrate in relative proportion. What this means for modern businesses is that both product assortments and their volumes change simultaneously in new and former locations, further compounding the complexity of demand forecasting. The Bakken region provides particularly telling evidence supporting this claim. When hundreds of people moved to western North Dakota, most of them were men, a phenomenon characteristic of oil field jobs. One of the region's grocery suppliers reported a spike in men's hygiene product orders, whereas female cosmetics did not have similar purchase increases. Issues such as these make supply chain functions like procurement (where contracts are often negotiated based on overall volume discounts) difficult for supply managers to address. In such cases, flexible contracts combined with the aforementioned flexworks might stave off the inevitable stockouts that arise from poor forecasting or demand sensing. Of course, this implies that the risks inherent in traditional supply chain management will be spread or shifted somewhat socialistically. Companies will be challenged to put the performance of the entire system ahead of short-term goals—a difficult recipe, to say the least.

Given that the Bakken migration took place in a country with a well-developed transportation and logistics infrastructure, we can expect that within months, supply chain managers will adjust to the supply/demand imbalance in toiletry goods by diverting inventory from other warehouses and recalibrating transportation. (However, if many companies do this simultaneously, we will see traffic jams like those in Williston.) As people from across the world continue to migrate in search of resources and better opportunities, we see much larger problems arising. For example, a sizable chunk of the Chinese migrant worker population still lives in the nation's rural inland. As opportunities arise along the coast, though, more and more able-bodied workers head east to pursue more lucrative careers. The result has been telling. In just a few years, the advent of a burgeoning middle class has clogged the nation's internal infrastructure, sent its property prices skyrocketing, and choked the environment with smog and other pollutants. This is the price of migration, especially when societies' other businesses, public infrastructure, and natural ecosystems cannot keep up.

This leads us to a second, and perhaps more daunting, trend noted by sociologists and economic geographers: humans' movement from rural areas into cities, a phenomenon known as urbanization. Numerous researchers have commented on the trend toward migration to large cities, a practice that has accelerated over the past decade. The McKinsey Global Institute conducted a study in 2012 that found that approximately one billion new consumers will emerge by 2025. Of these, roughly 60% will live in one of the 440 cities on Earth that can be classified as "emerging" in terms of their size and consumption. These cities are expected to deliver about half of the total GDP growth (which should be about $20 trillion) at that time.[8] Figure 2.4 shows World Bank predictions that by 2030, over 80% of the world's population will live in urban areas versus the 50% populating them today. The worldwide 50% mark was achieved for the first time in 2011.

Why are populations urbanizing? There are many explanations for why people migrate, but sociologists have narrowed the roots of rural-to-urban migration to three primary forces: rural flight, quality-of-life issues, and economic opportunity. To put these more colloquially, people are moving to cities (or creating new ones) because the role of humans in world agricultural efforts is diminishing in the new knowledge economy; because cities provide more interesting and valuable opportunities for needs fulfillment; and because, at a fundamental level, that's where the jobs of the present and future are and

---

[8] McKenzie Global Institute. (2012). "Urban World: Cities and the Rise of the Consuming Class," white paper.

will be. Of course, as a result, our concern is that global supply chains are not currently designed to be conducive to matching demand and supply in the urban environment due to traffic congestion, pollution, and customer service challenges. Most major U.S. cities' transportation infrastructures are already congested, even without taking into account the increased demands of urbanization. We address this subject in greater depth in later chapters, but it's worth considering

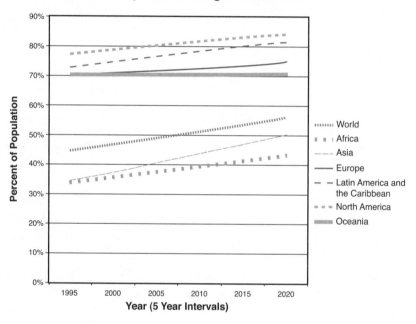

Figure 2.4 Percentage of the world's population living in urban areas

that as of 2010, over 20 major U.S. airports exceeded their cargo capacity—and no major airport construction has been planned to increase capacity.

The key questions are scary for current managers to consider. First, how do we service intensified concentrations of people within a geographic space when, as a result of this intensification, very little (or very expensive) space remains to store products? When designing the networks of the future in urbanized areas, conventional center-of-gravity models with intermediately positioned distribution centers won't suffice. Companies and industries need to investigate new urban-centric models of storage, scheduling, lot sizing, and customization. Related to this, the costs of real estate inside congested areas will skyrocket, but locating outside the congestion will result in unattainable delivery windows and missed or delayed shipments. Not to mention, the sheer cost of retail space will render current store designs obsolete due to their excessive space for stock. Additionally, in the most congested urban areas, such as London and Paris, many logistics delivery vehicles and inventory storage sites are prohibited by law from entering or passing through, making access much more difficult. How will these challenges be met and managed?

The Future Supply Chain Manager's Population-Oriented Agenda

Balancing supply and demand is the biggest challenge for world-class supply chain managers. However, in the face of changing populations, the time will come when addressing these issues with long-term planning will become a pipe dream. In the short term, adjustments can and should be made to SKU-level forecasts for key items. Investing in synchronizing supply chain management technology may reduce the costs of poor forecasting. For items with longer customer or supplier lead times, the sheer volume and sporadic nature of population changes is a potential hazard that will create great inefficiency for businesses. We see the following specific effects as the most damaging to the firm's supply chain management effort (and, therefore, they present the greatest opportunity for savvy managers):

- A shortage of supply in the optimal locations to satisfy extremely large-scale demand
- Different approaches to public investment in infrastructure across similarly crowded areas
- Difficulty in assessing where rapidly changing demand will come from
- Increased assortment due to population diversification within restricted geographic spaces (geographic demand heterogeneity)

- Shortage of advantageously located real estate and transportation assets to serve increasingly crowded areas
- Shortages of energy and water for use in conversion processes unless new sources are located and tapped
- Shortages of adequate retail store and stock space in crowded areas
- Insufficient port and airport capacity, creating expensive bottlenecks
- Problems with the accuracy of demand forecasting models for many products as customers live longer, use products differently, and consume earlier or later in life than ever before

Issues related specifically to increased consumerism and resource scarcity are addressed in greater detail in forthcoming chapters. For now, we will discuss how to prepare for the specific challenges associated with organic and migratory growth. Managers first need to narrow their focus to the potential effects that population growth and migration will have on the eight critical processes from the Global Supply Chain Forum framework. Table 2.1 lists each process and describes the potential adjustments that may be needed to address population growth, migration, and demographic change.

Table 2.1 Population Growth and Migration Implications on SCM

GSCF Process	Population Growth and Migration Implications
Customer relationship management (CRM)	Challenges:
	It's difficult to understand demand market segments and to devise metrics due to segment heterogeneity and constant migration.
	It's difficult to collect and examine customer information in time to make adjustments (data staleness).
	It's difficult to assess rapidly changing or highly diverse customer trends at two or more supply chain echelons without nearly perfect information visibility.

GSCF Process	Population Growth and Migration Implications
Customer relationship management (CRM) (continued)	Suggestions:
	Sharing collaborative demand information with downstream partners will become critical; employing integrative visibility software and collaboration tools is imperative.
	Shared and highly integrated databases with auto-collected customer preference information may be required to meet customer effectiveness metrics.
	Automate low-impact relationship management tasks to allocate resources to strategic relationships.
	Reward business customers who effectively bridge the gap between the focal company and new market segments.
Customer service management (CSM)	Challenges:
	It's difficult to understand customer service strategies by segment due to variations in cultural expectations within segments and/or segment membership fluidity.
	Call volumes may be more predictable but at very high volumes, and customers will have lower failure tolerances worldwide.
	Customer service staffing will retreat from low-cost labor locations and return to worldwide localization.
	Internal and external coordination in the customer resolution process will require more information sharing/mobility.
	Sales will often decline for little apparent reason, and the diagnosis will be more difficult and expensive.

GSCF Process	Population Growth and Migration Implications
Customer service management (CSM) (continued)	Event recognition may be difficult because the definition of "event" will differ globally.
	Suggestions:
	Decentralize monitoring and reporting functions to effectuate local handling.
	Develop worldwide standards for event recognition and resolution, but apply adjustments locally to meet cultural norms.
	Build a portfolio of CSM strategies to select from, and adapt best-fit solutions to local conditions.
	Enable customer self-service responses wherever practical, with strategic customer incentives for participation.
Demand management (DM)	Challenges:
	It's more difficult to collect demand data that is timely and relevant.
	It's difficult to forecast demand at all levels in the short to medium term due to population transitivity. Ideal forecasting approaches may vary widely across product-market scenarios.
	Information flow may become more complex due to dispersed collaborators.
	Different supply chain types are required for the same or similar products in different contexts.
	Suggestions:
	Increase the scope of vendor-managed inventory (VMI) and/or collaborative planning, forecasting, and replenishment (CPFR) in light of increased risk profiles.
	Leverage cloud computing technologies (or their replacement) to maximum capability in capturing and using information, as well as internally integrating supply and demand serving functions.
	Employ advanced technologies that sense changes in demand close to real time.
	Firms may need to retain consumer demographers and ethnographers to assist with end-user demand management and trends/forecasting.
	Develop global and local contingency plans for both inventory shortage *and surplus*.
	Shape demand through dynamic pricing and promotional strategies.

GSCF Process	Population Growth and Migration Implications
Manufacturing flow management (MFM)	Challenges: It's difficult to coordinate multinational flows into multiple facilities for production. Facility location models will under- or overestimate costs as demand shifts. Congestion and decaying infrastructure will create significant lead-time variability. Producing items to accommodate new market segments may require new materials and uncharted processes. Suggestions: Revise supply chain network designs (and use tools) for sensitivity to population dynamics. (Manufacture flexibly near demand locations, and be ready to shift.) Use short-term assets/leases/flexible operations, and focus on expected real estate costs. Forecast population expansion in critical locations, and invest in assets early. Avoid future/forecasted congestion bottlenecks when locating facilities. Seek public-private partnerships to develop infrastructure and security systems where demand is expected (rather than simply where it is now).
Order fulfillment (OF)	Challenges: Customers will place orders with greater assortment and volumes and will have higher service expectations. Cost-to-serve models will reveal many segments that are unprofitable or barely profitable in urban centers and rural areas. Shipping over distance may become nearly unfeasible if fuel prices persist upward and technology fails to keep pace.

GSCF Process	Population Growth and Migration Implications
Order fulfillment (OF) (continued)	Suggestions:
	Develop "flexworks" systems to react to demand and supply spikes in the short term.
	Urbanized vertical distribution cooperatives may ease the cost pains of localizing distribution in urban centers.
	Increased variability in product assortment inside geographic regions, when combined with expensive floor space, may require a "newsstand" fulfillment model with many touches/small shipments.
	Build fulfillment strategies that work well for both rural (rare) and urban (frequent) deliveries. May require a different blend of brick-and-click strategies than those used currently, based on geography.
	Invest strategically in pay-for-use cargo lanes early as they become available (and before prices settle).
Product development and commercialization (PD & C)	Challenges:
	It's difficult to implement early supplier involvement in design when SKUs are proliferating and within-line designs are highly differentiated.
	Ideation will necessarily need to involve multinational, multicultural teams.
	Sales force training, promotion planning, inventory deployment, and transportation planning will become necessary parts of the product design process, with integrated solutions required to compress costs.
	Suggestions:
	Collaborative technology for live-time design will reduce time and cost.
	Collaborate with advanced product engineering specialists for rapid prototyping and best-practice development.
	Phased global product rollouts will become standard and must be strategically based on input from all departments.
	Global flows for rollouts will necessarily include manufacturing, sourcing, and assembly at decentralized locations based on centralized planning.

GSCF Process	Population Growth and Migration Implications
Returns management (RM)	Challenges:
	Global cultures related to what constitutes a "normatively valid" return request will differ widely and require gatekeeping standardization.
	Disposition of reclaimed inventory will require many localized channels with managed relationships.
	Credit rules will vary widely based on local laws and norms.
	Suggestions:
	Take a clear position on what constitutes an acceptable return.
	Establish returns policies that stimulate customer confidence, but do not overburden the returns process.
	Understand your company's influence in the supply chain to garner suppliers' commitment to issue credits on returns.
	Recognize why customers are returning unwanted merchandise, and seek to remedy the problems.
	Flexworks should allow for misrouted or returned merchandise to reroute locally.
	Greater use of supplier chargebacks will alleviate credit pressures.
Supplier relationship management (SRM)	Challenges:
	It's difficult to develop long-term supplier relationships (especially in narrow commodity categories) due to demand fluctuations.
	It's difficult to leverage volume purchasing with a wider assortment and smaller SKU volumes.
	Supplier proliferation is a danger and can result in suboptimizing overall spending and compromising quality assessment.
	Increased competition for supply volume may disrupt continuity of supply.
	Supply/segment management teams may be geographically and/or culturally distant
	Total cost management may more frequently require considerations of global currency, tariff, and so on.

GSCF Process	Population Growth and Migration Implications
Supplier relationship management (SRM) (continued)	Suggestions:
	Supplier certification will be more complex but yield greater dividends due to geographic separation and supply competition.
	Manage supplier proliferation more frequently than traditional strategies via supply base audits.
	Focus on total cost of ownership even outside the strategic commodity category if quality and/or price are volatile.
	Make errors on the side of slightly longer contracts as needed, thereby swapping price risk for quantity risk.
	Create information connectivity/visibility wherever practical.

Population growth and migration present several distinct challenges to the process of customer relationship management. You might think that the greatest future challenges will rest with retailers and businesses that sell directly to consumers. We suggest that although these organizations will most certainly find themselves on the front lines of changing population dynamics, the reverberations will be felt throughout the supply chain to the point of raw-material extraction. Each organization's CRM process will reflect changes in customer tastes, volumes, and locations. These customers will bring not only distinctive tastes, but also their perspectives on how business should be conducted. This will require companies to be adaptive in the CRM process to negotiate terms that stray from convention.

Leading companies will also increasingly employ CRM software and powerful analytics to wade through the complexity of customer data. Although CRM software is primarily used today among retailers as they sort through consumer purchasing data, it will find increasing application in business-to-business settings, helping to illuminate trends, buyer tendencies, and market opportunities with distinct segments and individual customers. Firms operating in globally diverse markets and/or with widely assorted product lines will find it hard to do without.

In addition, companies' customer service management process will experience some of the greatest challenges with respect to addressing the macrotrend of population shifts. As the company's "face to the customer," this process will be forced to adapt to ever-increasing diversity of tastes, preferences, biases, and sensitivities. This translates into limitations on efficiency within company-customer interfaces. For instance, how many different languages must customer service personnel be prepared to accommodate? Beyond recognizing customer issues, how prepared are service representatives to address the problems? Although customer service expectations currently vary around the world, it seems probable that these will greatly homogenize and/or settle at the highest level of customer accommodation, which of course will become the global standard. Once excellent service is rendered in one company interaction in a particular setting, customers quickly become accustomed to heightened standards. It is unlikely that, in the globalized marketplace, many will be willing to settle for less.

Before they address customer service process issues, companies will experience growing pains as they try to better understand diverse customers and their expectations. What does a crisis look like for a given customer? What might be considered routine for one customer could be a major crisis for another. Supply chain executives will have to sort through the expectations, establish variable but appropriate service standards, and spell them out in the product-service agreements established with customers. This could present many challenges due to culture clashes and general lack of understanding from market to market. The leading supply chain companies will have boots on the ground in all key market venues, establishing systems to become prepared before full-scale penetration occurs.

Furthermore, forecasting changing consumer tastes as well as anticipating the quantities and locations of demand will prove challenging to companies that are fortunate to sell goods and services in emergent markets. More intensive sharing of sales data and promotional strategies among companies in the supply chain will feed complex forecasting models based on artificial intelligence/neural network platforms. These expert systems will incorporate the best of quantitative, data-driven techniques and blend the insights of managers and executives who closely watch the business.

Although firms must continue to seek improved forecasting techniques, companies gearing up for the future are also encouraged to devise more collaborative and flexible supply chains that reduce the dependence on forecasts. That is, more response-based systems will be devised in an effort to flex with the market dynamics. Supply chain initiatives like vendor-managed inventory (VMI) and collaborative planning, forecasting, and replenishment (CPFR) that put supply chain partners "on the same page" when it comes to fulfillment planning will gain great popularity. Yet beyond *responding* to changing demand, companies will employ more persuasive tactics to *shape* demand. By deploying tactics similar to Dell's "sell what you have" approach, companies will employ dynamic pricing and promotional strategies. This will direct customers toward products for which supply is great and away from items approaching stockout. Therefore, the options available to a customer at one point in time will likely change based on the supplier's ability to fill the order. Furthermore, as we have mentioned, the route the product will take from the plant to the end user depends on the supply chain assets most available at the time of order.

The manufacturing flow management and order fulfillment processes will face perhaps the greatest change of all the supply chain processes with the "population" macrotrend. Conventional practice in producing and distributing goods involves significant capital expenditures (CAPEX), with expectation of leveraging facilities for 20 or more years. Shifts in demand population will seriously challenge this convention in two primary ways. First, it will be difficult to acquire and sustain operations in the central business districts of growing cities. Property values, government restrictions, and congestion will combine to discourage companies from making significant "land grabs" in the cities. Rather, the downtowns will be regarded as safe havens for residential, office, and retail activity. Industrial activities like production and distribution will be relegated to the metropolitan periphery. Second, companies will be reluctant to assume mortgages on properties when the market landscape is changing in dramatic fashion. Companies will continue to entertain outsourcing (though not necessarily offshoring) through contract manufacturing and third-party logistics in an effort to alleviate this fixed-cost burden and provide greater flexibility. In fact, it is likely that large logistics providers will continue to expand their footprints in the supply chain, regularly performing value-added production activities close to the market.

Therefore, supply chain network designs will assume a very different character from their current composition, which embodies size and economies of scale as the driving forces. Flexibility and market access should supersede our fixation on cost economies, though flexibility will not be achieved "at any cost." Companies will become more open to flexworks and collaboration with outside parties—noncompetitors and competitors alike—to achieve a blend of high service and low costs. The opportunities for third parties to facilitate such collaborations on an independent, unbiased basis will be great.

The product development and commercialization process must devise the ever-growing assortment of products and services that a diverse market seeks. Gathering inputs for new products will require expanded channels of market data. Getting accurate "reads" on the market requires disparate sources. The company then must assess the market potential and determine which segments to pursue. This orientation is common today, but the level of difficulty will increase with rapidly changing demographics. Supply chain collaboration will prove essential for gathering product/service ideas and then executing a successful rollout.

The notion of centralized planning and decentralized execution in supply chain operations presents unique challenges in a hypersegmented market, where "one size fits one." The capacity of the centralized R&D department will be critical. Those stretched too thin will struggle greatly with the rapidly growing assortment of offerings. Companies will be forced to decide whether to pursue common product platforms that can be tailored to the individual needs of the local markets or to pursue a more decentralized strategy that affords local markets the opportunity to devise wholly unique offerings. It is safe to assume that costs will be higher under the latter scenario, yet the market relevance should be greater. These determinations will likely be made on a product-by-product and market-by-market basis.

As noted earlier, some portion of goods that are sold in the market are returned to the retailers, distributors, and manufacturers. These returned goods are sometimes welcomed (in the form of reusable or recyclable content) and other times they are not, as is the case with faulty goods, misused items, or simply buyer's remorse. Quite simply, returns are a fact of life. Supply chain managers should think about how to best accommodate their flow and generate financial return for the company. Too often, however, returns are regarded as an afterthought and a headache.

Population growth presents more than added volume to returns, but questions are associated with what qualifies as a "valid" return. Just as different cultures bring distinct expectations to the products they buy, it is possible, too, that they bring distinct expectations to the items they return. Can a well-used lawnmower be returned after a full season of use? If so, can the buyer seek a full or partial refund, a swap, or store credit? The answers are likely to vary depending on the market circumstances (the market's general expectations) and the value of the complaining customer. Companies must come to terms with how liberal they want their returns policies to be and the uniformity with which they want to apply those policies. A more liberal returns policy can boost top-line sales but also can increase costs and challenge bottom-line profits, so finding the right balance is key.

Although this scenario speaks primarily to consumer-to-business returns, the same determinations can be found in business-to-business returns. The company must decide how best to accommodate the acceptance guidelines, credit issuance, and efficient handling of returns for its business customers. For all accepted returns (consumer and business alike), it will become more critical than ever for the company to identify *why* unwanted returns are occurring. Is the product truly defective, or are customers ill-informed about the product's usage and performance? In the former case, steps should be taken to isolate the root cause of the defect and remedy the problem. In the latter case, perhaps the means by which the product is promoted and sold must be adjusted to better inform the customer. In the diverse markets of the 2020s and beyond, such opportunities for missteps are expected to increase dramatically, and a proliferation of global competition will be ready and available to pounce when failures arise.

A critical strategy for the future, then, will be to build appropriate and highly impactful relationships with supply chain partners. The implications for supplier relationship management reflect a composite of the many forces applied to the other seven business processes.

Given changing demand patterns, the array of suppliers with which the company interacts is likely to increase. Measures should be taken, however, to distinguish the most critical suppliers and to seek their assistance in absorbing the risks your company faces. Risk absorption might come in the form of flexible volume arrangements, commitments to rapid ramp-up, or product take-back agreements. To attain such provisions, it is probable that longer-term commitments will be sought from these "choice" suppliers. Given the amount of effective risk transfer found in these arrangements, it will be considered a good investment.

A "team" orientation with choice suppliers will manifest not only in supporting the quality and volume needs of the focal company, but also in harvesting market intelligence that the supplier can provide and through the innovation of products and processes. Product development and commercialization can be aided by the dedication of suppliers to providing product and market insights that can drive new growth. Furthermore, it should be noted that companies that choose to outsource production and distribution activities expand the responsibility of the SRM process, with transfers occurring from "making" provisions to "buying" them. When outsourcing becomes the preferred strategy, responsibilities shift from doing the work to managing the work. As the prospects for outsourcing (again, not necessarily offshoring) increase with serving a more diverse market, the scope of SRM activity will increase in kind.

Of course, these issues represent only a portion of those that the supply chain manager of the future will face. Other issues that emerged as we discussed our findings with executives were informative because they elicited additional questions but relatively few answers. Perhaps most interesting (and, in some cases, worrisome) were the questions related to the need to sustain an adequate rural presence in the face of burgeoning urbanization. To wit, what will become of the remaining rural areas in terms of supply of necessary products and services? How will supply chain systems be designed to serve a very small number of highly critical people living in outlying areas, especially given the expected rising fuel costs of the coming years? These are among the issues we will discuss and debate as the book moves on.

3

Global Connectivity and Socioeconomic Leveling

Whether you are a top-level executive or an undergraduate business student, chances are you have heard the term BRIC. The acronym stands for Brazil, Russia, India, and China. These countries are grouped not only because of their landmass and population size, but also because they share similar economic development characteristics and occupy comparable positions in the industrialization process. These nations do not yet occupy the same economic status as the United States, Germany, Japan, and other highly developed industrialized nations. However, the BRIC countries are poised for steep productivity growth—especially when you consider the rapidly accelerating conditions fostering local consumerism.

Consider Brazil, the country described by the acronym's first letter. With 192 million citizens, Brazil is the world's fifth-largest country in terms of population, behind only China, India, the United States, and Indonesia. Brazil is developing as an economic power because its massive population has become a vital consumer base for the world's goods and services. Its citizens' willingness to consume was tacitly recognized when the nation was named host of the world's two largest athletics competitions: the 2014 FIFA World Cup and the 2016 Summer Olympics. That makes it the first South American country ever to host both events, let alone having them back-to-back. Viewing FIFA's and the International Olympic Committee's historical choices, South American countries have in recent times been a relatively unpopular destination for the games. Yet Brazil's staggering economic growth has certainly changed their minds, and it's likely that soon, sports won't be the only thing feeling the country's commercial influence.

Economists dating as far back as Aristotle suggest that the leveling of a population's economic status is key to sustaining a healthy economy. Leveling represents the narrowing of a nation's monetary distribution such that more people have significant consumption power. Generally, this means that the state in question has a large, burgeoning, economically viable middle class. That's because, when customers enter their country's middle class, they tend to consume high-status goods at increased rates. To say that contemporary Brazil's middle class meets all of those criteria would be an understatement. In late 2011, the Brazilian government reported that its middle class had expanded to 95 million people. That's half of its entire population. Much of that growth occurred from 1999 to 2009, when 31 million people entered its middle class. Economists anticipate that, by 2014, just five years later, another 20 million Brazilians will achieve the same financial power.[1]

Brazil's middle class isn't just large—it's economically powerful. The Brazilian middle class holds an astonishing 46.24% of the national population's purchasing power. This statistic alone poses a slew of supply chain management issues as companies around the world are rushing to meet the nascent market's demands. The middle class also possesses 70% of the country's credit cards, and with credit so widely available, the demand for more statured goods is bound to grow. We also cannot ignore that, of all Brazilian Internet users, the middle class accounts for 80% of them, and many are shopping online. Just as American automakers of the last decade learned that they could not survive without competing in China, the online Brazilian market could emerge as the next consumer frontier. Companies that want to serve it need to understand its game-changing potential.

Brazil is just one example of global economic leveling happening today. Its middle-class income bracket alone is larger than most countries' entire populations. With more discretionary income at their disposal, more credit at their fingertips, and widespread Internet accessibility, it is inevitable that consumption will continue to surge.

---

[1] Tarrisse, Isabel. (2010). "Brazilian Middle Class Reaches 95 Million, Represents Over Half of Population." Brasil.gov Press Releases. Secretariat of Strategic Affairs of the Presidency of Brazil (SAE). "Brazil's middle class in numbers." (2010). Brasil.gov Press Releases.

But Brazil is not the only nation where economic leveling is happening. Internet proliferation is yielding worldwide access to product and service information. Whereas many international markets traditionally have been characterized by localized production and consumption, this kind of accessibility gives us reason to believe that their future counterparts will be much more globalized. If they do, globalized markets and growing populations will begin to unravel the assumptions that underpin our current supply chain systems. These forces will geographically scatter demand around the globe and thereby require longer, more sophisticated supply chains to balance supply and demand.

However, not everyone agrees that the world economies are, or will be, as globalized as some predict. Before we begin to address the supply chain challenges of the future, we need to understand the two most prominent perspectives of the globalization argument.

Is Globalization Real?

Since the United States' Industrial Revolution and then throughout much of the 1900s, the global economy was structured as somewhat of an oligarchy. A small number of nations produced the bulk of the world's goods and services, consumed the most finished products, expended the most natural resources, and held the most significant wealth. This was the world economy as most of our parents and grandparents knew it, and it was stable in this form for nearly a century. The preponderance of global commercial activity revolved around North America and a few European countries, with Japan bursting onto the scene in the latter part of the 20th century. Lesser economic presences were also emerging in South America and the Middle East's more developed nations, and Australia was also showing signs of life in international commerce. Even at the end of the 1900s, as shown in Figure 3.1, a very small percentage of the world's 200-plus nations represented almost all of its consumption and demand. In most cases, markets were still localized, and although global trade had always played a role (albeit limited), the vast majority of the world's commercial activity could be described as domestic.

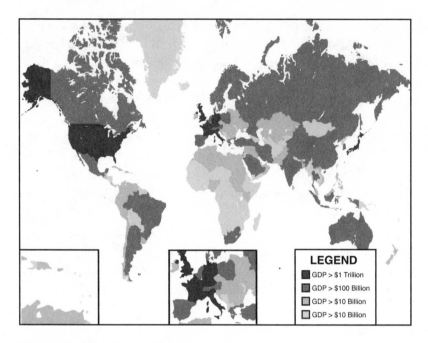

Figure 3.1 Global GDP, 1995–2000 means

Just before the turn of the 21st century, though, a number of extraneous forces converged to revolutionize global commerce. First, as described in Chapter 2, "Global Population Growth and Migration," many nations' populations began to grow nonlinearly and nonuniformly, with some nations rapidly outgrowing others due to organic growth, migratory growth, or both. At the same time, significant geopolitical barriers were falling, buyers and sellers were being granted greater market access via the Internet and global connectivity, and services were being outsourced—first to other companies and then to other countries. Suddenly, as shown in Figure 3.2, many more nations established global economic presence where it hadn't existed before, the BRIC countries among them.

Interestingly, these forces affected different nations in different ways. India suddenly became prosperous because of its population's connection with Western business ideals (often learned in Western business schools), as well as its citizens' willingness to work for wages much lower than those overseas. Eastern Europe became a viable commercial node after the Berlin Wall fell in 1989, and despite its lower-educated workforce, the region thrived because of its cost advantages. Technology made outsourcing to low-cost nations possible because workers could communicate in real time with their overseas employers. Outsourcing to these regions thus became a viable business strategy, but the work outsourced from one place to another would differ based on the labor pool's educational attainment. (Some nations could perform more socially sophisticated customer service management tasks, whereas others would be hired to perform labor-intensive manufacturing.)

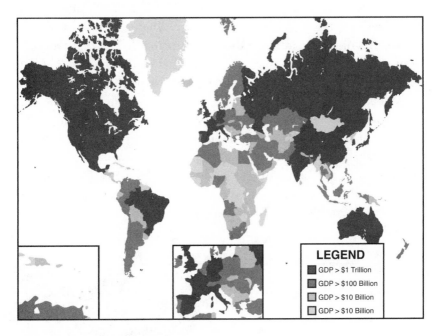

Figure 3.2 Global GDP, 2011

Thomas Friedman's 2000s books, *The World Is Flat* and *Hot, Flat, and Crowded*, fueled much public discussion about the forces that brought about these aspects of business globalization. In the books, which were highly touted by business leaders and regular readers alike, Friedman made several seemingly uncontroversial claims related to the world's rapidly increasing interconnectedness. In a nutshell, he associated Internet-enabled technologies like file sharing, weblogs, workflow software, Voice over Internet, and "Googling" with the aforementioned outsourcing and geopolitical smoothing trends. He concluded that these forces were responsible for radically decreasing the previous century's economic isolationism barriers. Friedman admitted that his writings' purpose had little to do with how to conduct global business activity per se. But many of the world's economists agreed with his basic premise: As technology diffused around the world and leveled the playing field, economic prosperity would soon follow in the nations and regions that best harnessed it.

Does evidence support Friedman's position? In the early 2000s, did the world suddenly become "hot," "flat," and/or "crowded"? At first glance, it would certainly seem so; we have already conceded the "crowded" aspect, and Chapter 4, "The Changing Physical Environment," has plenty to say about the Earth's being "hot." When we study Figure 3.3, we can see that, over the past two decades or so, GDP changes have been greatest in the areas encompassing BRIC nations, as well as some areas of sub-Saharan Africa. We could conclude that the world's economies were—and still are—rapidly leveling. The nations that were formerly economically powerful (those with the darkest shading in Figure 3.1) appear to be stagnating rather than growing at (remarkably) the same time as the new economic powers are taking flight. It only makes sense, then, that Friedman's lexicon is mostly true, and that the world could indeed become "flat" if it is not already. Right?

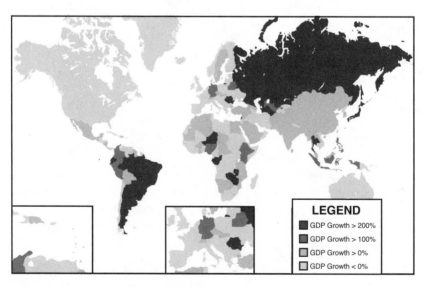

Figure 3.3 Change in GDP, 1995–2010

Alas, Friedman's work has not escaped criticism. Several authors opposed to his ideals soon joined the literary fray, armed with the one weapon they claimed Friedman lacked: hard data. Almost immediately following the 2005 publication of *The World Is Flat*, magazine columnist and George Mason University professor Richard Florida, along with some of his geographic science colleagues, illustrated the fallacies that can arise when conducting economic analyses of globalization using growth percentages instead of absolute numbers. Florida and his colleagues published an article in *The Atlantic* magazine. They pointed out that although populations are growing and technology is spreading to new parts of the world (especially those within Figure 3.3's darker shaded areas), these types of growth were not actually yielding much economic production or consumption. Nor did these areas produce noticeable patent or scientific citation growth, two of the leading indicators of economic development. In fact, the analysis performed by Florida et al. showed plainly that although economic activity was beginning to accelerate in developing nations, these countries had started off far behind their predecessors in terms of rote productivity and consumption. Their implication was that even quick and sizable growth would do little to meaningfully close the gap between the traditional powers and developing economies, at least in the near future. The authors were convinced that Friedman's globalization idea was essentially an anecdotally driven myth, but they did suggest that it was useful to consider as more meaningful development continued to occur.

Subsequent reviews of the Friedman school of thought arrived at similar conclusions. His two books became the focal point of scholarly circles' harsh criticism, which culminated when Harvard business professor Pankaj Ghemawat published *World 3.0* in 2011. In this book, Ghemawat proposed that the business world is not as globalized as many contemporary thinkers would like to believe. Citing data drawn from a variety of public sources, Ghemawat develops a compelling argument that positions the globalization conversation spurred by the Friedman books (and their advocates in the punditry) as nothing more than media hype. In so arguing, Ghemawat noted that only 17% to 18% of Internet traffic crosses international borders, that the world economy's export-to-GDP ratio is but 20%, and only about 20% of all equity investment is international. These statistics are far below what a Friedman proponent might expect. As a result, Ghemawat contended that the 2009 world could best be construed as "semiglobalized." Therefore, business entities needed to consider strategies that leveraged both national homogeneity *and* international differences to prosper abroad.

As authors of a book about managing the supply chains of the future, we are most interested in the current status and future trajectory of global demand and supply. The evidence presented by Friedman's detractors—Florida, Ghemawat, and numerous others—distills to a compelling argument against the current existence of a fully globalized world. But it is also entirely possible that history may judge Friedman as being more right than wrong, with the lone delinquent factor simply being the amount of time it will take for the world to achieve true global integration. With our interest piqued by this possibility, we conducted one more analysis, the results of which are shown in Figure 3.4. Here, we extended the most recent 15-year growth curve another 15 years into the future. That is, we took 2010's absolute GDP (the same data used to compose Figure 3.2) and applied the most recent population and GDP growth data available to see what might happen if the current state of affairs continued in straight-line fashion.

The results, and their implications for future supply chain managers, are quite interesting. Several modern international powers—like the United States and Canada, Europe, and the BRIC countries—could be expected to sustain their growth or stagnate, with China overtaking the United States as having the world's highest GDP. Many countries that surround these areas also see impressive gains. Take a look at the islands between the Pacific and Indian Oceans. While many of these had a GDP above $100 billion in 2011, by 2025 our projections show them to have surpassed the $1 trillion mark. The Middle East, South America, and Africa are also expected to sustain their impressive numbers.

Though the 2012 edition of planet Earth should not be construed as fully globalized by any stretch of the imagination, the forces Friedman described do seem to be having at least a marginal impact on global commerce, only a few years after his books' emergence. Furthermore, based on our own, very conservative forecasts, it appears that incremental increases over the next 15 years could reveal a "new world order" in terms of economic activity. Children in nations formerly disregarded as economic also-rans are witnessing consumerism as the Information Age provides worldwide consumers access to all kinds of product and service information. Like Friedman, we are speaking anecdotally, but consider that in some places in Africa, kids are introduced to cellular devices before their village even has physical infrastructure. Since there's also no electricity, they walk miles to charging stations and pay to recharge their phones.[2] In these parts of the world, technology is outpacing many other modern developments, and intermediate developments are being leapfrogged as the most advanced technologies show up in the most remote villages. Therefore, a new consumer generation is growing up around the world with perspectives toward consumption that businesses never would have dreamed possible before the turn of the century.

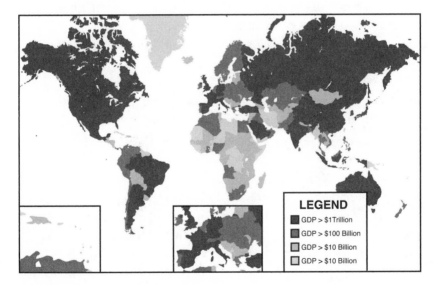

Figure 3.4 Global GDP, 2025 (projected)

[2] Steele, Chandra. (11 May 2012). "How the Mobile Phone Is Evolving in Developing Countries." PCMag.com.

Of course, any change in global economic power that will influence global demand patterns will also increase the strains on the world's natural resources and process inventories—things that are already under great pressure. In China, consumer beef eating has made water more scarce than usual, because beef takes a great deal more water to produce than rice and vegetables. Despite the fact that China has constructed over 85,000 reservoirs in the last 60 years, nearly 400 of its 600 largest cities suffer from water shortages. This trend can only continue as China's growing middle class demands more beef, more produce, and more of other natural resources. Therefore, these products must be produced in and/or moved from places with production excesses to places where shortages commonly occur. As a result of its problems, China has turned to high-quality beef exports from the South American country of Uruguay to sate its demand.[3] McDonald's has set a goal of having 2,000 restaurants in China by 2013 (as of 2011, it had 1,356). The fast food giant will look to Australian suppliers—not U.S.-based ones—to get beef for its Chinese restaurants.[4]

We see one big question—and it's one of our prevailing themes. What if one day every child in every developing country grows up wanting cheeseburgers, flat-screen TVs, and other production outputs their parents and grandparents never had access to and maybe never even dreamed of owning? What will this mean for the companies charged with delivering those goods in the right form, at the right place, and at the right time via their global supply chains?

We need look no further than the Middle Eastern country of Pakistan for a hint of the future. As of 2011, the Pakistani middle class accounted for 35% of the nation's population, or approximately 63 million people. Fascinatingly, the Pakistani median age is 21.1 years, which is far younger than the world median of about 28 years. Given this expanding and surprisingly youthful middle class, we would expect a different kind of Pakistani consumer to emerge—one who will have the most disposable income in his or her national history. When considered in aggregate, these new consumers would represent

---

[3] Peters, Mike. (25 June 2012). "China's appetite grows for meat from Uruguay." *China Daily: USA.*

[4] "Australian beef farmers set to benefit from McDonald plans to expand in China." (17 August 2011). MercoPress: South Atlantic News Agency.

a suddenly viable market segment possessing wealth not unlike that of modern-day Netherlands or the Czech Republic. As exuberant new consumers, the Pakistani middle class is starting to consume goods that reflect their youthful demand. In 2011, Pakistan saw sales volume and import increases in TVs (+28.6%), automobiles (+14.6%), and fast-moving consumer goods (+9.3%) versus its previous three-year period.[5]

In Nigeria, Ethiopia, and Egypt, African nations already among the world's top 15 most populous, converging GDP and population factors are slowly developing them into global consumer forces to be reckoned with. African incomes have yet to catch up to those of other developing countries, but many of today's Africans do have dispensable income—and, as with Pakistan, they are becoming experts at spending it. As of 2012, nearly 343 million Africans were considered middle class. Only four short years ago, they spent $830 billion on consumer goods alone, and that rate continues to grow. The International Monetary Fund predicts that, by 2030, these highly populated African countries will spend $2.2 trillion dollars a year.[6] Yet few global companies are ready and able to serve customers in these places. And the anecdotal evidence we collected from managerial interviews in preparing for this book suggests that the leaders of companies headquartered in developed nations are struggling to consider—even deigning to believe—that markets such as Pakistan, Egypt, Ethiopia, Nigeria, and even Paraguay will always present economically viable opportunities, even when more fertile masses of potential customers are nearby.

We believe that modern global firms ignore such nations at their own peril, and that the way to succeed in these kinds of markets is through adequate forethought related to supply chain design. Although the world is not yet flat, it *is* flattening, and modern companies need to start developing plans to serve an ever-broadening customer base if they want to remain prosperous.

---

[5] Ahsan, Afnan. (May 2011). "Business and the Middle Class in Pakistan." Planning Commission: Government of Pakistan. "Pakistan: Framework for Economic Growth." Planning Commission: Government of Pakistan.

[6] Hatch, Grant, Pieter Becker, and Michelle van Zyl. (2011). "The Dynamic African Consumer Market: Exploring Growth Opportunities in Sub-Saharan Africa." Accenture.

The forecasted interconnectedness of the world's commercial systems presents a multitude of challenges for managers seeking to deliver products optimized for efficiency and effectiveness. Many factors are affecting demand in previously infertile markets due to two forces in concert with the aforementioned population changes: Internet proliferation in places where it was previously largely inaccessible, and disposable income influxes to these same places as a result of increased GDP.

While Internet commerce and dot-com companies were exploding onto the international scene in the 2000s, Africa was only just receiving the technology that would make access to the World Wide Web possible. It wasn't until 2009 that African-owned Seacom installed an undersea fiber-optic cable that connected East Africa to Europe and parts of Asia.[7] Meanwhile, in southern Africa, the broadband market is woefully underserviced but still expects to haul in $19.08 billion by 2017,[8] a 405% increase from 2010.[9] In fact, in the period between 2000 and 2011, the percentage of Africa's population on the Internet increased by 2,988%. This usage statistic tops all continents, but other areas, like South America and the Middle East (regions with notable growth in Figures 3.1 through 3.4), aren't far behind. Africa still makes up only 6.2% of the world's Internet users, as shown in Figure 3.5. Nevertheless, its astronomical growth, combined with GDP and population projections, shows that the Internet will bring wealth to these countries, which will, in turn, encourage the Internet's further propagation.

What will Internet propagation mean for companies seeking to do business over the next quarter century? Many businesses, especially smaller ones, have always been localized and will continue to be. But for the majority of commercial enterprises, the Internet represents the best, and perhaps lone, source of worldwide demand generation. Until the early 2000s, shopping was almost strictly a local

---

[7] "East Africa gets high speed web." (23 July 2009). BBC News.

[8] Miniwatts Marketing Group. (2012). "Internet Users in the World." Internet World Stats.

[9] Moyo, Admire. (13 July 2012). "Southern African broadband market to hit $19bn." ITWeb: Enterprise.

phenomenon. But just a decade later, we now search for goods world-wide—and can compare specifications, quality, and prices of offerings located continents apart in seconds. Notwithstanding the extent to which this capability has reduced businesses' ability to commit consumer arbitrage, these issues have massive implications for global supply chain design. After all, it's one thing to find buyers for your goods in a faraway country. It's another thing entirely to develop an economically viable capability to serve them with the accuracy, speed, and service that match their down-the-street retailer.

2011 Worldwide Internet Users

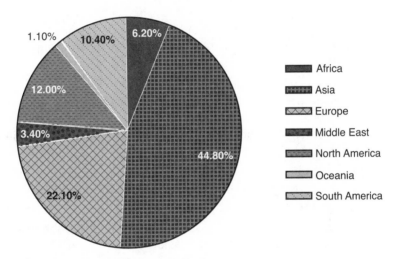

Figure 3.5 Worldwide Internet users, 2011

We believe that prominent demand shifts will happen as a function of population growth, Internet access, and the accruing wealth in traditionally dormant markets around the world. Based on these factors, we can deduce that supply and demand are poised to drastically slip out of alignment in the foreseeable future in locations like Brazil, Pakistan, Egypt, Nigeria, and Paraguay, among others. Each of the eight GSCF supply chain processes therefore is susceptible to risks associated with global economic leveling. We will address them in turn.

Economic Leveling and Connectivity Issues for Future Supply Chain Managers

As we have noted, the balancing of supply and demand is both precarious and essential to business success. Populations are growing and migrating, but they are also becoming more interconnected and economically level. Along with the leveling of production and consumption power comes a leveling of consumer expectations for what constitutes quality products and service. We see the following as key issues related to the connectivity and leveling of global demand centers, for consideration in supply chain planning efforts in the forthcoming years:

- Developing a significant online selling presence will be almost mandatory to succeed in mature or highly competitive industries.

- Customers will become more homogenous worldwide in terms of tastes, preferences, and price sensitivity as time goes on. They will be less homogenous within populations, nations, and segments in the short term, therefore requiring greater assortment.

- Many products will become commoditized earlier in the life cycle, so competition based on logistics and supply chain services will serve as a critical differentiator.

- Global visibility of offerings will require the expansion of supply chain networks into places never before considered and will lead to some of the few remaining growth opportunities in goods industries.

We differentiate the issues related specifically to increased global consumerism and connectedness from those that are associated purely with population ecology. Future supply chain managers are advised to consider these issues in supply chain network design and demand planning to better effectuate DSI. Table 3.1 lists each process and describes its potential implications.

Table 3.1 Global Connectivity and Economic Leveling Implications for SCM

GSCF Process	Global Connectivity/Economic Implications
Customer relationship management (CRM)	Challenges: Customer segmentation within new and emerging nations will be challenging to interpret and execute. Matching the optimal product mixes to different global settings will require much research and understanding of local/domestic cultures. While demand for products around the world will become more homogeneous, challenges will remain in conducting business across different cultures, languages, and standards. Traditions of competition and differing legal systems in foreign markets may make collaboration and relationship management difficult concepts to execute. Many transaction-based economies may be unfamiliar with the ideas and practice of supply chain management across multiple firms. Suggestions: Customer segmentation will have to consider both current and anticipated future spending growth in addition to design tastes. Use current and future data mining and artificial intelligence technologies to analyze and isolate profitable target markets abroad. Benchmarking across cultures and in-depth research in the new market will reveal new segments and opportunities and help match the right product/service to new segments. Training employees in the cultures, languages, and business traditions of emerging economies will open doors to new relationships and build business opportunities. Educating partner firms in the new markets on supply chain concepts and practices will help them evolve into effective partners. Product and service agreements should be short-term and simplistic until new global relationships evolve to maturity. Companies that are quickest to learn how to sell effectively in radically different markets will gain advantage.

GSCF Process	Global Connectivity/Economic Implications
Customer service management (CSM)	Challenges:
	Customer service strategies must accommodate the unique requirements of a growing and increasingly demanding middle class in many new markets.
	Response procedures for service disruptions will prove difficult to establish across distinct cultures and business systems.
	Demanding customers from foreign cultures will be intolerant of trial-and-error in efforts to remedy service problems.
	Legal systems in emerging economies may not support or may be in conflict with traditional Western business concepts such as warranties, liability, insurance, terms of sale, and guarantees.
	Suggestions:
	Understand the criticality of customer service and the forms of service expected in each market setting.
	Devise customer service expertise that is specific to each new market, in accordance with provisions established through the customer relationship management process.
	Build customer service call center procedures tailored to meet the cultural and legal requirements of emerging market segments. Include technologies that can automate and tailor solutions for a vast array of market differences.
	Recruit and educate service personnel staff who can serve different cultures and respond flexibly to changing demands.
	Conduct customer service audits early and often upon entering new markets to gain a foothold on successes and respond effectively to failures.
Demand management (DM)	Challenges:
	Anticipating demand in wholly new markets is particularly difficult because historical data is lacking.
	Demand variability will be great across an array of emerging markets in different geographic locations with different infrastructures, business traditions, and expectations.
	The reliability of information flows can be questionable in emerging markets, creating more variability and costly inventories to protect against shortfalls.

GSCF Process	Global Connectivity/Economic Implications
Demand management (DM) (continued)	Supply chain planning may be strained across disparate locations for supply, production, and logistics, increasing the need for additional resources and time to plan properly.
	Supply chain flexibility is challenged when distribution operations stretch over large geographic areas. Long delivery lead times may make it difficult to rapidly transition to a change in demand.
	Suggestions:
	Building and improving grassroots systems for collecting and disseminating demand information for new markets will be critical to matching demand and supply in highly variable environments.
	To improve information flow about demand, ensure that the lines of communication are as expedient and reliable as possible. This could mean investing in improved information systems technology that can transcend language and connectivity difficulties associated with emerging markets.
	Marketing strategies will need to be constructed with existing or planned supply chain assets more in mind; you can't sell what you can't deliver profitably.
	Flexible procurement and production systems will have to be implemented to respond to increasing and highly variable demand-and-supply situations.
	Forecasts must be changed and adapted frequently to assess the status and health of emerging new markets in realistic terms.
	Do not enter new markets without establishing a thorough procedure to synchronize supply and demand planning, including allocating additional market-specific resources to the task.
	Contingency management systems will have to be extremely robust to quickly respond to increased demand variability and to fulfill service expectations with minimal disruptions. Artificial intelligence systems may be used to recognize changes in demand patterns and implement fulfillment actions without human intervention.

GSCF Process	Global Connectivity/Economic Implications
Manufacturing flow management (MFM)	Challenges: Economies of scale can prove elusive in manufacturing for emerging markets. Producing in distant locations will challenge flexible accommodation of market demand. Implementing "pull" strategies in centrally located manufacturing facilities distant from markets is less attainable. Emerging markets will experience growing regulations that can prove disparate from nation to nation. Global standards in manufacturing capabilities will vary greatly when operations are established in several different settings. Suggestions: In absence of economies of scale, look to manufacture different, yet similar products in a single facility to gain economies of scope. Explore regional manufacturing and distribution strategies that group similar production requirements and needs in a single regional location. Consider decentralized management systems that can concentrate on and tailor solutions for varying regions, including becoming experts in meeting different legal and regulatory requirements in emerging markets. Employ strategies that best accommodate the local market conditions, with an understanding of profit contribution and potential associated with different strategies. Manufacturing flexibility will prove critical in accommodating different market needs and ramping up volumes in fast-growing markets. Employ metrics that measure flexibility in volumes and product type. Use standard processes and equipment with limited automation to ensure a wide range of upside and downside production flexibility in manufacturing plants. Establish global best practices, and ensure that they are shared and implemented where appropriate.

GSCF Process	Global Connectivity/Economic Implications
Order fulfillment (OF)	Challenges:
	Logistics and transportation networks are lacking or deficient in many untapped markets.
	Urban congestion and insufficient infrastructure may prevent reaching new customers in emerging markets.
	Rules and regulations for distribution and transport can vary widely across settings.
	Economies of scale gained through large distribution lot sizes can prove elusive in serving emerging markets.
	Long transportation links result in long lead times and high variability.
	Data standards can vary across regions and national settings.
	Suggestions:
	Build new logistics delivery networks to new and often austere locations in emerging markets.
	Understand the market's transportation, storage, and distribution regulations. Hire local experts, as needed, to ensure compliance and track necessary data elements.
	Provide input to the CRM team to inform and influence order fulfillment aspects of product-service agreements.
	Abandon traditional order fulfillment practices that lack transferability and appropriate application in the new market.
	Benchmark performance against key competitors.
Product development and commercialization (PD & C)	Challenges:
	Customers with different tastes and interests seek distinct products that meet their unique needs.
	Companies often seek to apply uniform strategies for product development and commercialization in disparate locations.
	Companies often believe that they can change the local culture and overestimate their ability to impose their will on the market.
	Costs can vary greatly from setting to setting, making it difficult to determine a single best way to approach the market.

GSCF Process	Global Connectivity/Economic Implications
Product development and commercialization (PD & C) (continued)	Suggestions: Develop competence in market sensing. Understand customers across settings, including using virtual and pattern recognition technologies to differentiate product and service needs. Leverage the Internet to ascertain market developments and trends; including establishing culturally distinct websites and interactive portals for product development in emerging markets. Seek out and employ local expertise in product development and commercialization efforts. Utilize in-country test markets and prototypes to reduce the risk of rollouts. Trade and sell information on how to produce products in situations where local manufacturing capabilities exist and only a limited logistics footprint is desired. Explore local alternatives for production and distribution. Balance against the loss of control and centralization.
Returns management (RM)	Challenges: Since returns are often managed as an afterthought, standards and procedures for accepting returns are lacking. Difficulties in forecasting demand can result in excess inventories that are often returned to vendors. Rules and regulations can vary for the collection, storage, and handling of used materials and end-of-life products. Many emerging economies lack sufficient waste-management systems and may not have established reverse supply chain procedures or policies. Suggestions: Understand how returns fit into the business strategy in serving the focal market. Be proactive and assertive in stating what qualifies as an acceptable return. Establish the terms of credit for returns, and implement returns policies in the CRM process. Identify secondary markets in the emerging economies that do not dilute the primary market and forward supply chain.

GSCF Process	Global Connectivity/Economic Implications
Returns management (RM) (continued)	Devise reverse-logistics systems that serve customers and ensure the best possible value yield for the company.
	Develop and build reverse-logistics systems in emerging economies where they do not exist, including the use of futuristic collection devices such as interactive kiosks and robotic collection vehicles to collect products and materials and the end of use.
	Recapture, recycle, and reuse scarce materials and resources in emerging economies where lacking waste management systems have failed to do so in the past.
Supplier relationship management (SRM)	Challenges:
	Sourcing strategies must include new and different criteria for supplier evaluation based on geographic reach and diversity in local tastes.
	Supply bases will almost necessarily grow in complexity due to striations in local demand by price and quality.
	Supplier relationships will be critical for gaining knowledge of local markets and will not be completely controlled by the focal firm.
	Suggestions:
	Apply logic similar to that employed in CRM to study and segment customers to the SRM process for suppliers.
	Incorporate key suppliers of services into the SRM, PDC, and MFM processes.
	Seek the advice of suppliers that are versed in conducting business in the markets of interest.
	Devise agreements with suppliers that minimize the risks associated with entering new markets and that leverage the local development of supply solutions.
	Reward suppliers that prove effective in supporting market successes and managing risks.
	Invest in and encourage the development of new supply sources and methods by local suppliers, including the development of technologies to discover and create new materials.
	Due to the dynamic changes and growth in emerging markets, picking the initial set of strategic supply partners is critical. Companies should be prepared for relationships to evolve over time as demand changes.

Customer relationship management is at the forefront of addressing globalization and socioeconomic leveling. As supply chain managers learn to conduct business among an emerging set of nations, they will be forced to adapt to new ways of approaching markets and the prospective customers that embody these markets. Western companies cannot expect that their counterparts will embrace the beliefs and practices that are brought to the conversation, nor should the non-Western companies simply roll over; their emergence among the global business elite validates them. Rather, a convergence of values, priorities, understanding, and practices will spell victory for firms trying to navigate a flatter world.

Calculating where to place speculative bets in prospective customer relationships presents the greatest challenge. Companies will face countless such investment opportunities, but knowing with whom to work closely and develop extensive, mutually intensive relationships is key. Rather than relying on historical precedent, supply chain managers will be pressured to identify choice prospects among the masses. Beyond sales and profit potential, however, "choice" customers are those that offer the best competitive position and allure through their influence in the market. They will possess knowledge, technology, and other valuable resources. They will prove compatible as business partners, but they may require considerable development and investment. To wade through these complex determinations, companies must employ advanced methods of data mining and artificial intelligence analytics to isolate the most promising targets for pursuit.

Conducting business with companies in emerging markets will be ripe with uncertainties, however, because the sheer number of unforeseeable circumstances in working with new partners could prove debilitating. The customer service management process will be forced to imagine the realms of possibilities and identify prospective issues in product and service provisions for which no precedent exists. That said, product-service agreements must be entered into with one's eyes wide open, understanding that close relationships will call for extensive handholding with customers. Beyond the basic provisions, the firm must be prepared to offer knowledge about navigating complex regulations, different languages, currency risks, divergent terms of trade, assorted or nonexistent information systems, and a host of cultural differences.

The more extensive the relationship, the higher the stakes and the more that can go wrong, so the need to act on customer knowledge and appreciate the risks involved is clear. Yet here too, advanced information technologies can aid the cause by providing databases populated with essential customer data that supports responsive, attentive service. Supply chain event management systems should be employed to detect small departures from acceptable service parameters before they result in major problems and complaints. Beyond merely dealing with problems when they occur, however, you can use simulation technologies to conduct scenario planning.

Among the most anticipated scenarios is the imbalance in supply and demand. With consumption on the rise, patience with shortages and stockouts will be minimal. Demand management will place a premium on flexibility, because forecasts will be highly susceptible to error in new markets. Positioning inventory in the emerging market can be costly and, by its mere presence, can discourage a company from gaining intimate knowledge of customer issues and buying habits. Rather than leveraging inventory as an insurance policy, companies are encouraged to collect and disseminate critical demand information. Information technologies can help here, too, but companies are encouraged to develop grassroots understanding of market matters and individual customers. This understanding can be leveraged in improved forecasting techniques. The qualitative inputs of people on the ground and close to the market will prove most adaptive to rapidly changing markets, as opposed to relying on data-driven methods that emphasize historical market developments.

All companies can expect, however, that it will take some time to gain comfort in newly emerged markets. The flexibility espoused by the demand management process will be called on to close the gap of demand management capabilities. Along those lines, flexibility in manufacturing is central to providing supply chain flexibility. Yet manufacturing products in distant locations complicates flexible response to disparate market needs, because variety in products and packs overwhelms most production systems. Manufacturing systems designed for large-volume production and bulk packaging struggle when facing a completely different set of market circumstances. Consider, for instance, North American health and beauty supply manufacturers accustomed to producing shampoo in 23-ounce bottles. This quantity might supply a typical North American consumer for a month or longer. However, the manufacturer finds that consumers in India prefer to buy shampoo in single-use packets, and they are willing to pay only a few pennies. Rigid manufacturing systems designed to produce large lot sizes will struggle to accommodate the Indian market—particularly if production occurs half a world away. The transportation cost alone from a factory any distance from the local market would usurp the expected purchase price. Yet production in the local market is challenged by a lacking production infrastructure, dwindling water resources (as described previously), and frequent power outages. The widespread blackouts that occurred on two consecutive days in July 2012 wiped out power for more than half of India's 1.2 million-person population.

The question of *where* to manufacture products to serve emerging markets will continue to challenge companies. Though manufacturing is among the most value-intensive steps in the supply chain, companies over the past two decades have searched far and wide for the lowest-cost location in which to perform these operations. Often they outsource to distant locations. Low-cost locations are defined largely by the cost of labor. U.S. firms sought the skills and favorable economics of Mexican labor in the latter years of the 20th century. More recently, China has become the manufacturing center for everything from whimsical tchotchkes to high-tech consumer electronics like the Apple iPhone. A study conducted by AMR Research indicates, however, that 56% of supply chain executives surveyed indicated that the total landed costs of their products increased markedly as a result of offshore operations.[10] This result can be attributed to the increasing cost of doing business in China associated with rising labor costs, higher material costs, and appreciation in the Chinese currency. Along with these direct economic movements, the added complexities involved, and longer and more variable lead times, losses

---

[10] "How Hybrid Sourcing Can Lower Costs." (1 March 2011). *Materials Handling & Logistics*.

in visibility and control combine to increase inventory holdings and impair service.

The future will hold some fascinating developments that could offset these forces. Expect the formation of regionally tailored manufacturing campuses, designed with excellent manufacturing flexibility, to accommodate different market needs and ramp up volumes in fast-growing markets. Competing campuses will race to see how many days it takes to increase output by 50%, or how many hours it takes to tool for a completely new product. Perhaps most exciting is the development of radical new manufacturing technologies such as 3-D printing to capture maximum production flexibility with a more limited logistics footprint. 3-D printing is a reality today for simple products with limited volume. The question is how long before these radical technologies support more complex items in market volumes at competitive speeds.

Like manufacturing flow, order fulfillment can also be especially challenged by socioeconomic leveling and the exploration of new markets. Economies of scale in order picking evaporate when orders involve small quantities, like cases or "eaches" (individual items), as opposed to pallets. Similarly, economies in transportation in emerging markets means effective utilization of motorbikes, as opposed to large trucks and railroads. Value stream map analyses of distribution operations in emerging markets illustrate that it is in the final stretch of the supply chain (from distribution center to retail) that service implodes and costs explode. Solving this "last mile" problem will only grow in importance in the coming years as the frequency and urgency of the problem increase and the world becomes more urbanized and congested.

Look for the triumphant return of two technologies that have fallen out of favor in recent years. Automated storage and retrieval systems (AS/RS), such as robotic cranes and vertical carousels, gained popularity in the 1980s and 1990s as a way to handle large volumes with minimal human engagement. The application of these technologies faced challenges, however, in accommodating mixed pallet loads, which became increasingly common among large retailers that could demand them of their suppliers. The automated equipment was designed to process full pallet loads and enjoyed limited flexibility.

Some companies shuttered the technology despite the sunk investment. Pressures to support urban populations in crowded downtowns will encourage the construction of high-rise facilities that consume a small footprint. The capability of automated facilities to provide flexible order fulfillment will be essential in this development.

Supporting this flexible accommodation will be passive radio frequency identification (RFID) technology. RFID was all the rage in the early 2000s. Supply chain superpowers like Walmart, Metro AG, and the U.S. Department of Defense established aggressive RFID mandates that they later retracted to various degrees. Vendors resisted firmly when they realized that the tags and readers were quite expensive and not achieving perfect read rates. Continued development of the technology and increased scale are helping to improve both the economics and capabilities of RFID. Paired with AS/RS, RFID provides smart and agile order fulfillment.

Logistics networks will adapt to serving emerging markets too. For instance, distribution facilities might be located in unconventional locations, like atop parking structures and multifamily housing units. Delivery modes might also evolve in interesting ways, including using microshipments to reach dense urban areas, parachute airdrops to reach remote rural areas, or solar-powered watercraft to traverse inland waterways.

Innovation is not limited to the production and distribution of goods dedicated to rapidly emerging markets, because the products and their development will call for new approaches. The Internet will continue to expand as a portal for ascertaining market developments and trends. As indicated earlier in this chapter, the Internet more than any other mechanism serves as the great leveler in our global economy. Devising culturally distinct websites will be critical for providing a relevant and meaningful interface with customers for product development in emerging markets.

The 3-D printing technology mentioned earlier will support the rapid development of prototypes before it enters mainstream production service. The proposition of creating a tangible and functional mockup of a product concept in minutes will prove invaluable, especially as product variety grows to serve an increasing array of markets. Perhaps even more radical is the notion of developing product technologies and products that can adapt to different markets characterized by distinct cultures and local tastes. Products that reconfigure easily and operate differently based on the customer's needs empower the manufacturer and customer to achieve the ultimate in flexibility. The question then becomes at what cost such capabilities are worthwhile.

Another supply chain process that will see the impact of global connectivity and socioeconomic leveling is returns management. Developing markets are often viewed as lacking sustainability awareness, but this is likely to change dramatically in the coming years. This is particularly true as people make the connection between the consumption of materials, energy, and water and the degradation of our physical environment, scarcity in natural resources, and quality of life. Customers in rapidly emerging markets will be quick studies in these dynamics. This will encourage companies to employ life cycle analysis, assuming greater responsibility for materials and goods throughout their life cycle. Companies also will try to have these materials and goods "reenter" the system for multiple life cycles (subsequent use through recycling, refurbishing, and/or repurposing). These firms will build reverse-logistics systems in emerging economies and exploit the benefits and profits of doing so. Since convenience is ordinarily a deciding factor in such systems, collection devices such as interactive kiosks and robotic collection vehicles will collect products and materials at the end of use. Such devices have been used for many years to collect used beverage containers in the United States where deposit systems exist. Their use is expected to expand, as will the ease and functionality of the collection devices.

The final supply chain process that will see the impact of the changing market environment espoused by emerging markets and improved global connectivity is the supplier relationship management process. Like CRM, SRM must race to try to understand the culture of operating in a foreign environment where norms can differ greatly from the home market. Much focus is directed at determining how to win over the hearts and minds of "choice" suppliers that can help the focal company navigate the treacherous waters of emerging market competition. Beyond identifying these select suppliers, we recommend making them a part of the success and rewarding them, in turn, for their contributions. In some cases, this might require formal strategic collaboration and even investing in suppliers that prove most instrumental in navigating emerging markets successfully. As with all the macrotrends presented in this book, we subscribe to the theory that supply chain management is a team effort. Companies that seek the expertise and engagement of the best suppliers and customers, respectively, will outperform firms that believe they can go it alone. This belief is more firmly reinforced in a world that is ever more flat and crowded. Hot? Well, we address that next.

4

The Changing Physical Environment

$$Cl + O_3 \rightarrow ClO + O_2$$
$$ClO + O_3 \rightarrow Cl + 2O_2$$

These expressions, while foreign to most of us, are simple statements describing one of the most profound occurrences of our age. In basic terms of chemical reactions, together they explain the destructive relationship between chlorine and oxygen in our atmosphere. When industrial chemical particles get released into the air, they float into the stratosphere, where they are exposed to ultraviolet radiation. These ultraviolet rays then break apart the chemicals and release chlorine atoms that destroy ozone molecules. Ozone in Earth's stratosphere serves as the planet's protective shield from the sun's ultraviolet radiation (UV-B and UV-C). When the ozone is depleted, more UV-B and UV-C radiation reaches the Earth's surface. Higher levels of UV-B exposure have been conclusively demonstrated to result in greater incidences of skin cancer and cataracts in humans. A hole in the ozone above Chile is suspected of increasing skin melanomas by 56%.

Because the current and recent levels of ozone depletion represent radical deviations from past data, they appear to be an unnaturally occurring phenomenon. A preponderance of scientists has pinpointed industrial activity as a major culprit in this scenario. Is ozone depletion the dastardly deed of a diabolical scientist looking to doom the Earth and its inhabitants? Not at all. The introduction of chlorofluorocarbon (CFC) chemicals dates back to the 1920s, when General Motors Chemical Company, working jointly with DuPont Chemical, sought an alternative to ammonia-based refrigerants. Although effective as refrigerants, these substances were known to be toxic and generally unsafe when improperly contained. This called for some sort of solution that preserved the benefits of CFCs while curbing their side effects.

In the mid-1920s, noted industry research scientist Thomas Midgely, Jr. and his team devised the solution—a synthesis of dichlorodifluoromethane that came to be known as Freon, a brand introduced by DuPont. Freon, a seemingly inert gas, would become the primary refrigerant for air conditioning and refrigeration systems for decades. CFCs also found common usage as degreasing solvents and propellants, like those employed in aerosol cans and fire extinguishers. Freon was feared to be a hazard on the ground. Several cases of lead poisoning and a handful of deaths had been attributed to lead exposure at DuPont's New Jersey production plant for tetraethyl lead (TEL). Nevertheless, CFCs' atmospheric hazards were years away from detection. Unbeknownst to the scientists, the new compounds had lasting, negative effects on the planet well beyond their lifetimes. Believing in the inertness of the chemicals with which he worked, Midgely famously poured TEL over his hands and inhaled TEL vapors from an open bottle for a full minute in a public demonstration of its innocuous nature. Midgely later suffered multiple bouts of lead poisoning and poor health before his premature death.

The science connecting CFC use with ozone depletion began yielding conclusions in the 1970s. Early reports were considered mere measurement errors. In a landmark 1976 study, however, the influential U.S. National Academy of Sciences reported the ozone depletion hypothesis as strongly supported by the scientific community. By the 1980s, proof of an ozone hole over Antarctica emerged, and satellite imagery confirmed its presence and an alarming rate of depletion. Governments convened and started taking steps toward phasing out and, ultimately, banning CFC production and usage, first in aerosols and later in all forms.

Though CFCs were banned in most developed markets, their production continued at DuPont until 1993. It is reported that production continues in China and Brazil, with black markets perpetuating the distribution and use of the chemical in many parts of the world. However, even if the use of CFCs completely halted today, they would continue to plague the ozone. It is estimated that it takes five to seven years for a CFC molecule used on Earth to reach the stratosphere. Once there, it can last for almost a century, taking out up to 100,000 ozone molecules during that time.[1]

What has replaced the role once filled by CFCs? Hydrochloro-fluorocarbons (HCFCs) serve as the primary refrigerant in commercial and household uses, representing a multibillion-dollar industry in 2012. Although they are believed to be up to 98% less damaging as ozone-depletion agents, they are regarded as potent greenhouse gases (GHGs). As a result, HCFCs are now seeing phaseout provisions around the world. The United States and other developed markets are scheduled to ban HCFC production and imports by 2030, with lesser-developed countries expected to follow by 2040. Hydrofluoro-carbons (HFCs), which contain no chlorine or bromine, are now hailed as the successor to HCFCs, though they too are regarded as damaging greenhouse gases.

Such is the story of many innovations. The transitional scientific developments that solved one problem created others. In the case of environmental impact, short-term human benefit often creates long-term scars on our natural environment that imperil humanity's future. It would be unfair to label the creators of these innovations as villains, but the perpetuation of the innovations' use *once the hazards are uncovered* is less defensible. Midgely never sought to be known as having "more impact on the atmosphere than any other single organism in Earth's history," as environmentalist author J.R. McNeil has depicted him. But ignorance is a not an acceptable excuse, and modern organizations are increasingly held accountable for their actions and the impacts of those actions on the people and environment around us.

Supply chain management, given its broad and holistic realm of influence, is neck-deep in environmental responsibility. Our supply chains reach every aspect of business engagement and interface with the natural environment throughout the product life cycle. This includes designing products/services, supplying raw materials, transporting, conversion/production, distribution, use, and post-use collection, including recycling/remanufacturing/reuse/disposal. In light of

---

[1] "Stratospheric Ozone Depletion by CFCs." (2012). *Encyclopedia of Earth.*

the far-reaching effects of manmade operations on the physical environment, and the inverse effects, understanding the implications of supply chain strategies and operations is critical. Should we really be concerned that whales are getting sunburns? Certainly, we should be concerned, but several direct business implications are tied to how we use the environment and how it responds to our actions. If those who cannot remember the past are condemned to repeat it—or so the saying goes—industry cycles and tolerances for imperfections will be shorter and more strict in the future.

This chapter reviews how economic activity impacts the environment. We subsequently consider how these impacts will influence companies and the supply chains in which they operate.

The Environment and You, You and the Environment

An inescapable reality is that with economic activity comes a consumption of natural resources and the residues of that consumption. Everything we use and consume comes from the Earth. This simple observation is lost on many people. Do not be confused by terms like "synthetic," "composite," "alloy," and "artificial flavors." These terms simply refer to the blending of natural elements into combinations that in some way exceed the capabilities of the raw elements, or match the capabilities more affordably. Once extracted from the Earth, raw materials are converted into usable materials, components, and, ultimately, the products we know and love. Products might be used immediately, like perishable food items, or remain in the "usage" stage for decades, like a Boeing 737 aircraft.

One residue of consumption is the product itself after it fulfills its useful life. At what point can someone else use the product next? Does it have any resale value? Can it be refurbished, recycled, or repurposed? Otherwise, disposal in dumps and landfills is the most common fate for spent merchandise. Aside from the product, its packaging materials can undergo the same review of options. Increasingly, firms are seeking to extend the useful stage of products and their supporting materials in the life cycle and to keep them in play for successive life cycles. After the U.S. government released new emission standards in 2004, Ford expanded its "Recycle Your Ride" program to include models from 1995 to 2003. This program awards customers up to $2,300 in credit toward a new vehicle if they turned in their old one for recycling purposes—not a bad deal for cars that could be as much as 17 years old.[2] Apple's MacBook Pro laptop line can sustain nearly 1,000 charges, keeping the product in its useful stage of life for a considerable time. However, when a user exhausts the battery, it can be submitted to Apple for recycling. In return, the customer receives a gift card for the laptop's residual value.[3]

Sadly, the residuals of economic activity do not begin and end with spent materials that are too often destined for landfills. Pollution of the air, water, and ground accompanies most sourcing, manufacturing, and logistics activity. The opening to this chapter addressed the emission of CFCs, which once spewed egregiously into the air and, eventually, the atmosphere. The primary culprits of air pollution are the burning of fossil fuels and coal, both of which serve as sources of greenhouse gases yet remain essential ingredients in today's industrial activity. Combustion engines running on fossil fuels are responsible for emitting carbon dioxide, particulate matter, and often an array of other pollutants, including sulfur dioxide, nitrogen oxides, and carbon monoxide. Greenhouse gases trap heat on the Earth's surface and lower temperatures in the troposphere. Even though many developed nations around the world have instituted pollution controls, such as the U.S. Clean Air Act and the EU's Air Quality Directive, the integrity of our air continues to be compromised. The American Lung Association finds that more than half of the U.S. population resides in areas with unsafe levels of smog and particulate pollution. It is estimated that 80% to 90% of Europe's urban population is subjected to particulate matter (PM_{10}) that exceeds World Health Organization (WHO) guidelines.[4]

The problem is much worse in China, where air quality enforcement is lax. It is estimated that only 1% of China's urban population

[2] Recycle Your Ride Program. (24 June 2009). Ford Motor Company.

[3] "Get an Apple Gift Card for your old device." (2012). Apple.com.

[4] Air Quality in Europe, 2011 report.

enjoys "safe air" by modern standards, with pollution in Beijing rated as 16 times worse than that in New York City. The WHO reports that the airborne particulate levels in the industrial north of China are 20 times greater than its guidelines for acceptable air quality. Some areas have pollution so dense that the cities cannot be seen by satellite. Should the Chinese government elect to take stringent action on air pollution, however, the tide could turn immediately.[5] Such dramatic changes in policy can occur rapidly if global pressure redirects central planning from growth to sustainment. Figure 4.1 illustrates the harmful particulate matter (PM) present across different world regions. Harmful particulate matter is a result of factory, power plant, and automobile emissions and can create health problems if inhaled in large quantities. According to Figure 4.1, China's east coast has the highest concentration of harmful PMs.

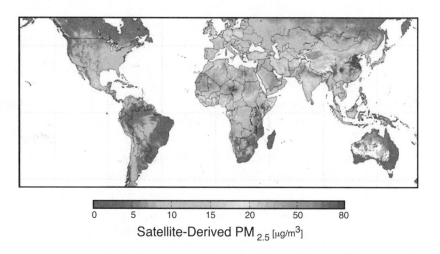

Satellite-Derived PM$_{2.5}$ [μg/m^3]

Figure 4.1 Harmful particulate matter concentrations[6]

Given our dependence on fossil fuels and the accelerated pace of economic activity in developing regions, the degradation of air quality is expected to worsen before it improves. The WHO estimates that

[5] Hays, Jeffrey. (2008). "Air Pollution in China." Facts and Details.com.

[6] Voiland, Adam. (22 September 2010). "New Map Offers a Global View of Health-Sapping Air Pollution." NASA.gov.

2.4 million people die each year from air pollution. The Organization for Economic Cooperation and Development (OECD) predicts that poor air quality in the world's cities will lead to 3.6 million premature deaths *per year* by 2050. Air pollution also contributes to climate change. Figure 4.2 shows how climate change will heat up the United States in the coming decades.[7]

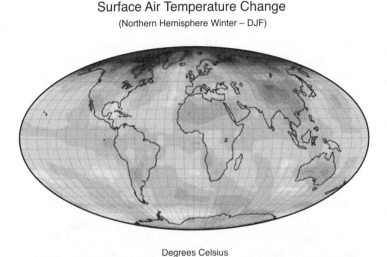

Surface Air Temperature Change
(Northern Hemisphere Winter – DJF)

Degrees Celsius

-8.00   -6.00   -4.00   -2.00   0.00   2.00   4.00   6.00   8.00

Figure 4.2 Climate change

Though alarming, this number of premature deaths from air pollution pales in comparison to the death rate associated with scarce and unsafe water today. Many world regions face significant potable water shortages, and more than 5 million people die each year from waterborne diseases. As shown in Figure 4.3, in 2010 significant portions of North and South America, as well as eastern Africa and northwest

---

[7] Youngman, Betsy, Mark Chandler, Linda Sohl, Mark Hafen, Tamara Ledley, Steve Ackerman, and Steve Kluge. (January 2010). "Envisioning Climate Change Using a Global Climate Model." Science Education Resource Center (SERC) at Carleton College.

and southeast Asia, faced severe water shortages. The lower pane of the figure extrapolates these shortages based on the climate change trends shown in Figure 4.2. The result is quite serious: Many nations will be looking to import potable water in the next 20 or so years, and few areas will have surplus to offer. Additionally, as shown in Figure 4.4, much of the available supply is currently or will be contaminated. The United Nations Environment Program points out that currently, a child under the age of 5 dies every 20 seconds from water pollution-related disease. The problem is greatest in the cities of underdeveloped regions, where sewage and wastewater contaminate the potable supply. Again, recalling the maps shown in Chapter 2, "Global Population Growth and Migration," the areas with the greatest growth and lowest GDP are also those with the poorest water supply and quality. Interestingly, as discussed in Chapter 5, "Geopolitical and Social Systems Disruptions," these are also the same areas where the greatest natural resource stocks remain, so they will become the next frontier of global competition.

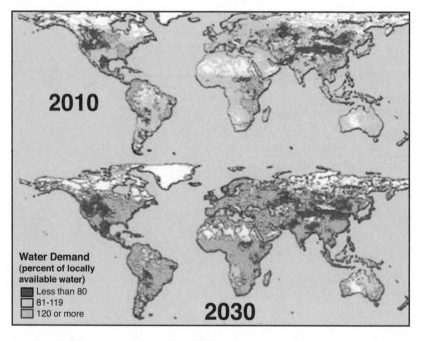

Figure 4.3 Future water supply degradation

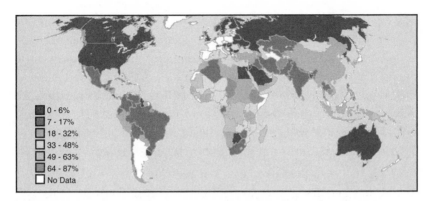

Figure 4.4 World regional lack of access to safe drinking water, 2012

Figure 4.4 shows the percentage of each country's population that does not have access to safe drinking water.[8] The water shortage is greatest in Africa. For a potable water supply that faces imbalances in supply and demand, the OECD estimates that demand will increase by more than 50% by 2050 and that as much as 40% of the world's population will live in areas of severe water stress. These instances show that natural resource scarcity isn't just attributed to overuse and overproduction; pollution is also a major part of the problem. These problems will contribute to both future supply chain disruptions and resource security issues.

We find these air and water pollution statistics particularly alarming because they relate to everyday occurrences, as opposed to the less frequent "disasters" that claim news headlines. In 1989, the 300-meter-long oil tanker *Exxon Valdez* ran aground in Prince William Sound off the coast of Alaska. The accident spread between 25 million and 32 million gallons of oil over 11,000 square miles and 1,300 miles of coastline. The accident also generated worldwide attention and resulted in more than 38,000 litigants and immeasurable damage to the region's ecosystem, which remains impaired today. This disaster

---

[8] "Human Development Report 2004." (2004). United Nations Development Program (UNDP). Tables 7 and 33.

was superseded by the BP *Deepwater Horizon* oil spill of 2010 in the Gulf of Mexico. It was perhaps the first such disaster that ordinary people could watch unfold over the course of its three-month duration in real time on their personal computers and handheld devices. A U.S. White House commission report blamed BP and its partners for making cost-cutting decisions that led to the blowout. The commission also indicated that unless significant reform in industry practices occurred, a similar incident might occur again elsewhere.

Less visible to the naked eye, but growing in size and awareness, is what has become known as the "Great Pacific Garbage Patch." It consists of plastics, chemical sludge, and other debris that is trapped by the current of the North Pacific between the U.S. West Coast and Japan. Since the patch is not visible from the sky or in images taken from space, its size is impossible to estimate with any accuracy. Estimates range from 700,000 square kilometers to more than 15 million square kilometers (or 270,000 square miles to 5.8 million square miles). The latter estimate would represent just over 8% of the Pacific Ocean's area, or double the size of the continental U.S. The sources of the garbage are believed to be both land-based and shipping vessels. Cruise ships are often targeted as a primary source of such waste, because a large ship carrying 3,000 passengers generates 8 tons of solid waste per week.[9] But industry practices fueled by an outraged public have led to better alternatives than ocean dumping.

Scientists believe that garbage patches of similar composition exist in most of the world's oceans. Though they may be out of sight, they do not leave us out of harm's way. The most direct impacts are felt by marine life, which can ingest the long-lasting plastics. These often contain organic pollutants like polychlorinated biphenyl (PCBs), dichlorodiphenyltrichloroethane (DDT), and polycyclic aromatic hydrocarbons (PAHs). The food chain is then affected when species like jellyfish consume these toxins and then are eaten by larger fish. The impact on humans, while difficult to measure, cannot be dismissed.

Back on terra firma, soil contamination from a variety of sources impairs our ability to live off the land. Indiscriminate use of pesticides,

---

[9] Bluewater Network, 2000.

solvents, and other heavy metals; corrosion of underground storage tanks; the dumping of oil, fuel, and industrial waste; and surface water contamination contribute to soil infertility and the contamination of precious water aquifers. Soil contaminants can also vaporize, introducing carcinogens into the air. These hazards are correlated strongly with the level of industrialization and the intensity of chemical usage. One estimate suggests that 10% of China's cultivatable land is unsafe for agricultural purposes, with much of this land in economically developed areas.[10]

In total, manmade activity impacts our natural environment considerably. The various pollutions are sometimes seen and directly affect our daily existence. In other cases, they take years or decades to reach us in some substantive way. They all relate to the economic pursuit of trade, with many implications tied to our patterns of usage and consumption. With the emergence of an ever-growing class of global consumers, the taxes placed on the Earth will increase. The chains that supply, produce, and deliver the goods demanded by the world's consumers will have to incorporate a life cycle perspective, assuming accountability for the direct and indirect impacts of the products and services they market. The next section addresses the forces that shape a company's environmental posture—its position on environmental stewardship.

Environmental Pressures on Supply Chains

Four broad forces affect a company's environmental posture: customer demand, supply, the public, and governments and their policies, as shown in Figure 4.5. The following sections describe each force and explain their implications for supply chain management.

---

[10] Qi, Xu. (29 January 2007). "Facing Up to 'Invisible Pollution.'" ChinaDialogue.net.

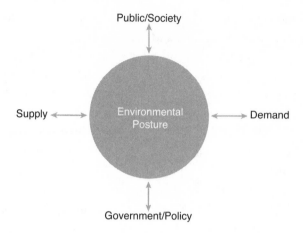

Figure 4.5 Drivers and consequences of environmental posture

Customer Demand

Customers should be the first source of inspiration for environmental action in our supply chains. Providing products and services that fulfill customers' environmental expectations has top-line implications—an opportunity to grow the business. Increasingly, companies are embracing a "green" imperative brought forward by business customers and consumers. Prominent efforts have been made by such heavyweights as Starbucks, Walmart, Hewlett-Packard, Ford, and IBM. Walmart has set far-reaching environmental goals to be supplied completely by renewable energy, create zero waste, and sell products that sustain people and the environment. Currently Walmart is falling far short on most of these goals. (It is closest on the second item, with reportedly 80% of the company's waste staying out of landfills.) However, the setting of such ambitious goals is not intended to only serve a corporate responsibility agenda, but also to serve as good business. CEO Mike Duke was quoted in 2012 as saying, "We've done all this (sustainability initiatives) because it is the right thing to do for the generations that will follow us. But sustainability is also the right thing to do for our business."[11]

---

[11] Walmart's Global Sustainability Milestone Meeting, 18 April 2012.

Supply Capability

Supply capability refers to the company's ability to meet customer demand through both internal and external sources. The environmental impact of supply operations is something that no company can avoid. Even the most innocuous of operations will impact the natural environment. The supplier relationship management (SRM) process seeks to form appropriate relations with suppliers so that the needs of both the buying and selling party are met through the trading relationship. Similar to CRM, segmentation is essential for customizing the relationship, as needed, to ensure that balance among inputs and outputs is found in the arrangement. It is impossible for large firms managing a multitude of business relationships to manage all partners as "choice." Therefore, selectivity is required to determine how many resources should be directed to distinct suppliers or groups of similarly valuable suppliers.

When determining whether to "make" or "buy" manufactured items in the supply chain, companies often measure the transaction costs associated with outsourcing. Transaction costs are associated with managing an outside company to act as an agent of the focal firm, to align its interest with yours. When opportunity presents itself in the form of an outside party and is regarded as an irreversible threat, the focal company will feel inclined to "make" (insource) the item. When transaction costs are low, however, the company elects to outsource. Companies seeking to shift the burden of environmental stewardship to other supply chain partners soon realize that this strategy offers little refuge. The practice of outsourcing (and, often, offshoring) operations does not present a buffer. Think back to when talk-show host Kathie Lee Gifford's clothing line became associated with sweatshop labor conditions in Honduras in the mid-1990s. Just as apparel makers could not run away from poor labor conditions, manufacturers and retailers cannot escape responsibility for environmental stewardship in the supply chain—particularly when their brand is on the product label. Critics claim that manufacturers in developed regions are outsourcing not only their production operations to China, but their pollution as well. With this in mind, companies are trying to ensure that life cycle impacts are minimized.

As we will elaborate later, natural resource scarcity and the natural environment are intimately entwined. The preface to this book explores the case study of Coca-Cola in the Indian market, along with the ensuing "water wars" that followed among the soft drink giant and the communities housing the bottling operations. But not all scarcity issues are so well documented. We return to water for one of the more pronounced scarcity problems. We've all heard that "there are plenty of fish in the sea," but that's not the case anymore. Shark and bluefin tuna populations are disappearing at an alarming rate due to overfishing. Their populations are 80% to 90% lower than in 1970. At current depletion rates, there is expected to be only 10 to 12 years' supply of bluefin, and fewer than 30 years of orange roughy, another popular entrée item. Both species are slow to mature but are in great demand. Also, the "efficiency of seafood" (in terms of a measure called "feed conversion ratio") is challenged, because large quantities of feed are required to achieve relatively little yield. This is particularly troublesome when you consider how Asia's rapidly growing economies rely on seafood as a primary source of protein. Farm-raised species like catfish, tilapia, and carp are looked toward as more sustainable options.

The upsides of environmental stewardship in supply include the harvesting of innovation and leveraging sustainability as a motivating force for continuous improvement. As for innovation, suppliers are increasingly considered rich sources of new-product ideas and process breakthroughs. Former Procter & Gamble CEO A.G. Lafley famously set the company's objective to attain more than 50% of its marketable innovations from outside the company. This was despite the fact that P&G employs more than 9,300 researchers and spends $2 billion each year on internal R&D. Despite these immense resources, it was believed that casting the net more widely to existing and prospective suppliers could yield more and diverse ideas.

Companies are looking to continuously improve their supply chain operations, often in ways that reduce environmental impact. The implementation of strategies geared toward making the business lean, green, and sustainable is gaining rapid adoption. Lean practices seek to reduce *muda*, the Japanese term for waste. The muda reduced through lean practices includes the following areas:

- Transportation
- Inventory
- Motion
- Waiting
- Overprocessing
- Overproduction
- Defects
- Untapped knowledge and creativity

Reducing these wastes reduces environmental impact and costs. Effectively implementing the manufacturing flow management (MFM) and order fulfillment (OF) processes creates lean results in the sourcing, production, and delivery of goods. The company processes only the goods that customers demand, *when* they are demanded.

Public/Social Impacts

The perspectives of outside stakeholders are commonly integrated into today's business decisions. These stakeholders can be citizens living in the communities in which the company operates, the families and friends of employees, nongovernmental organizations (NGOs), and a host of other nonaffiliated parties who have an interest in the company's actions. Conventional business practice was to draw as little attention from these outside parties as possible. Nothing good could come from such meddling. As noted in the discussion of supply, if your brand is associated with the final product, society will hold you accountable for the actions of your suppliers, as they relate to the environment or any other social ill. Avoiding newspaper headlines was the goal.

Fast-forward to the present. Newspapers, while still serving as an important "beacon of truth," are too slow in reporting news and are losing readership, especially among "millennials," who find flipping through pages tedious. Rather, online reports and social media dominate. Social media has no editors, censors, or buffers. Grassroots movements on Facebook and Twitter are the latest worries that keep corporate executives up at night. While they try to slumber, groundswells can mobilize overnight from person to person in ways that were unimaginable until the mid-2000s. Consider that even though Coca-Cola consistently has one of Facebook's most popular fan pages, the company does not maintain the site or control the content or comments posted. With more than 900 million Facebook users worldwide, anticorporate campaigns go viral around the world quickly and at no expense. Increasingly, customers are filing complaints on companies' Facebook pages. If the companies fail to respond (as often happens), this reflects poorly on the offending company, and exodus follows. Cadbury faced a tsunami of opposition to its use of palm oil in its chocolate candies in Australia and New Zealand in 2009. Palm oil supply had been linked to deforestation and the loss of orangutan habitats in Southeast Asia.[12] Volkswagen UK posted a seemingly innocuous message on its Facebook fan page on January 1, 2012, asking fans what they would like to see from the company as a New Year's resolution. Greenpeace UK organized a concentrated response that yielded hundreds of pro-environmental postings. These examples speak to the changing landscape in customer service management, the supply chain process responsible for anticipating customer issues and addressing them. Manning a toll-free phone line is no longer sufficient to stem a tide of customer complaints and reverse customer sentiments.

Smarter companies are learning not to run away from social media and the wrath of customers, but to embrace the medium. U.S. grocery retailer Safeway tries to respond to every customer complaint posted to its Facebook page, some of which exhibit an environmental interest. Rail company CSX embraced the "Earth Month" of April in 2012 by launching a Facebook page called "Environmental Pursuit" to test fans' "green IQs" and stress the company's pro-environmental messaging.

Environmental Regulatory Considerations

When all else fails, the final source of inspiration for environmental action is government mandate and regulations. This "reactive" posture rarely leads to growth in the top or bottom line. Furthermore,

---

[12] Fitzsimmons, Caitlin. (21 August 2009). "Cadbury bows to people power, drops palm oil." Ecosalon.com.

waiting for rules to be imposed spawns little inspiration for innovation through improved means of serving customers and/or enhanced cost competitiveness through environmental stewardship.

Though companies often struggle to quantify the value of pro-environmental action in terms of customer impact or internal cost savings, they sometimes strive to advance the state of the art in an effort to differentiate themselves. This is particularly true in product and service areas that are commonly viewed as commoditized, or industries where competition is largely driven by price. Chemical giant Dow demonstrates commitment to sustainability that greatly exceeds government mandates. Still others may seek to advance environmental action as a way to precede impending legislation and perhaps influence the rules, essentially creating the standards to which their peers must adhere.

Even though no single supply chain process is dedicated to ensuring adherence to the full array of government policies, actions tied to all eight of the key business processes carry implications for proving that the company is an upstanding, law-abiding corporate citizen. The reality is that the days of wreaking havoc on the environment, dumping, and running are over in most developed regions of the world. Someone is always watching, and the price of violating environmental laws, industry standards, and public expectations continues to escalate. Integrity throughout the implementation of the supply chain processes is the norm, because ignorance is no longer an acceptable excuse.

Environmental Challenges for Future Supply Chain Managers

Changes to the physical environment are threatening to knock out of balance many of the world's ecosystems, including the global commercial ecosystem. These changes are trickling down to the industry and firm levels of operation, where supply chains are beginning to struggle to achieve balance in supply and demand. The following are key issues related to the physical environment that should be considered within supply chain strategy and planning efforts in the coming years:

- Greater accountability in companies' environmental performance among all stakeholders, including customers, end users, regulators, suppliers, communities, and even shareholders
- Market opportunities for innovative companies that can devise products and services that perform as well as or better than competitors' offerings, with reduced environmental impact
- Harsh and lasting negative responses when companies fail to live up to their environmental obligations under the scrutiny of the market and regulators
- Advantages that will stem from early adoption of alternative fuels and technologies, which will reduce environmental impact and/or comply early on with anticipated regulations

The challenges associated with physical environmental change are numerous and have the potential to greatly affect each of the eight GSCF supply chain processes in the coming years. Future supply chain managers are advised to consider the ramifications of environmental change on supply chain management to better integrate demand with supply. Table 4.1 matches each process to its environmental implications.

Environmental issues affect each of the eight supply chain processes significantly. We'll begin by discussing the impacts on customer relationship management, which is focused on forming effective, profitable relationships with customers. Segmentation of the market is an essential step toward forming relationships that meet the needs of distinct customers while ensuring profitability for the company. An important realization is that not all customers of the future will view environmental stewardship as a primary concern relative to matters of product performance, delivery assurance, and price. One major consumer goods company currently distinguishes "greenies" (those who favor environmentally friendly products) from "nevergreens" (consumers who are opposed or even hostile to environmental messaging). We expect these trends to continue for the next couple of decades, until and if the recognition of the global climate crisis becomes imperative. As indicated earlier, customers can be an instrumental force in directing companies to more environmentally benign products and processes.

Table 4.1 Physical Environment Implications for SCM

GSCF Process	Physical Environment Implications
Customer relationship management (CRM)	Challenges:
	Customers will have disparate views on environmental stewardship. Some customers will place high value on environmentally benign practices, and others will not.
	Environmental actions are not integral elements of value propositions in conventional supply chains.
	It can be difficult to understand where investments in environmental provisions should be made.
	Quantifying the value of environmental benefit for the firm and its customers can be challenging.
	Customers sometimes shift their environmental "burdens" to the supplying company.
	Suggestions:
	Collaborate with customers to reduce total environmental impact.
	Distinguish customers' environmental expectations.
	Understand the economics of environmental stewardship in product and service provisions. Where is it free, and where does it call for investment?
	Where are premiums required for environmental stewardship? What are customers willing to pay for?
	Segment customers based on their environmental dispositions, and develop appropriate product-service agreements for the distinct segments.
Customer service management (CSM)	Challenges:
	It can be difficult to anticipate environmental issues, but these can have a big impact on the business and customers of the focal firm.
	It's difficult to assess which environmental risks are imminent and require imperative response.
	Customer service personnel are not universally prepared for environmental matters.
	Customer service assessments often lack measures of environmental performance.
	Unrealized environmental hazards can leave some second-guessing the steps taken to prevent them.

GSCF Process	Physical Environment Implications
Customer service management (CSM) (continued)	Suggestions: Identify potential environmental problems and disasters. Conduct failure modes and effects analysis (FMEA) to recognize potential events calling for immediate attention. Conduct customer service audits that include consideration of environmental aspects in the provision of goods and services. Serve as a consultant to customers on environmental matters.
Demand management (DM)	Challenges: Imbalances in supply and demand can result in disappointed customers and unnecessary costs. An absence of contingency plans can impair service and damage the company's image and marketability. Inventory can be a wasteful and expensive form of risk management. Emergency reactions can be extremely costly and potentially ill conceived. Suggestions: Incorporate greater flexibility in operations that allows for more response-based supply chain operations. Rely on shorter forecasts to minimize the risk of forecast error and oversupply. Devise contingency plans for environment-related supply-demand issues.
Manufacturing flow management (MFM)	Challenges: It can be difficult to measure the environmental impact of manufacturing processes. Conventional manufacturing practices and measures can impair advances that incorporate environmental stewardship. Environmental considerations and regulations are regarded as constraints on productivity. Suggestions: Enhance manufacturing flexibility to reduce speculation and waste.

GSCF Process	Physical Environment Implications
Manufacturing flow management (MFM) (continued)	Incorporate environmental measures (carbon footprint, emissions, energy consumption, water consumption, hazardous-material usage, material waste) into process assessments.
	Determine push/pull boundaries that assign manufacturing activity across the supply chain that minimizes environmental impact.
	Integrate environmental stewardship into continuous-improvement programs.
Order fulfillment (OF)	Challenges:
	Logistics networks are designed for service and cost objectives. Environmental considerations traditionally are not factored in.
	Transportation is the activity that consumes the greatest energy and generates more pollutant emissions than any other activity.
	Suggestions:
	Design logistics networks that minimize environmental impact.
	Collaborate with logistics service providers and other shippers to reduce total environmental impact.
	Use more fuel-efficient and lower-emission modes of transportation.
	Implement energy-reduction measures in warehouses and distribution facilities (such as LEED certification).
	Improve the consolidation of loads to reduce trips and empty transit.
	Employ environmental measures in process assessment.
	Reward service providers for improvements in environmental performance.

GSCF Process	Physical Environment Implications
Product development and commercialization (PD & C)	Challenges:
	Conventional wisdom suggests that environmentally friendly products cost more.
	Short-term decision making does not accommodate life cycle analysis.
	It can be challenging to determine the demand for "really new" products for which history is not helpful or insightful.
	Incorporating innovative new materials in products can prove risky to quality and environmental management.
	Suggestions:
	Incorporate total life cycle analysis into product design decisions.
	Design products for extended use.
	Design products (with reusable and recyclable content) for multiple life cycles.
	Seek supplier and customer inputs that can reduce environmental impact.
	Factor environmental impacts into the go/no-go decision for new products.
	Involve environmental experts on product development teams.
	Incorporate environmental performance into the make-versus-buy decision. (Can an outside party produce the item at a lower environmental impact?)
	Devise commercialization channels that uphold the environmental beliefs of the focal company.
Returns management (RM)	Challenges:
	Reverse material flows are often managed as an afterthought.
	Post-use considerations are rarely integrated into corporate or supply chain strategies.
	Gatekeeping practices lack consistent standards and practices, allowing noncompliant returns to occur.
	Secondary markets for returned merchandise are not fully explored and developed.
	Suggestions:
	Seek to minimize unwanted returns (defects), and learn why these returns are occurring.

GSCF Process	Physical Environment Implications
Returns management (RM) (continued)	Collaborate with customers and service providers to reduce the total environmental impact of returns.
	Design supply chain configurations that account for the collection of used and recyclable materials. (Opportunities may overlap with existing distribution provisions for product deployment.)
	Employ advanced analysis tools (network analysis, transportation management system [TMS], route management) to manage reverse flows.
	Establish agreements with customers and suppliers that clearly establish protocols for returned merchandise and crediting.
	Adhere to standards for accepting returns and handling them.
	Explore secondary market alternatives that reduce write-offs and disposal.
	Employ best practices in disposing of materials when disposal is imminent.
	Incorporate environmental consideration in continuous-improvement efforts with returns.
Supplier relationship management (SRM)	Challenges:
	Competition among suppliers is often based only on service, quality, and cost.
	Suppliers often do not know what is expected of them in the way of environmental performance of products and processes.
	Environmental "burdens" are sometimes shifted from the focal company to suppliers.
	Suggestions:
	Collaborate with suppliers to reduce the total environmental impact.
	Incorporate environmental measures and assurances in supplier qualification and certification programs.
	Add environmental performance to supplier scorecards.
	Reward suppliers for improvements in environmental performance.

Once customer segments are defined, the company must devise value propositions that resonate with the distinct segments. Assessing customer opinion and ensuring relevance to distinct segments is essential to drawing up relationships that serve the needs of buyers and suppliers. A caveat to anyone considering green messaging toward customers is to bring it forward with sincerity and integrity. "Greenwashing," disingenuous concern for the environment associated with a featured product or service, can (irreparably) impact a company or an entire industry.

Where customers are not properly informed about the environmental risks they will face, the supplying company needs to provide this expertise. While suppliers will be expected more than ever to have expert knowledge of the materials and products they provide to customers, imparting the complete array of risks that customers might face in using the product is an activity at which many firms would balk. However, there is potential for the supplying firm to serve as a consultant on matters of environmental risks—to fully inform customers of potential risks and even to anticipate possible consequences. Incorporating failure modes and effects analysis (FMEA), a common tool used in continuous improvement, into customer service arrangements helps illuminate events that could pose harm and challenges to the customer company.

In addition to anticipating potential environmental challenges, suppliers can implement environmental stewardship in their assessments of customer service performance. Did the firm maintain a proactive posture to events? When events occurred, were they remedied to the customer's satisfaction and in an acceptable time frame? Furthermore, what can be gleaned from the situation to prepare better for future occurrences? These questions are commonly asked in the customer service management process, but they are rarely applied specifically to matters of environmental concern.

Demand management finds itself at the heart of balancing supply and demand within and across companies. When supply exceeds demand, a company finds itself with excess inventory, which is a problem in itself. From an environmental perspective, however, the excess inventory is but one form of waste embodied in the imbalance. Materials were wasted in generating the excess inventory. Energy was also consumed in extracting, processing, and transporting the materials.

Emissions were generated in these activities as well. Therefore, the pallet of unwanted merchandise represents just one manifestation of the supply-demand imbalance.

To better maintain balance—and to make it easier to achieve the balance—companies will be forced to underscore flexibility in their operations so that they can rely less on speculative forecasts and more on actual demand. Some managers use the term "endcasting" to refer to the use of actual demand to drive supply chain execution, as opposed to the use of long-term forecasts that are highly speculative.

To accommodate customer demand in a responsive manner, manufacturing flexibility is key. The manufacturing flow management process determines just how much flexibility is warranted to meet customer demand and the company's return on investment. When flexibility is free, companies should embrace every last bit of it. However, when a premium is required to enhance flexibility (such as by cross-training employees or acquiring new equipment or information technology), you must determine how much and what forms of flexibility need to be embraced. This determination is not static, however, and requires continuous review.

The order fulfillment process results in particularly high environmental costs, especially in light of the energy consumption and emission generation found in transportation. Transportation in the U.S. alone consumed nearly 14 million barrels of oil per day in 2007.[13] In the late 1990s, transportation in the U.S. exceeded manufacturing activity as the leading contributor to greenhouse gas emissions, exceeding 2 billion metric tons of carbon dioxide emissions in 2007. Warehouse operations of the future will also be a leading source of energy consumption and emission generation, leading many companies to consolidate their logistics networks and reduce the impact of each individual facility.

Although collaborations among suppliers and customers are fairly common in pursuit of lean-ness, recent developments illustrate a new dimension of collaboration in the supply chain—horizontal collaboration among competitors. As noted in the discussion of strategies to

---

[13] Bureau of Transportation Statistics. (2012). *Pocket Guide to Transportation*. Also U.S. Department of Energy, Energy Information Administration.

avert traffic congestion in Chapter 9, competitors are sharing trucks and warehouse space to serve common customers. Sharing capacities means that fewer half-empty trucks and warehouses are employed, removing redundancy and waste from the companies' operations. Europe, with its more progressive stance toward the environment and higher fuel costs, is seeing higher levels of collaboration. In one such example, JSP and Hammerwerk are co-bundling loads shipped from the Czech Republic to Germany, with reported transport cost savings of 10% and carbon dioxide reductions of 30%. Companies like Kimberly-Clark and Colgate-Palmolive are paving the way for similar collaborations in the United States. More collaborative practices among competitors are expected in the future, particularly with fuel price increases.

Determining whether a new product or service would meet customers' environmental interests and fulfill the company's business needs is the work of the product development and commercialization process. PD&C receives the customer input of the CRM process as well as the capabilities of internal departments and external supplies to assess the viability of new offerings. For most companies, new offerings and new markets represent the best opportunities for growth. For companies seeking relevance among youth, upper-income, and more highly educated market segments, the pressure is greatest to devise environmentally friendly products. These market segments tend to identify most closely with environmental messaging and seek out these products and services.

Increasingly, companies are examining the total life cycle of the products they produce and distribute. Life cycle analysis factors in the environmental impact of all activities, from raw-material extraction, through manufacturing and distribution of goods and services, to use and even post-use stages, including collection, remanufacturing, recycling, or disposal. Measurements like total cost of ownership (TCO) are also employed as a way to encourage holistic management of materials beyond their initial use.

An effective returns management process is required to efficiently collect used and recyclable materials for subsequent life cycles. Unfortunately, the economics of future material flows will be highly inconsistent with those found in the forward deployment of product. Whereas full pallet-loads of homogenous (similar) products are distributed in the forward channel, the reverse channel consists of odds and ends that are usually poorly contained and lack the original packaging. This will increase as customer segments diversify around the globe. Handling and transport of returned goods will be significantly more challenging. Adding to the challenge will be the lack of visibility and the inability to predict "demand" for returns.

For these reasons, returns flows will be harder than ever to integrate with forward flows and often will simply be ignored by management. They can represent significant costs, however, with returns reaching as high as 40% of sales for some goods, particularly those sold online. Furthermore, returns provide closure to one life cycle and the requirement for subsequent cycles. Strategic thinking therefore is required to manage returns. Given their strategic importance, wholly separate channels are often devised for returned goods. Specialized service providers are often called on to support the collection and flow of returned goods. One such third-party logistics provider (3PL), Genco ATC, has devised its business model on the premise of "product life cycle logistics," providing focused support for reverse logistics.

Reduced environmental impact in products and services often calls for the input and involvement of outside parties in the supply chain. Customers are one such source of innovation, and so are suppliers, university researchers, research firms, and consultants. The supplier relationship management process seeks to identify the suppliers that possess the greatest potential to innovate. Suppliers demonstrating the most promise for new and valuable developments in products and processes are those that receive the best prices, terms of trade, and other forms of relationship nurturing.

Segmentation of suppliers will be virtually mandatory to identify suppliers that pose the greatest environmental hazards through the materials they provide or by virtue of the operations they perform. These suppliers require the greatest scrutiny on environmental performance. Provisions such as supplier screening, qualification, and certification might be required to ensure environmental safety and integrity. Increasingly, supplier scorecards will need enough granularity to convey the importance of supplier compliance and performance in light of agreed-upon standards and should lend opportunities for environmental innovation.

Our purpose in this chapter is not to encourage tree hugging, unless you are already so inclined. Instead, we want to help establish the intertwined linkages between supply chain activity and the future environment on which it depends. Virtually every action we take has some impact on the natural environment in which we live and on which future generations depend. Meeting the needs of the present without impairing future generations' ability to meet their needs calls for immense creativity and problem-solving ability. To those engaged in such endeavors, however, it is fun and rewarding. And with such consideration and action, we could all breathe a little easier.

5

Geopolitical and Social Systems Disruptions

Mrs. Crosby's is a popular local cantina located in Ciudad Acuña, a Mexican village just across the U.S. border from Del Rio, Texas, and only a three-hour drive west of San Antonio. Walking into Mrs. Crosby's is like stepping back in time. The wooden floors and furniture, antique brass and ceramic tile, and adobe walls with arched doorways (which are sometimes adorned with sombreros) create the aura of an Old West movie set. "Ma Crosby," as the place has been known by regulars, for over 80 years attended to an enigmatic mix of local Mexican blue-collar workers, American oilmen, tourists, ranchers, and a sometimes-boisterous detachment of U.S. military officers from a nearby airbase. In fact, the café used to see so much *American* business, from gringos crossing the border in search of a good time, that local native and country music legend George Strait featured it in his comic cowboy ballad "Blame it on Mexico." Strait's lyrics described one night's festivities there as including too much guitar music, tequila, salt, and lime, which led to the unfortunate early departure of the singer's potential love interest. Apparently, a short trip to Mexico was to blame for the protagonist's mischief, hangover, and subsequent aloneness.

Unfortunately, mounting numbers of Mrs. Crosby's customers have been blaming Mexico for other, much more serious transgressions in recent years. Whereas crossing the Rio Grande in search of fiesta had been a longstanding tradition for many neighboring Texans, many now stay home in fear of the increased violence in the area stemming from drug cartel activity. Shootings, theft, and other violent crimes in recent years have discouraged potential patrons from spending their downtime south of the border. Some local Americans see the problem as a product of the Mexican government's blatant disregard for their safety. Some patrons suggest that police "look the other way" when night falls and are largely uninterested in quelling street violence in and around the Ciudad. More than a few regular customers from the Mexican side of the river lament that Mrs. Crosby's now often looks more like an empty warehouse than a once-bustling and festive saloon.

It would be a gross understatement to say that the clashes between the drug cartels, law enforcement officers, and innocent bystanders along the U.S.–Mexican border have adversely impacted the local economy in recent decades. U.S. citizens working and living near the border have long sought refuge from life's predicaments at Mrs. Crosby's, but many no longer cross into Mexico because they fear for their lives. In the period between 2006 and 2010, drug cartel violence killed an estimated 28,000 people near the southern U.S. border.[1] The problem has become extremely difficult for the Mexican and American governments to collectively manage and has in fact recently become a point of friction between the two nations during trade discussions. However, these neighboring partners are not alone in their preoccupation with drug-related trade disruption. The demand for illegal narcotics generates billions of illicit and untaxable dollars for dealer networks worldwide. According to recent United Nations estimates, drugs classified as opiates, including heroin, yield more than $65 billion of illegitimate revenue annually based on current retail prices. The cocaine market alone could be worth nearly $85 billion. Though the illegal drug supply chain extending to Texas from Latin America has operated for decades, historically it has been considered more of an inconvenience for the U.S. and Mexican governments than an international threat to commerce. But since the 1980s, crime, violence, and intimidation have slowly yielded way to economic forms of hostility.[2] In spite of the apparent efficacy of the North American Free Trade Agreement (NAFTA), the national governments of the

---

[1] Burnett, John. (16 August 2010). "Mexico's Drug War Hits Historic Border Cantina." npr.org.

[2] Sterling, Eric E. (1 March 2012). "The War on Drugs Hurts Businesses and Investors." *Forbes*. Retrieved 27 July 2012 from www.forbes.com/sites/realspin/2012/03/01/the-war-on-drugs-hurts-businesses-and-investors/.

bordering nations seem unwilling or unable to do much to control the violence.

Pragmatically speaking, drug-related conflict certainly depresses trade along the southern U.S. border. But it also symbolizes a larger and more systemic problem affecting cross-border trade worldwide: the lack of geopolitical efficacy between many economically codependent states and nations. In the case of Ciudad Acuña, the drug wars themselves are undoubtedly important to resolve from the social and security standpoints of the locals. But they also are a microcosm of situations where businesses reliant on cross-border trade for survival are adversely affected by their national government's inability—or unwillingness—to address larger-scale social and diplomatic tribulations. In many cases, national governments' inactivity in solving localized societal issues inhibits the flow of goods and services between willing buyers and sellers across borders. The businesses that serve those nations as producers and consumers suffer accordingly.

To be clear, the chaos along the Rio Grande emanating from the drug trade is but one example of where a geopolitical problem— defined here as *a conflict in the interests between two or more geographically distinct government entities*—disturbs, interrupts, or inhibits a global supply chain from optimal performance. Generally speaking, domestic governments are not well designed to address localized commercial problems affecting businesses, especially during foreign dealings. In a way, the lack of government capability to foster micro-level economic exchange should be unsurprising. Most legislative bodies are arranged in the pursuit of multiple and sometimes countervailing objectives, only some of which are explicitly economic in nature. In the U.S., for example, the nation's founders provided seminal guidance for administering the federal government in the form of a mandate to "promote the general welfare" of the nation's citizens. But this mandate can be interpreted as including multiple economic and noneconomic (social or security-related) directives, and often a government's multiple missions conflict with one another. As a result, governing bodies sometimes act to directly address one type of concern at the expense of another (which draws the ire of the latter's strongest proponents). In modern times, this occurs most noticeably when the governing body in question seeks the advancement or preservation of social objectives, at the plausible expense of economic gains.

For example, the U.S. state of Arizona recently instituted strict—and controversial—immigration laws intended to curtail the influx of Mexican citizens moving into the state illegally. The new laws implicitly allow for the racial profiling of "Mexican-appearing" citizens and noncitizens alike during ordinary traffic stops. The result, intended or not, is that persons of Hispanic appearance can be legally intimidated, regardless of their legal citizenship status. In response, Mexico's central government has fought stalwartly against Arizona's new laws.[3] The laws appear to be reaching their desired outcome. Surveys indicate that over 100,000 persons of Mexican descent intend to leave the state (or have done so already), with fear of persecution or mistaken deportation cited anecdotally as a leading reason. Many of those leaving the state are believed to be legal U.S. citizens.[4] Some Arizona businesses are suffering economically due to the pursuit of the social objectives by the Arizona legislature, because of either a shorter supply of affordable labor or a reduced customer base.

Sociopolitical issues such as immigration have great potential impact on firms' ability to balance supply and demand and therefore turn a profit. For instance, on the supply side, businesses and farms across the southern U.S. have long survived—or even thrived—based on their ability to reliably attract workforces from the legal and illegal Hispanic labor pools. These workers are often willing to accept laborious positions that other demographic groups shun. However, this labor source is effectively being decimated in Arizona and a few other

---

[3] Davila, Vianna. (28 June 2011). "Fear of violence hurts Acuna business." mySanAntonio.com; "Mexico Joins Suit Against Arizona's Immigration Law, Citing 'Grave Concerns.'" (23 June 2010). FOX News; Reilly, Mark. (2 July 2012). "Late-night violence hurting downtown business." *Minneapolis-St. Paul Business Journal.*

[4] Myers, Amanda Lee. (22 June 2010). "Evidence suggests many immigrants leaving Arizona over new law." *Austin American-Statesman.* Associated Press; Tyler, Jeff. (18 May 2010). "Hispanics leave AZ over immigrant law." *Marketplace* (American Public Media); Stevenson, Mark. (11 November 2010). "Study: 100,000 Hispanics leave Arizona after immigration law debated." Associated Press. MSNBC.

states that have enacted parallel legislation.[5] In one notorious incident, the state of Georgia in 2011–2012 enacted laws aimed at aggressively reducing its illegal immigrant Hispanic worker population, ostensibly to "free up jobs" for American-born manual laborers. This action created a shortage of people to pick Georgia blueberries, melons, and other leading cash crops, and very few workers of any ethnicity (legal or otherwise) applied for the suddenly vacant positions. As a result, many thousands of bushels of produce died on the vine, devastating the annual supply market. Similarly, on the demand side of the equation, businesses such as restaurants, doctors' offices, auto repair shops, and shopping malls in southern Arizona are suffering the same fate as Mrs. Crosby's, only on the other side of the border. Though the problems associated with illegal immigration in Arizona and other border states are economically significant in terms of their influence on local demand and supply, they represent governments' inability to address macro-political problems on a micro-level scale. Returning to the illegal drug scenario, *Forbes* magazine writer Eric Sterling observed recently "…drug organizations depend on corrupting border guards, customs inspectors, police, prosecutors, judges, legislators, cabinet ministers, military officers, intelligence agents, financial regulators, and presidents and prime ministers. Businesses cannot count on the integrity of government officials in such environments."[6] The lesson is that these are not simply disagreements between different groups of citizens, at or near a national borderland. They are societal systems dilemmas—related to immigration, corruption, and social neglect—between multiple national governments. There are many noteworthy instances where such problems contribute to the decline in a local or national economy.

The drug feuds overwhelming Mexico and the American southwest are emblematic of how toxic blends of government conflict, foreign policy, and illegal activity can harm a company or industry's chances of survival. Mrs. Crosby's isn't the only business that has seen its operations interrupted because of external factors that are

---

[5] Ozimek, Adam. (21 June 2011). "Georgia's Harsh Immigration Law Costs Millions in Unharvested Crops." *The Atlantic.*

[6] Sterling, Eric E. (1 March 2012). "The War on Drugs Hurts Businesses and Investors." *Forbes.*

symbolic of greater political fissures. Problems such as terrorism, organized crime, diplomatic hostility, institutionalized corruption, and potential nationalism of foreign assets all are potential barriers to effective supply chain management when governments allow them to go unchecked or are simply unable to mitigate their risks.

The geopolitical and social systems risks we are concerned with encompass a wide and deep spectrum of activity, ranging from national government to individual levels, across high/low ranges of potential conflict and outcomes. At one end of the spectrum, we consider that large-scale conflicts between nations, such as wars and embargoes, are rare but can devastate a global supply chain when they do occur. At the opposite end, we see evidence that more constrained international issues such as cargo theft and open-seas piracy often present one-off, individualized threats that are highly disruptive to a particular shipment or situation. These threats are more easily mitigated by the involved companies via individual or government interaction. Most cargo theft involves valuable goods that can be resold on the black market.[7] Following a single incident, subsequent shipments can be rerouted or additional security provided.

Our goal in this chapter is to unpack the most salient geopolitical and social systems issues from across the spectrum and to devote space to uncovering potential solutions to the most pressing problems facing the future supply chain manager. However, nations and governments conflict with each other daily, and in hundreds of different ways. Given our current objectives, which are centered on identifying and addressing the opportunities and threats posed to the supply chains of the future, we focus on three particular aspects of the geopolitical panorama that present the most salient conceivable supply chain impacts. First, given that we are greatly concerned with supply and supply management, we address the potential (and already realized) impacts of commodity hoarding by governments on integrated supply chain management. There is already evidence that microeconomic trade via the supply chain is being inhibited by macroeconomic policy related to scarce materials, in situations where national governments are electing to hoard or stockpile key raw materials. This topic

---

[7] Burges, Dan. (2012). *Cargo Theft, Loss Prevention, and Supply Chain Security*. Waltham, MA: Butterworth-Heinemann.

is explored in the next section. Related to this trend, we are also concerned with the impacts that moderate-level intergovernment conflicts could have on future supply chains, in the form of export restrictions. As tensions between governments escalate, the embargo or complication of goods transfers to and from nations becomes important for companies to consider in their supply chain design. Second, given these issues, and considering them in light of the aforementioned global connectivity, we also address the potential impacts of widespread electronic network failure, particularly due to deliberate action (such as cyber attacks) on the part of governments or terrorists. The reliance of modern firms on electronic information systems presents a potentially critical weakness that must be addressed if they are to ensure supply continuity. Third, given that some critical commodities are becoming *extremely* scarce either locally or worldwide, we briefly consider the possibility that major military conflicts between nations and/or individual terrorism groups will inhibit both future supply and demand, and we evaluate a selection of the most probable of these scenarios. Contemplating these types of geopolitical risks provides a basis for both opportunistic advantage seeking and threat mitigation for companies in the coming years.

Commodity Hoarding and Export Restriction: The China Syndrome

The Earth is endowed with many natural resources that for all practical purposes are nonrenewable, but that are also basically "required" to sustain the human race. In addition, though some renewable resources such as grain or freshwater are relatively abundant worldwide, they sometimes exist in limited quantities in different locales. In spite of these supply restrictions, natural resources are often widely and voluminously demanded. As a result, throughout history political units have tended to organize themselves in ways that best facilitate their acquisition. Consider as a simple example that most cities in Scandinavia and Australia historically developed along coastal regions. This occurred at least in part because much of the interior land of these nations is untenable for growing crops due to weather and terrain. The indigenous peoples in each case located themselves near a reliable food supply (such as fish) and where they could most easily receive water shipment of resources brought back from abroad. However, for scarce but highly demanded resources, especially those that are nonrenewable, the "creation of availability" has often led to significant conflict between political units. Students of history can recall many instances where resource shortages have created disputes or even wars over finite but very important resource stocks. The Roman Empire conquered foreign lands to capture both servants and food supply, for example. In recent years numerous countries have warred over increasingly limited stocks of petroleum. (But often the underlying reason has been cloaked in a social cause, given that the taking of life for the sake of resource acquisition is often considered unpalatable within "civilized" society.)

When political entities such as states or nations control a preponderance of a key commodity's supply, political tensions with others often arise. The production of oil by dictatorships, and the correlated behaviors of the OPEC countries that produce and control its supply, provide the most obvious modern example. Similarly, even as we were writing this book, one of China's state newspapers released a report affirming that the country had begun stockpiling its reserves of several rare-earth metals needed by other nations to produce industrial machinery.[8] Countries stockpile resources as a strategy to create geopolitical leverage, and this behavior both strengthens the holding nation and weakens others. For example, China accounts for an overwhelming 90% of daily world rare-earth metals production, and it holds 23% of the world's rare-earth reserves.[9] The stranglehold that the Chinese have on the rare-earth metals market insures the Chinese people against external economic threats. It also serves as a direct threat to others seeking to do business with Chinese companies or their supply chain partners. And rare-earth metals aren't the only commodities China is stockpiling. According to an Asian coal analyst,

[8] Currie, Adam. (12 July 2012). "Market Focused on Chinese REE Strategic Reserves." *RARE EARTH Investing News.*

[9] "China warns its rare earth reserves are declining." (20 June 2012). BBC News: Business.

the country had coal reserves of up to 9.5 million tons in the summer of 2012.[10] Oil and coal are two of China's main sources of energy, and for a country with such enormous domestic demand, any stockpiling is bound to affect worldwide consumption.

Some economic indicators suggest that the current growth of China's economy is slowing. If that's the case, China may be stockpiling commodities to have near unchecked price control down the road. Therefore, scarce resources would act as a hedge against recession. If the Chinese government controls highly sought commodities, it can also regulate how much it exports at a time, thereby manipulating demand in its favor and allowing it to drive up prices in the process. Although we certainly don't predict that these circumstances will lead to warfare in the next quarter century, they definitely put the world in a tenuous geopolitical situation. Revisiting Malthus, unless we see some sort of groundbreaking innovation that eliminates the need for these commodities, businesses and countries will be forced to buy key raw materials from the Chinese. But they won't want—or be able—to pay monopolistic prices. The European Union, the United States, and Japan have all implicated China on such charges in recent years, but it has defended itself by claiming that the measures are necessary to adjust to falling market prices.[11] Already we can see quarrels developing among countries that rely on these commodities. And, lest we appear prejudiced, it should be noted that the amassing of critical resources for geopolitical benefit is hardly confined to China. Much as China hoards palladium, tungsten, and zinc, other nations also hoard key resources and use them to barter for various national strategic considerations. Table 5.1 lists the 23 nonrenewable natural resources that are expected to become highly or extremely scarce in the next 20 years. Each of these plays a key role in producing highly demanded goods and services. The table also estimates their remaining global share by country, based on the 2012 U.S. Geological Survey.

---

[10] Bradsher, Keith. (22 June 2012). "Chinese Data Mask Depth of Slowdown, Executives Say." *New York Times*.

[11] www.manilatimes.net.

Table 5.1 Scarce Nonrenewable Resources and Known World Locations

Resource	Global Production, 2011 (in Tons)	Probability of Depletion by 2030*	Common Uses	Locations of the Largest Remaining Stores[12]
Cadmium	21,500	Nearly certain	Batteries, paints, plastics	China, Korea, Japan
Gold	2,700	Nearly certain	Electronics, wire, jewelry	China, Australia, U.S.
Mercury	1,930	Nearly certain	Scientific instruments	China, Kyrgyzstan
Tellurium	Unknown; less than 100	Nearly certain	Alloys, solar panels, semiconductors, CDs	Japan, China
Tungsten	72,000	Nearly certain	Alloys, munitions, lubricants, lighting	Democratic Republic of the Congo
Cobalt	98,000	Very high	Aircraft engines, cutting tools	Democratic Republic of the Congo, Russia, Canada
Lead	4,500	Very high	Automotive batteries, steel structures	Australia, China, Russia
Molybdenum	250,000	Very high	Steel and cast-iron alloy, metal powder	China, U.S., Chile
Phosphate rock	191,000	Very high	Phosphoric acid, fertilizers, animal feed supplements	Morocco, Iraq, China
Platinum group metals	399,000	Very high	Emission reduction catalyst, bulk chemical manufacturing	South Africa, Russia
Silver	23,800	Very high	X-ray films, jewelry, electronics	Peru, Poland, Chile
Titanium	186,000	Very high	Paint, paper, plastics, aerospace	China, U.S., Germany
Zinc	12,400	Very high	Alloys, agriculture industry, chemical industry	Australia, China, Peru
Chromium	24,000	High	Stainless steel, heat-resistant steel	Kazakhstan, South Africa
Coal	7,229[13]	High	Energy, electricity	U.S., Russia, China[14]

Resource	Global Production, 2011 (in Tons)	Probability of Depletion by 2030°	Common Uses	Locations of the Largest Remaining Stores[12]
Copper	16,100	High	Building construction, electronics, transportation	Chile, Peru, Australia
Indium	640	High	Liquid crystal displays (LCDs), solders, alloys	China, Korea
Iron ore	2,800	High	Iron, locomotives, paper clips	Australia, Brazil, Russia
Lithium	34,000	High	Ceramics, glass, batteries	Chile, China
Magnesium	780	High	Packaging, transportation	China
Natural gas	193 billion cubic meters	High	Heating, electricity	U.S., Russia, Iran[15]
Nickel	1,800,000	High	Stainless steel, nonferrous alloys, electroplating	Australia, New Caledonia, Brazil
Oil	4,028[16]	High	Transportation, fuel	Saudi Arabia, Venezuela, Iran[17]

° Nearly certain = 97% or greater; very high probability = 95% or greater; high probability = 90% or greater

12 U.S. Department of the Interior, Mineral Commodity Summaries, 2012.

13 Coal Statistics. (2011). The World Coal Association.

14 "Coal Matters: Global Availability of Coal." The World Coal Association.

15 BP Statistical Review of World Energy, 2011.

16 Ibid.

17 Ibid.

As shown in the table, numerous countries are participating in the resource arbitrage game to ensure the future safety and life quality of their people. China figures in prominently, holding the majority of the remaining quantities of cadmium, gold, and mercury. All these resources are becoming extremely rare and play a significant role in manufacturing and technological innovation processes. In addition, China holds major stockpiles of titanium, zinc, indium, and magnesium, which are needed for paints, LCDs, and thousands of metallic machine parts. Additionally, China controls over 90% of the annual production of rare-earth metals used in high-tech items such as computer monitors, communication devices, and military night-vision goggles. China has placed export controls on what the Chinese consider to be "their" mineral resources. Clearly, China will wield awesome power in terms of the future of manufacturing unless alternative deposits of many of these materials are discovered. Some scientists suspect that the ocean floors may be tapped in the pursuit of alternative sources.

Other materials, such as tellurium and tungsten, are also in drastically short supply and are also unevenly and heterogeneously deposited around the globe. Each plays a huge role in modern manufacturing processes. Many of these and other critically short resources are located inside the borders of highly unstable nations such as the Democratic Republic of the Congo, Kyrgyzstan, and Kazakhstan. Or they are in countries that typically deal poorly with Westernized partners due to severe cultural differences or historical conflicts (Russia, Iraq, Iran, Saudi Arabia). Clearly, the advantages to a nation holding scarce and badly needed resources are many. Yet many nations holding scarce resources are also among the poorest on Earth. The U.S. Central Intelligence Agency tracks the resource positions of all the world's nations. Several nations that are relatively low in terms of annual GDP output actually score highly on latent resource holdings. Often, this occurs because the country in question lags in the economic development cycle to such a degree that resource extraction or refinement is impossible. In some cases, the nation's political environment is volatile enough that external partnerships for the purposes of extraction are untenable. We see such situations as presenting great opportunity for developed nations over the coming quarter century if the political barriers can be overcome.

Table 5.2 highlights several such situations where the "right partnership" with an underdeveloped nation could yield surprising benefits to first-world nations or multinational enterprises. Nations such as Gabon and Kazakhstan are rapidly developing infrastructures that will allow for future partnerships to be built for such commodities as oil and natural gas. Others are less developed and currently remain hostile to outside partnerships. The CIA estimates that the Central African Republic, Mali, and Democratic Republic of the Congo possess some of the richest undeveloped resource stores on Earth, but historically they have been plagued by civil unrest and internal violence. As the world becomes more resource-strapped and economically leveled, these nations will rise in relative power if they can leverage their untapped resource bases. Firms competing in industries that rely on these resources for survival will face a serious dilemma. They can create a disruptive innovation that allows the resource in question to be eliminated from product designs. Or they can strategically partner with foreign allies (or governments themselves) that can provide sufficient access to the focal commodity.

Table 5.2 Resource-Rich But Underdeveloped Nations

Nation	World GDP Rank	Key Natural Resources
Gabon	61	Petroleum, diamonds, manganese, uranium
Kazakhstan	64	Major petroleum deposits, natural gas, copper, uranium, zinc, gold, molybdenum
Namibia	86	Diamonds, copper, uranium, gold, lithium, cadmium, tungsten, zinc
Bosnia/Herzegovina	104	Coal, copper, iron ore, zinc, nickel
Kyrgyzstan	157	Significant gold and rare earths, coal, oil, natural gas, mercury, bismuth, zinc
Burma	158	Coal, precious stones, antimony, zinc, copper
Mali	166	Bauxite, manganese, copper, tin, gold, uranium
Central African Republic	179	Diamonds, uranium, gold, oil
Democratic Republic of the Congo	190	Petroleum, tantalum, copper, diamonds, gold, silver, zinc, uranium, natural gas

Source: CIA World Factbook 2012

If the actor seeking a supply of a scarce resource is a national government, a third but more unsavory option exists: taking the needed commodity by force. However, unlike ancient times, the first resort in the modern age for acquiring scarce resources is rarely to exercise military force. Typically, today nations enter into economic agreements that are agreeable to both parties. The purchase of resources by foreign countries is a growing theme. Over $1 billion in resources currently is purchased each day via market exchanges or private transactions. However, this has made some companies in resource-rich countries fearful of foreign purchase of their raw-material resources, and this could significantly disrupt the local company's supply chain. For example, Australia blocked the purchase of one of its ore mining companies by a Chinese firm. Australia is also currently in the middle of a controversy over the purchase of a major coal mining company by a U.S. purchaser.[18]

Alternatively, fears that national control will be surrendered are counterbalanced in many situations by export restrictions. Restrictions on exports of key raw materials can be problematic for domestic supply chains, whether or not the resources in question are renewable. Consider Argentina, one of the world's leading corn exporters.[19] Countries and companies around the world use several forms of corn to make food products, antibiotics, livestock feed, oil-based products, artificial sweeteners, and even adhesives.[20] The U.S.-based Corn Refiners Association estimates that about 4,000 products in a typical American grocery store have some sort of corn ingredient. With so much depending on a single input, when a country like Argentina sets ceilings on its corn exports, the global market is bound to suffer. The Argentine government insists that it does so to "guarantee affordable local food supplies and help tame high inflation."[21] But when drought or other unforeseen disasters strike elsewhere, as they did in the United States in the summer of 2012, foreign farmers struggle to maintain production, and manufacturers must seek supply elsewhere. When "elsewhere" is a country like Argentina, which has a corn export

[18] *Wall Street Journal*, August 2011; Voeller, 2010.

[19] Capehart, Thomas. (28 May 2012). "Corn Trade." United States Department of Agriculture: Economic Research Service.

[20] "Corn." Iowa State University: Center for Crops Utilization Research.

[21] Burke, Hilary and Alejandro Lifschitz. (16 July 2012). "Argentina to approve more corn exports; 'Plant corn, boys,' president says Monday." *Grainews: Practical production tips for the prairie farmer.*

quota of 7.5 million tons,[22] the increased demand and limited supply send prices soaring. Some Argentinean farmers are pressing the government to end the export quotas so that they can increase their output.[23] By way of analogy, others are circumventing the wheat ceiling by choosing to produce barley instead.[24] Finding a viable substitute for corn would be useful in the same way.

In summary, supply chain managers of the future will often find themselves battling the competition for not only customers, but also scarce resources. As with many supply chain tasks, the development of key relationships will be critical, especially when it appears necessary to avoid export quotas or to navigate internal conflict within a supplying nation. We expect resource hoarding to expand significantly in the next 25 to 30 years as well, as more and more resources become scarce due to increased consumption based on population growth and economic leveling. We present advice for future supply chain managers at the chapter's conclusion.

Government Risks and Considerations

In addition to the strategic constraint of resources by governments, supply chain managers of the future will face increasing additional diplomatic and sociopolitical threats that will inhibit the effectiveness and/or efficiency of their systems. Entire books could be written about these subjects, but our research leads us to believe that three types of such future threats possess likelihood/magnitude profile characteristics that warrant consideration here. First, in many nations, the pervasive and entrenched corruption of local and national government officials has long given potential foreign market entrants pause. In many cases, government officials abuse their power in highly coordinated ways to gain personal benefit, and this endangers

---

[22] Walsh, Heather. (18 April 2012). "Argentina Meets About Extra Corn Export Quota, Group Says." *Bloomberg*.

[23] Gonzalez, Pablo. (23 July 2012). "Argentine Corn Growers Urge Export Cap to Boost Crop 60%." *Bloomberg*.

[24] "Argentine farmers changing from wheat to barley to avoid export taxes." (21 July 2012). MercoPress: South Atlantic News Agency.

the long-term viability of the supply chain network in multiple ways. All nations are corrupt, just not equally so.

To judge the risks of corruption on a global supply chain venture, supply chain managers should assess both the pervasiveness and arbitrariness of the illicit activity. Arbitrariness can be thought of as the ambiguity or complexity associated with navigating the nation's illicit social systems. For example, in India and Russia, a variety of ever-changing bribes, kickbacks, and other unethical practices are regarded by many as accepted methods for a foreign business entity to succeed. In places like Mexico and Chile, the "rules of the game" are just as pervasive but are more explicit.[25] Supply chain managers should consider pervasiveness and arbitrariness together when assessing their supply chain partnering strategy in a foreign nation. As arbitrariness increases, firms may want to establish joint ventures with partners rather than locating wholly owned distribution or production facilities there or, better yet, avoid engaging supply chain partners there. As pervasiveness increases, in situations where the partner is of critical interest, the best move seems to be creating and maintaining an arm's-length relationship, with several backup suppliers in development if possible.

Corruption is at least to some extent an inverse function of income (in that officials in poorer nations have greater incentives to divert resources for personal gain). Therefore, managers should be aware that corrupt practices are most likely to take place when they are partnering with a resource-poor nation. The Corruption Perception Index (CPI), published annually by Transparency International, captures this phenomenon. Figure 5.1 shows a world map of its most recent CPI. The lighter shaded countries received the highest scores in the CPI, reflecting freedom from corruption. The darker shaded areas are likely to be most problematic for managers seeking to take supply or serve customers there. Notably, the least-corrupt areas according to the index include North America, Western Europe, and Australia. Areas in which to exercise extreme caution include Venezuela, Iraq,

---

[25] See Rodriguez, Peter, Klaus Uhlenbruck, and Lorraine Eden, "Government Corruption and the Entry Strategies of Multinationals," Academy of Management Review, April 2005, for a highly rigorous treatment of this subject.

the Baltic-area former Russian states, Burma, and the areas around the eastern horn of Africa (such as Sudan and Somalia). We expect less relative corruption to occur worldwide as populations diversify and economies level; however, a number of problem spots such as these will remain threats in the future.

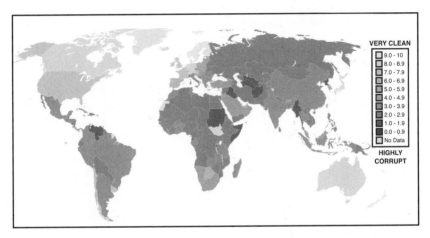

Figure 5.1 Corruption Perception Index, Transparency International (2011)

A second and related concern pertains to the possibility that foreign governments can either explicitly or effectively nationalize the assets of a foreign business within their borders. In many cases, domestic governments have nationalized businesses' property without compensation to the former owners. For instance, in 1971, Libya famously nationalized the local supply chain assets of British Petroleum in response to Britain's failure to protect it from Iranian aggression. Such situations would obviously disrupt the supply chain significantly and would cost the entrant significantly in terms of lost physical assets. In recent years, the nationalization of scarce resources such as petroleum has increased in frequency. We expect this behavior to accelerate as governments increasingly squabble over badly needed resources that are coming into short supply. Nationalizations are most likely to occur when resource prices are high (or suddenly become high), when corruption is high, when the local government is run under an extremely socialist system, and/or when that system provides for relatively weak checks and balances versus the chief government executive (president, prime minister, monarch).[26] Supply chain managers should assess these issues before undertaking large and expensive market-entry maneuvers in the coming years, while adjusting carefully for the relative global scarcity of the commodity or finished good in question.

Third, and perhaps most important for supply chain managers to consider in the short to medium term, is the pervasiveness of uncontrolled illicit trade of counterfeit and knockoff goods in the supply-and-demand markets. The manufacture and sale of counterfeit finished goods has exploded over the past two decades. It is expected to continue in the future due to lack of customs enforcement in combination with lax intellectual property laws in many low-cost-labor nations where manufacturing occurs. In 2009, the U.S. value alone of fraudulent finished goods was over $260 million, across a wide variety of sectors, from footwear to electronics to jewelry.[27] The following year the Office of U.S. Trade published a list of the primary sources of counterfeit goods in the U.S. market:

- Algeria
- Argentina
- Canada
- Chile
- China
- India
- Indonesia
- Pakistan
- Russia
- Thailand
- Venezuela

However, the report also noted that intellectual property laws were strengthening across Eastern Europe and several other world regions, indicating a glimmer of hope.

---

[26] Guriev, Sergei, Anton Kolotilin, and Konstantin Solin. (Spring 2011). "Determinants of Nationalization in the Oil Sector." *Journal of Law, Economics, and Organization*.

[27] "Growth in Counterfeit Goods Shows No Signs of Abating." (24 April 2010). *Supply Chain Digest*.

However, not all of the worries surrounding counterfeiting are centered on the U.S. finished-goods sector. Fraudulent materials are introduced at all levels of the supply chain, all around the world, every day. Counterfeit parts often are manufactured and shipped to free-trade zones worldwide for assembly into finished goods. Copyrighted intellectual products are a popular vehicle, because they represent low up-front investments for criminal enterprises. Many pirated or fake goods are currently sold online. We expect this trend to explode as criminals become more sophisticated at web design and electronic commerce and as worldwide economies flatten. High-tech and medical-device markets are another significant venue for criminal activity due to the products' design similarity and high price points. Even the U.S. military is feeling the effects of counterfeiting. A 2012 investigation by the U.S. Senate Armed Services Committee found that over 1,800 cases of counterfeit electronic parts had been purchased and incorporated into weapons systems. We expect the trend toward counterfeiting to flourish as customers from around the world increase their participation in global commerce.

Tangible and Virtual Intentional Disruptions

It would be impractical to try to provide full coverage of the incidence of manifest physical and virtual conflict in a supply chain primer. But we believe that a few notes related to political conflict pertain significantly to our assessment of future supply chains. Some futurists and political scientists are predicting potential wars over primary resources such as water, oil, and food in the future. In the pursuit of scarce resources, conflict has occurred many times between nations and cultural units throughout history. In some cases, such conflicts take the form of traditional wars, whereby political entities literally battle over key commodities in the name of survival. As an example, the Sudan, which is divided into northern and southern regions, has long endured conflict and civil war based on its former colonization as well as its racial and religious divisions.[28] Although ruling positions,

---

[28] Raftopolous, Brian and Karin Alexander. (2006). "Peace in the Balance: The Crisis in Sudan." Institute for Justice and Reconciliation.

elite statuses, and demographic differences are all significant in the Sudan's complicated history, so too are the resources that the two sides have clashed over. The land is rich in natural resources—oil and water in particular. Both regions seek to establish economic and political stability, and both need control of the resource-rich areas to do so. Tribes wage civil war against one another. Neither the Sudan nor South Sudan intends to give up the fight for the borderlands that both economies need to survive—nor do they intend to compromise. The battles started in the mid-1940s, and they continue today.[29]

We can easily envision two types of wars that have great potential for future supply chain disruption. The CIA has already noted that shortages of basic human needs—particularly food and water—are on the horizon. Given their salience to human existence, they provide significant motivation for full-scale conflicts in the future. We can particularly envision scenarios in which industrialized nations using mass quantities of water for manufacturing purposes become the targets of poorer nations needing water for human survival. Relatedly, due to the lowering of aquifers stemming from global climate change, food is becoming relatively harder to produce in mass quantities. Therefore, nations may begin to war over supplies of both food and the water needed for its irrigation in the next 20 years. Alternatively, more humans on Earth consuming more goods also equals increasingly massive amounts of waste by-products, the most significant of which is garbage. Chapter 4, "The Changing Physical Environment," introduced the "Great Pacific Garbage Patch," which we believe has the potential to annihilate an entire aquatic ecosystem if allowed to perpetuate. However, it is likely that many nations will come together and form agreements to police ocean dumping in the name of saving the food fish supply in the Pacific. If this occurs, and garbage volumes increase in proportion to the growing population, the potential for "garbage wars" also exists. Some futurists believe that full-scale battles will be fought over which nation is forced to serve as a region's garbage dump. Such conflicts are already appearing in locales such as Chicago, where they are currently being fought on the battlefield of politics, rather than with guns. But there is no guarantee that less

---

[29] www.upi.com/Business_News/Energy-Resources/2012/05/03/Sudans-on-brink-of-all-out-war-over-oil/UPI-16581336078729/.

civilized and more distressed nations (with less or nothing to lose) will react similarly.[30]

However, it is not always the case that an international conflict will take place between governments. Sometimes, small groups of actors become disconcerted with imbalances in wealth, perceive inequities in standards of living, or for other reasons seek to act violently to bring about social or economic change. In other words, though a terror act typically is executed against individuals within a society, it is often done to achieve broader political goals. Most of us are well aware of the incidences of terrorism that have received publicity since the 9/11 crisis in New York, Washington, D.C., and Pennsylvania over a decade ago. Yet we only rarely or unceremoniously consider terrorism when conducting supply chain planning. Figure 5.2 shows the terrorism incidents that have occurred since the year 2000. Not coincidentally, some of the areas we've been speaking of all along in the Middle East and Africa have seen the greatest occurrence rates. Logically speaking, incidences of terrorism should decrease as the planet levels into broader economic equality. However, the concern we share with future supply chain managers is that the proliferation of terrorist-enabling weapons worldwide will provide more opportunities for such criminals to act. Though the likelihood of such attacks is small, and of their success smaller, we encourage supply chain planners to consider world terror hotspots when designing future networks. We also emphasize that these may not be the same places that we all grew up dreading. When citizens of any nation become financially repressed, they eventually lash out at those who have more. As a result, it will be important in the future to consider the safety and security provided by some traditionally stable nations such as Greece and Spain, once their financial paths following the 2009–2011 recession are better determined.

Generally speaking, if any subsequent reaction to the 9/11 attacks was productive for global supply chain managers, it was the resultant heightening of security awareness worldwide. The systems that were enacted following the tragedy to protect people have also proven to be largely effective at protecting goods and materials inventories.

---

[30] Pellow, David N. (2004). *Garbage Wars: The Struggle for Environmental Justice in Chicago*. Cambridge, MA: MIT Press.

However, in the same time span, as we've mentioned, the Internet has proliferated greatly. Savvy would-be terrorists have to some degree concluded that they can do as much or more damage through cyber attacks on social, political, and financial institutions. The widespread impact of viruses, worms, and other bugs, as well as direct attacks on highly targeted institutions (through hacking) appear to be the terrorists' next frontier. Critical systems such as power grids, intranets, dams, and credit scoring systems are all vulnerable targets and will be for the foreseeable future. Given that the supply chain trades as much or more in information and financial flows as it does physical transactions, supply chain managers should be highly cognizant of this growing threat in the coming years.

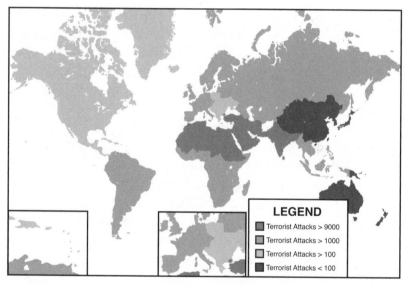

Figure 5.2 Incidents of terrorism, 2000 to present

Geopolitical Challenges for Future Supply Chain Managers

Changes to the geopolitical environment will threaten the efficacy of many of the world's increasingly globalized supply chains in the future. As supply-and-demand networks lengthen and markets diversify in location, it is possible that many different types of conflicts will present themselves as hazards to efficient and effective supply chain processes. Though a great number of geopolitical issues constantly affect world commercial activity. We see the following as key issues related to the geopolitical environment that may be particularly problematic for businesses seeking to optimize supply chains over the coming two to three decades:

- Shortages of petroleum-based fuel needed to transport goods will become common. Shipping costs and risks will therefore rise unless alternative sources are embraced, possibly leading to faux-regionalization or localization of some markets.

- Import/export restrictions on critical commodities may periodically force expensive supply chain redesigns.

- Commodity hoarding by nations seeking political advantage may shorten product life cycles and diversify supply requirements, leading to stock-keeping unit (SKU) proliferation.

- Full-blown international conflicts are possible in the next 20 years if innovation to replace some critical commodities (fuel and minerals) within high-demand product or process designs fails. Later, in 20 to 30 years, conflicts are also possible over the acquisition of basic necessities (food and water) or disposal of by-products (such as garbage and nuclear waste).

- Intentional disruption, violence, and terrorism risks will skyrocket as commodities become increasingly scarce. The effects will be proportional to the extent that local/national governments are incapable of addressing them or are willing to turn a blind eye.

- Cyber terrorists represent an equally threatening risk. They may succeed in corrupting supply chain systems that promote visibility of product and/or facilitate shopping/payment.

- Counterfeiting and black/gray markets will destroy supply chain value propositions if they are left unchecked or remain undetected.

- Regulatory risks have always existed in supply and demand market locations, but regulations of the future may be applied more aggressively and/or arbitrarily based on local perceptions of foreign businesses' home nation. Similarly, corruption in foreign governments will always present risks to foreign supply chain assets.

As nations develop economically, they present relatively less political risk to supply chain partners due to economic investment and inertia. We expect the economic leveling of many nations to reduce such risks substantially. However, the challenges associated with geopolitical conflict stemming from resource-based conflicts of interest are numerous and can greatly affect each of the eight GSCF supply chain processes in the future. Future supply chain managers are advised to increasingly consider geopolitical risks as potentially significant to their global supply chains and to develop contingency and/ or crisis plans that address critical demand and supply points. Additionally, geopolitical risk should increasingly figure into supply chain network design, especially at more distant echelons, as new products are being developed and old ones reconfigured. Table 5.3 lists each process and describes some projected potential geopolitical change implications. As shown in the table, the implications of geopolitical risk affect each area of the GSCF and therefore influence how supply chain managers of the future should conduct business. In the area of customer relationship management, managers cannot ignore how the potential activities, policies, and restrictions created by governments will influence their business relationships with customers and supply chain partners. For example, firms must consider the geopolitical risk in the market locations they select. What seems to be an advantageous location on the surface, based on initial cost-and-profit analysis, may not be lucrative once changing geopolitical risks are included in the decision. For instance, even as recently as 2007, U.S. oil companies in the Caribbean saw their assets seized during nationalization activities of Venezuelan leader Hugo Chavez.[31] Similarly, as population growth and resource scarcity increase, we expect that governments will increasingly restrict, interfere with, or even seize foreign business entities in their country. Therefore, firms should select supply chain partners who are adept at tracking and even influencing geopolitical policy and regulations in the target country where end customers are located. One way to avoid additional risk in a volatile region is to use capacity sharing agreements for transportation and production with partners who already have infrastructure in the country. Doing so

---

[31] Crooks, Nathan and Corina Pons. (April 2012). "Exxon gets disappointing $750 million after Venezuela seizure." *Bloomberg News*.

avoids further investment and risk. In the future, managers must also expect geopolitical conflicts and build contingency plans for limiting the impact of potential wars, seizures, or restrictions placed on their operations. The ability to virtually extract information and pre-plan for the evacuation of resources and personnel in the event of political upheaval or war should be considered part of the cost of doing business in a transforming world.

Table 5.3 Geopolitical Change Implications for SCM

GSCF Process	Geopolitical Implications
Customer relationship management (CRM)	Challenges:
	Demand market risks magnified by political and legal uncertainty will lead to suboptimized customer selection and poorly specified relationship management metrics.
	Cost-to-serve will become blurred due to security requirements and political risk (nationalization, enforceability of sales agreements).
	New customer opportunities may appear potentially lucrative until import/export regulation issues are considered.
	Regulations and legal issues may adversely affect cost-to-serve in hidden or ambiguous ways.
	Suggestions:
	Market location must be factored into customer segmentation criteria due to potential geopolitical trade risks.
	Account management teams should be constructed with the customer's national culture in mind and be trained on current, relevant geopolitical issues.
	Adopt total landed cost perspectives toward customer selection and service capability.
	Write product/service agreements with legal enforceability in both the home and host nation in mind.
	Enlist local supply chain partners to assist with local regulations pertaining to customers. Immerse expatriate employees in local cultural training.
	Approach select noncompetitors about the possibility of capacity-sharing agreements for transportation and production.

GSCF Process	Geopolitical Implications
Customer service management (CSM)	Challenges:
	Disruptions (both intentional and accidental) as well as regulatory risks will increase the likelihood and magnitude of customer service failure events.
	Key products or parts may become difficult to repair or replace due to commodity stockpiling in an important supply location.
	Regulations and legal issues may adversely affect cost to recovery in hidden or ambiguous ways.
	Export/import restrictions and customs seizures may prevent the ability to provide customer service to key customers.
	Suggestions:
	Establish customer service companies in politically "neutral" locations to address service failures in affected nations in the event of international political conflicts.
	Strategically and incrementally expand and diversify supply base and service center locations to hedge against political commodity hoarding impacts on recovery.
Demand management (DM)	Challenges:
	Valid information for making demand and supply projections may be more difficult to come by as resources become scarce and political entities take more active control of markets.
	Limited fuel and transportation capacity may make variability reduction and flexibility to meet demand harder to achieve.
	It may be difficult to identify network bottlenecks due to political differences in seemingly similar supply chains.
	Vendor-managed replenishment strategies may struggle in import/export-constrained situations.
	Suggestions:
	Conduct robust supply chain risk analyses that illuminate avoidable risks associated with supply/demand uncertainty and vulnerability.
	Work with supply chain partners to collect information and identify network bottlenecks and constraints to serving demand.
	Implement thoroughly vetted supply chain risk strategies that hedge risks through supply chain flexibility, such as taking positions in "safe harbor" locations.

GSCF Process	Geopolitical Implications
Demand management (DM) (continued)	Conduct demand execution plans (such as sales and operations planning) that incorporate the substitutable capacities of supply, manufacturing, and logistics resources around the world.
	Work with in-country market experts to identify hidden demand variability created by political activities, restrictions, and volatility.
Manufacturing flow management (MFM)	Challenges:
	Counterfeit goods introduced into the supply chain may compromise product quality and are not controlled by all governments.
	Unforeseen embargos or export restraints may yield stockouts of key raw materials needed by manufacturing plants.
	Intentional disruption of goods and information inflows due to political activity may interrupt or delay manufacturing lines.
	Manufacturing assets are at risk of shutdown or nationalization by local officials or stakeholders.
	Low-cost labor outsourcing to foreign countries during the past two decades has placed large production capacities in regions that face great geopolitical risks.
	Companies are likely to resort to "push" strategies and to bolster inventory levels under speculation of manufacturing disruption.
	Suggestions:
	Work actively with local and national host governments on programs to reduce market subversion and increase security.
	Design networks with adequate degrees of freedom (or migrate to flexworks) to address sudden facility immobilization.
	Design supply bases with adequate degrees of freedom. Activate supplier development programs to hedge against supply volume shifts or losses of key suppliers.
	If affordable, consider shadow plants in nearby nations or divide capacity across borders.
	Build future manufacturing plants and capabilities that reduce or even eliminate manufacturing infrastructure. Trade in production knowledge and information, and limit investment in actual manufacturing capacity in geopolitically volatile areas.

GSCF Process	Geopolitical Implications
Order fulfillment (OF)	Challenges:
	Fuel cost volatility and increases may challenge current transportation networks' economic viability more frequently. Shifting to alternative modes such as rail networks may be expensive and may lack the needed infrastructure and capacity.
	Import/export restrictions may emerge that would require immediate network redesign and new transportation flows.
	Terrorists/saboteurs and violent locals will tend to attack network links rather than nodes due to security challenges.
	Cyberterrorism poses a constant threat to in-transit inventory visibility and status.
	Import quotas are likely to tighten during geopolitical conflicts.
	Customs inspections and increased scrutiny of operations can introduce long and variable delivery lead times.
	Suggestions:
	Develop flexworks to address fuel issues.
	Investigate public-private partnerships to develop alternative transportation capacity, such as rail and inland water transport.
	Lobby governing bodies to lift restrictions and increase transportation investment.
	If affordable, implement shadow information technologies.
	Contract with and actively engage in security management. Take this function in-house if security concerns threaten core competencies and the execution of vital operations.
Product development and commercialization (PD & C)	Challenges:
	Intellectual property protection suffers during times of geopolitical conflict. Quick counterfeiting is possible, with commensurate value deterioration.
	Cross-national collaboration with foreign subsidiaries, suppliers, customers, and research organizations is hindered due to political tension, conflict, and policy incongruence.
	Rules and regulations for entering new markets impart resistance on product launches.
	Differing technological standards and laws create product proliferation and inhibit the implementation of common technologies.

GSCF Process	Geopolitical Implications
Product development and commercialization (PD & C) (continued)	Suggestions:
	Enact intellectual property security initiatives, and practice selective distribution early in product life cycles.
	Use highly encrypted private cloud space for collaboration with foreign entities and to coordinate solutions to disruptions.
	Lobby and work with foreign governments to prevent disruptions to product launches, to receive technical licenses, and to prevent counterfeiting of intellectual property. Be prepared to offer incentives and offsets to gain support.
Returns management (RM)	Challenges:
	Fraudulent returns are possible where black/gray markets exist.
	Policies for managing waste streams and end-of-life products are often inconsistent or absent.
	Potential contamination and quality issues arise where mismanaged returns flows are reintroduced to the forward supply chain in countries and regions that lack sufficient controls.
	Increased potential exists for active geopolitical activity and regulations related to returned goods and waste streams.
	Suggestions:
	Careful gatekeeping at the outset of the returns process could reduce inadvertent loss. Shift to more conservative returns policies in higher-risk locations.
	Implement RFID and future advanced technologies to track and identify the firm's products and to eliminate counterfeit goods from the reverse supply chain.
	Increase security and inspection of returned goods and materials in locations where policies and controls are lacking.
	Build networks and practices now that will proactively prepare for increased regulation and returns policies abroad.

GSCF Process	Geopolitical Implications
Supplier relationship management (SRM)	Challenges:
	Supply markets will carry additional risks associated with national political interests at multiple tiers in the supply chain.
	Supplier segmentation will become even more difficult due to origin nations' risk factors (raw materials capacity constraints and volatility, most-favored-nation status, political tensions).
	Supply market complexity will grow as multiple nations with different risk factors participate, leading to more bottleneck and strategic (expensive to assess) commodity contracts.
	Suggestions:
	Open-book costing should be utilized wherever possible. Written contingency supplier plans with a broader supply base may be necessary.
	Adjust global sourcing decisions based on global import tariffs and restrictions across multiple boundaries in the supply chain.
	Build excellent relationships with intermediaries in third-party nations to circumvent commodity export restrictions and with first parties to gain access to strategically stockpiled goods.
	Explore the potential of supplier-owned and -managed inventory that can transition risks to strategic suppliers.

In the area of customer service management, supply chain managers need to preempt customer service failures and potential disruptions created by predictable geopolitical instability or conflict. The costs of complying with regulations or legal requirements in a host country may make it difficult to repair or replace key products or meet customer service expectations for delivery time and location. Therefore, managers should factor in the acquisition of systems and technology to establish better communication links with customers, to give them information on delays and hopefully prevent lost sales. In addition, they must work with partners to negotiate settlements, comply with customs laws, and settle legal disputes that delay effective logistics operations related to serving their customers. Establishing a customer service center in a neutral location or country to address service failures in affected nations may also help mitigate customer service problems during international political conflicts and crises.

Orascom Telecommunications in Egypt did so well before the 2012 revolution. Additionally, in the future, geopolitical limits on exports and imports, as well as hording of resources by foreign entities, may lead a firm to diversify its supply sources and service locations to hedge against the effects of hoarding or political restrictions in a particular location.

For demand management, managers need to understand how geopolitical action will impact demand variability. They will have to work with supply chain partners to proactively predict and take actions to mitigate demand-related risks. As political restrictions increase in the marketplace, achieving the supply chain flexibility needed to meet demand will become more difficult. In addition, it will be important to collect information about limited transportation capabilities and network bottlenecks created by government action in the market. Firms will need to work with governments to try to reduce policies and restrictions that influence demand for their products. They also will need to work with local supply chain partners to find creative solutions to meeting demand within the regulatory environment. Strategic audits that identify avoidable risks associated with demand variability will need to be conducted. Such an analysis will help a company pinpoint areas where conducting business is too risky due to uncertainty. It also will help the company concentrate on areas where the impact of geopolitical activity can be minimized or at least managed. In the future, supply chain management may take on a much more political role. Some markets or at least market access may be entirely controlled by governments that intend to protect their own national interests and economy. Supply chain managers must be able to negotiate with governments, offer incentives, and make concessions to gain access to government-controlled markets and the lucrative demand for their products.

In the area of manufacturing flow management, supply chain managers need to consider and plan for possible disruptions to manufacturing capacity due to action or inaction by geopolitical actors. In particular, the last several decades have seen a major outsourcing of capacity abroad in search of lower labor costs. However, this has left a vast amount of manufacturing capacity for major global firms in areas of the world that have the potential for future geopolitical instability or disruption. Therefore, managers should consider working with host governments to reduce capacity subversion and increase security at plants. In addition, firms should consider reducing these risks by repositioning or relocating some of this capacity to more stable regions or countries. Firms should also aim to design their future networks to avoid possible geopolitical shutdowns or seizures. Finally, firms should analyze their supply base to see what risks their suppliers' manufacturing facility locations pose to the flow of supplies to their own plants.

In future decades, managers may need to consider more radical hedging strategies that include shadow plants in nearby nations where manufacturing capacity can quickly be relocated. Or they may need to divide capacity across borders and suffer short-term cost increases to hedge against potential geopolitical disruption in lower-cost locations. Additionally, firms must embrace technology and seek to reduce manufacturing infrastructure size and cost. Doing so will minimize the risk of loss of such investments if the assets are lost due to political activity and seizure. The ability to quickly mobilize and relocate manufacturing capacity may be a measure of future supply chain flexibility. In addition, firms of the future may seek to trade more in manufacturing knowledge and information. They may limit their actual investment in manufacturing capacity and assets in the geopolitically volatile areas of a transforming world.

Order fulfillment in the future is expected to take place in an environment marked by increased geopolitical activity and turmoil. This will increase variability in transportation lead times, make delivery times uncertain, and increase the cost of order fulfillment. Heightened fuel price volatility is expected as nations vie for limited fossil fuel resources; increased transportation costs will be the result. Additionally, nations may employ increased import and export restrictions that limit the current ability to transport goods. Politically motivated activists and terrorists may destroy transportation lines and disrupt vulnerable in-route shipments that possess limited security. Therefore, the supply chain managers of the future must consider logistics network redesigns and product flows that limit risks and costs and reduce transportation flows in politically volatile areas. Reducing order fulfillment distances, increasing in-route security, and downshifting to slower and less costly transportation modes may be trends in the coming decades. These changes will require increased investments from public and private sources to build new infrastructures and security systems to protect product flows in a more dangerous transportation pipeline. In the future decades, firms may also need to consider more in-house security to protect product flows related to their core competencies and the execution of vital operations. Such security is already starting to be necessary for ocean vessels that traverse areas such as the Malacca Straits and Red Sea, where modern-day pirates target the flow of goods through key logistics chokepoints.[32]

Geopolitical actions and inactions also will make product development and commercialization more difficult in a transforming world. For example, lack of enforcement of global agreements and political tensions will make it difficult to keep new products from being counterfeited and from intellectual property from being stolen in an unstable environment. Additionally, gaining technical licenses and import approvals for new products will be more difficult in countries where political activity is aimed at protecting local markets from foreign companies and where political tension has positioned the company as being connected to a disfavored foreign regime. Such restrictions will also make it more difficult to conduct cross-border research with supply chain partners for new products and disrupt the ability to work in development teams for new-product launches. In the future, firms may be forced to practice more selective distribution of new products early in their life cycle to prevent loss of intellectual property in regions where geopolitical tension or lawlessness exists.

In addition, firms may have to be prepared to increase communications security related to new product and technology efforts. They may need to use highly encrypted private cloud space for collaboration with foreign supply chain partners and scientists to continue development efforts and to coordinate solutions within geopolitical barriers. Finally, firms may need to increase political lobbying activity with foreign governments in a future filled with geopolitical tension. Such activity will help prevent disruptions in new-product launches and prevent loss of intellectual property. However, firms may need to be prepared to offer incentives and offsets to foreign entities to gain market access and ease geopolitical tensions. For example, firms in

---

[32] Gardner, Frank. (13 March 2012). "Dangerous Waters: Running the Gauntlet of Somali Pirates." BBC News Online.

the aircraft industry have dealt with the geopolitical difficulties of selling military aircraft to foreign countries for the last several decades. It is not uncommon for manufacturers such as Lockheed Martin, Boeing, and Northrop Grumman to offer elaborate offsets or side deals to bolster the foreign country and make a major aircraft sale. This can include ensuring that jobs and technologies are transferred to the foreign nation.[33] Similarly, consumer-goods manufacturers may be exposed to increased scrutiny in selling their goods abroad in future decades and may have to engage more directly in political activity and offer similar offsets to ensure open markets for their goods.

Returns management and reverse logistics also are not immune from the influence of geopolitical action or inaction. Many countries do not currently possess the infrastructure or policies to manage waste streams emanating from their economies. As such, some countries have become a dumping ground for end-of-life products such as electronic waste from computers and other high-tech electronic devices, which have extremely short life cycles. However, loss of control and limited policies for managing these returns can and has resulted in contamination and quality issues in the supply chain. For example, counterfeit goods may be returned for credit when they cannot be properly identified as fraudulent products. Additionally, in the case of computer waste sent to China, large quantities were melted down. The lead that Chinese companies recaptured was reintroduced into jewelry that was unknowingly (and sometimes fraudulently) sold in the U.S. These contaminated products resulted in an outcry from U.S. consumers in 2006 following the death of a child in Minnesota who swallowed a piece of contaminated jewelry.[34] Such risks have also resulted in increased tracking and inspection costs for companies as they attempt to manage the risk of dangerous returns in an inconsistent and often unregulated environment.

---

[33] Wayne, Leslie. (16 February 2003). "A Well-Kept Military Secret." *New York Times* Online.

[34] Fairclough, Gordon. (12 July 2007). "Lead Toxins Take a Global Round Trip: E-waste from Computers Discarded in West Turns up in China's Exported Trinkets." *Wall Street Journal.*

In the future, it is expected that countries will increase their labor safety practices and environmental pollution standards, making it much more difficult to manage the returns management and reverse supply chains abroad. Additionally, geopolitical tensions and increased regulation may result in harsh penalties for companies that pollute or do not properly manage waste streams and returns abroad. Therefore, companies would be smart to build returns management and waste management systems in advance of future political policy and to meet the reasonably high standards expected by society. Future policy by foreign governments concerning the management of hazardous wastes and the disposal of products may result in higher penalties and costs from making adjustments to the supply chain. It would be a better idea to proactively build a more sustainable system before such regulation is passed.

Finally, supplier relationship management will be greatly affected by growing geopolitical tension and activities in the future. In particular, firms should expect that supply markets will carry additional risks associated with national political interests and policies being implemented across multiple tiers of their supply chains. Increasing resource scarcity and congestion, created by increased population growth and congestion, will cause foreign governments to be more actively involved in regulating and protecting their home markets. Such activity will make it difficult to maintain supplier relationships and operations without violating such policy. Additionally, analyzing, segmenting, and selecting suppliers will become more difficult in the future due to ambiguous risk factors such as political tensions, raw-material constraints, and most-favored-nation status.

Overall, supply complexity is expected to increase as more suppliers enter the global market and bring with them a greater variety of host-nation policies and regulations to understand. This will lead to additional bottlenecks and increased costs in assessing supplier risks in future contracts. Therefore, firms will have to adjust their global sourcing decisions to account for geopolitical and regulatory risks at multiple tiers in their supply chains. In addition, wise firms will begin building excellent relationships with intermediaries in third-party nations to mitigate or even circumvent commodity export restrictions. They also will continue to work with suppliers and foreign governments to gain access to strategically stockpiled supplies and natural resources that are being restricted from trade. Modern organizations should also explore the idea of allowing foreign strategic suppliers to maintain ownership and manage inventories abroad, as long as possible, to limit the risk of geopolitical activity against their assets in the transforming world.

Part II

Macrotrend Implications for Supply Chain Functionality

6

Implications for Supply Chain Planning: Demand and Supply Uncertainty

As we stated at the beginning of this book, our overarching purpose is to connect multiple environmental forces that impact (or will impact) human society to the future practice of supply chain management. Therefore, we hope to help business organizations deliver the customer value that defines their missions. More specifically, our goal is to help you understand how the confluence of human population growth and migration, global economic leveling, physical environmental change, and world geopolitical dynamics will affect the efficiency and effectiveness of supply chains designed to create time, place, and form utility for customers. In modern business organizations, these types of utilities are delivered when their supply chains can reliably provide goods and services that impart customer value.

It often surprises business leaders to find that customer satisfaction is not solely, or even primarily, about offering quality goods and services at a fair price, or by creating and marketing offerings that have differentiated features versus those of the competition. Value creation is also highly dependent on the focal organization's ability to unite the goals of buyers and sellers within the interfunctional relationships that typify world-class supply chain operations. The efficacy of these relationships hinges on the supply chain's key players, among which are the functional areas of supply chain planning, procurement, goods/service production, and logistics. Each of these functions is necessary in isolation, and they also must work well together for value delivery to occur. The four functions appear in the original version of the popular Supply Chain Operations Reference (SCOR) model of supply chain functionality.[1] Managers and academics often call this the "plan, source, make, deliver" sequence.

Consistent delivery of value is the foundation of effective, trusting relationships between functions in the supply chain. In essence, the company's ability to achieve integration among these four essential operational areas is integral in generating confidence in the company's ability to fulfill its role in the supply chain, to be a competent partner, and to attract favorable attention from customers and other stakeholders. This is especially true as product offerings themselves become more complex and/or difficult to differentiate within highly competitive industry settings.

The macrotrends we identified in Part I, "Global Macrotrends Impacting the Supply Chain Environment," are exciting to consider, because they yield a wealth of opportunity for businesses of the future to consider, primarily in the form of new potential markets. Yet, as described in Chapters 2 through 5, these same forces also may inhibit organizations' ability to maintain high-performing supply chains. They could potentially disrupt how the eight GSCF processes link the four critical functional areas and thereby lead to service problems, supply interruptions, and, ultimately, customer dissatisfaction and lost business. The concern we have for future organizations is that macrotrend-driven process disruptions can meaningfully disable the plan, source, make, deliver operational sequence in the medium to long term and thereby erode hard-earned customer advantages. Customers who fail to extract value from one supplier's offerings tend to search for substitute value from another source in the short term and replace the failing partner in the medium to long term. Beyond losing business on individual accounts, companies risk disappointing clusters of customers or, worse, gaining a reputation as a high-risk/ low-reward supply chain partner.

Part II, "Macrotrend Implications for Supply Chain Functionality," Chapters 6 through 9, examines the specific impacts of the macrotrends on the four-stage sequence of the supply chain operations functions. This chapter looks at the impacts that demand and supply

---

[1] The SCOR model was originally developed by PRTM Consulting and is endorsed by the Supply-Chain Council as a supply chain benchmarking and diagnostics tool.

uncertainty stemming from the macrotrends have on the supply chain planning function. Chapter 7 addresses the issue of resource scarcity and its impacts on the organization's sourcing/procurement function. Chapter 8 considers how the goods and services production function is and will continue to be hampered by the macrotrend-related impacts. It focuses on how critical flows within the manufacturing environment will be further disrupted in the future. Chapter 9 describes how congestion and decay occurring within the physical infrastructure of many nations will challenge the transportation and logistics managers of the future.

In summary, we suggest that the macrotrends will challenge supply chain process execution across the four key operational areas of the supply chain over the next 20 years or so. The problems should not be insurmountable if future organizations engage in proactive planning. In fact, we estimate that the macrotrends, considered as a whole, will even present strategic opportunities for future market differentiation. This can occur if companies thoughtfully manage the problems and address these problems before competitors do. This chapter begins by looking at the anticipated supply chain planning issues that macrotrend forces will cause. Then it describes some steps that companies can take to mitigate their negative impacts while taking advantage of the opportunities that will arise.

How Supply Chain Plans Improve Performance

With great fanfare, the Chevy Volt was launched onto U.S. automobile dealership floors in late 2010. The Volt boasted a unique, electricity-supported-by-gasoline engine technology.[2] Chevrolet anticipated it would sell close to 10,000 Volts in the U.S. during the 2011 fiscal year. However, the maker's original estimates fell drastically short of expectations when only 7,761 customers who visited dealers in 2011 left with a Volt. This didn't bode well for the company's initial 2012 projection of 45,000 units. Indeed, through the

---

[2] Chevrolet Volt. (2012). "Model Overview." Chevrolet.com. Retrieved 7 August 2012 from www.chevrolet.com/volt-electric-car.html.

first two months of 2012, Chevy had sold only 1,700 more units—far behind planned sales.[3]

As a result, early in 2012, many of the company's workers were furloughed as Chevrolet waited for demand to catch up with supply. Beginning in March 2012, Chevrolet executives decided to halt Volt production for five weeks, citing high inventory levels.[4] The problem started at the demand end of the supply chain, where American consumers demonstrated an unexpected reluctance to purchase electric-based automobiles in general. The problem was exacerbated at Chevy when a Volt that had been involved in a collision caught fire three weeks after the accident. A media firestorm ensued, with anti-electric-vehicle activists vociferously proclaiming Volts to be unsafe.[5] The public, suddenly wary of the Volt's new and unusual technology, hesitated before renewing its interest in GM's flagship new product. The Volt was later deemed to be safe by the U.S. National Highway Traffic Safety Administration, and in fact earned its difficult-to-achieve Five-Star Safety Rating. However, the negative publicity spread in early 2012 dramatically affected Volt sales at the showroom for nearly two months. Interestingly, following a change to a California law that allowed electric-motor cars to drive in the high-occupancy highway lane, and as news of the safety rating slowly spread, sales of the Volt rebounded significantly during the summer of 2012. By the end of July, the company had sold nearly 11,000 units—a 40% increase *over the entire previous year*—and dealers became more worried about keeping units in stock than in holding excess, unsellable inventory.

The Chevy Volt example illustrates the first of our four forward-looking hazards to effective supply chain management in the face of world macrotrends: the inability to optimize supply chain operations due to high demand and supply uncertainty. Best-practice supply chain companies have been investing heavily in different forms of supply chain planning for over a decade. They have kept two simultaneously pursued but (traditionally) countervailing goals in mind: reducing overall supply chain system costs while maximizing customer

---

[3] Hill, Brandon. (5 March 2012). "GM to Suspend Chevy Volt Production for Five Weeks, Cites Soft Demand." *DailyTech*.

[4] Ibid.

[5] Lutz, Bob. (12 January 2012). "Chevy Volt and the Wrong-headed Right." *Forbes*.

service. In an ideal scenario, a business would begin each day with no inventory; receive exactly what is needed to fulfill that day's demand; manufacture and sell exactly what the customers require; deliver in perfect time, place, and condition; and conclude the day with no inventory. Of course, lead times are long and uncertain, and customers and suppliers invariably fail to behave in the highly predictable ways that such a fanciful system would require. So in many cases companies hold inventory in one or more forms as a measure of insurance against customer service failures and stockouts.

In the consumer-goods world, for example, it is nearly impossible for a company to make a perfectly accurate demand forecast. In the case of the Volt, forecasted demand was significantly less than expected in the product's early stage of the life cycle, leading to drastic measures. Abundant models, techniques, and equations are available for managers to use in predicting demand. However, just as many or more uncontrollable variables can wreak havoc on forecasts, and these can greatly disrupt the supply chains that are designed to follow through on predicted demand. Indeed, in some scenarios, manufacturers and retailers alike have found it best to dispense with forecasting. Instead, they simply produce their wares after, and only after, actual demand is recognized. Regardless of the system employed, inaccuracies in the volume, assortment, and/or location of demand and supply usually cause the supply chain to suffer and costs to rise. Current and future companies must walk a tightrope given the demand and supply fluctuations we predict for the future. Too much product can lead to excess costly inventory, whereas too little can lead to equally (or more) costly stockouts. We expect, as a result of the macrotrends we have identified, that these problems will only accelerate in the coming two decades as demand and supply diversify, migrate, level, disappear, and are otherwise disrupted.

The Supply Chain Planning Function

The supply chain planning function includes planning for both demand and supply so that a business can meet future requirements. This function works to achieve the smallest plausible inventory holdings possible to meet demand, because storing any leftover materials or finished goods saps valuable financial and human resources. However, in many organizations, the concern overriding inventory costs is the modern philosophy that no customer should ever place an order that isn't fulfilled perfectly. In many cases, customer service becomes the supply chain manager's primary, or sole, objective. However, this implies that perfectly balancing supply with demand is in reality an unrealistic goal. Even the best supply chain planners don't carry out this balancing act perfectly. They equalize demand and supply with the smallest possible amount of error, which is measured financially as an aggregation of estimated stockout costs and inventory carrying costs. To think of it another way, the best supply chain planners are those who can best address the demand and supply uncertainties that exist within the system and minimize their financial impact on the company.

Based on this logic, depending on a product's strategic role for the company and its associated supply and demand market characteristics, one of three types of supply chain systems is planned and implemented. The first of these, an *anticipatory* system, is used when product demand and supply are relatively predictable and stable, so the competitive focus is placed on cost minimization in the system. In an anticipatory system, the supply chain's activity is triggered by an initial forecast, which leads to the procurement of materials and manufacture of a product in advance of actual demand. Large-volume procurement and long manufacturing runs reduce direct costs of goods sold, and lean production and logistics can be implemented, all of which facilitate savings that can be passed along to customers. The dark side of an anticipatory system is accumulating finished-goods inventory. If customer tastes change or forecasts are wrong, the company can be stuck with unwanted product and may have to take drastic steps to liquefy the assets.

Alternatively, a *responsive* system is typically used when variability in the demand for a product is high. Here, the focus is typically more on customer service and satisfaction than on cost savings. In the responsive system, the supply chain process is initiated by an actual customer order, and the source, make, and deliver functions are executed after the fact. The idea is to hold as little inventory as possible and to react quickly when an order is placed. There is an implicit risk of customer stockouts if the needed materials cannot be acquired in time, but the trade-off is that few inventory carrying costs accrue. Planning-based systems generally are inadvisable in such situations. Instead, "agile" systems are created that allow high responsiveness in a very short time. However, agile systems are inherently expensive, and customers tend to absorb a portion of their costs. In the modern, highly customer-focused era, a purely responsive system is sometimes too risky to be palatable for some product scenarios. Due to the costliness of uncertainty in the supply chain and the severe repercussions associated with disappointing customers, a hybrid system has emerged. It mitigates the risks of highly responsive systems by delaying the product's commitment to a final form or location. This system, known as *postponement*, allows both manufacturers and customers to hold a smaller amount of partially finished or transported inventory in advance of demand (as in the anticipatory system). The final value is added to the product only following the actualization of that demand (as in the responsive system).

The role of modern supply chain planners is to correct for the errors that inevitably occur in these systems due to demand and supply variability. If both demand and supply could be predicted perfectly, both systems would operate at 100% effectiveness and efficiency. However, this rarely happens, so demand managers have a number of tools with which to "shape" demand to meet available supply. In the short term, these typically include several marketing-based solutions to shift demand for one product to another. These can include pricing or promotional techniques, or geographic postponement, which locates finished product near but not at several final consumption points. It allows final locational diversion to meet exact demand quantities when they occur. In the longer term, more process-oriented solutions such as sales and operations planning (S&OP) and visibility programs are effective in anticipatory systems. Pull systems such as Kanban and form postponement are used in responsive systems.

However different they may be, the anticipatory, responsive, and postponement strategies also have a number of aspects in common. They are all designed to minimize cost while maximizing service, and they are all linked inextricably to demand and supply quantities. Most importantly, their effectiveness is highly susceptible to major shifts in demand and supply quantity and assortment variations. More important, though, is the concept that supply and demand can almost always be brought into closer alignment if managers constantly emphasize doing so, even in the face of short-term hardships. Earlier in the book we introduced the Demand-Supply Integration (DSI) model, which illustrates how important it is to align these perspectives, because the long-term benefits far outweigh the startup costs of doing so. Companies that successfully implement DSI often develop exemplary supply chain processes and customer service proficiency that exceed those of competitors.

For example, careful study would reveal Dell Computer to be a DSI pioneer. When Dell was founded in the 1980s, it applied a "sell what you have" strategy to its operations that quickly put it at the forefront of personal computer sales. One story related to demand/supply misalignment illustrates this fact particularly well. In late 2003, Dell's operations were disrupted by a U.S. West Coast dockworkers' strike that shut down an integral part of its supply chain. It was through this channel that Dell received its cathode ray tube (CRT) desktop monitors. Since Dell was using a minimal safety stock strategy, it was unable to fulfill customer orders, and supply fell out of alignment with demand. But Dell's supply chain planners were prepared for the crisis. Instead of telling its consumers that their computers would be on backorder for the holiday season, Dell offered to upgrade its orders to flat-screen monitors, thereby shaping its demand. This effectively changed the PC market overnight, because Dell's competitors were unprepared to sell flat-screen monitors at the same margins. By having a DSI contingency plan in place, Dell circumvented its potentially disastrous bottleneck and transformed the entire monitor market in the process.[6]

We see the future business climate as being impacted greatly by the world macrotrends we describe. Therefore, there is much cause to believe that the DSI that enables supply chain-based competitiveness will be greatly affected over the next two decades by the confluence of factors this book addresses. The population and economic shifts, geopolitical issues, and environmental concerns we describe will all affect the demand and supply of critical materials and finished goods companies will manufacture and sell over our time horizon of study. The following section examines the complexities associated

---

[6] Stank, Theodore P. and John T. Mentzer. (17 December 2007). "Demand and Supply Integration: A key to improved firm performance." *Industryweek*.

with supply and demand uncertainty in the transforming world, as well as what demand managers should consider doing about it.

Macrotrend Demand/Supply Impacts: Supply Chain Planning Considerations

As the supply chains of the future increase in complexity due to the macrotrends we describe, future supply chain planners will need to make a number of adjustments. We propose that five different threats to supply chain performance will result from the macrotrends' influence, and each will cause a different array of problems for planners. These issues will threaten both demand and supply but will do so to different degrees and in different ways. However, we also suggest that wherever there is a threat to an organic system, there is also usually an opportunity to gain competitive position by solving it. Table 6.1 aligns the expected disruptions with both opportunities and threats emanating from the macrotrend impacts. If organizations pay thoughtful attention to these issues' impact on relevant demand and supply markets, we hope planners can leverage these issues competitively as they devise future supply chain strategies. We conclude this chapter by summarizing the visions presented in Table 6.1, with an eye on generating supply chain planning considerations for supply chain planners and managers moving forward.

Table 6.1 Macrotrend Impacts, Supply Chain Implications, and Planning Considerations

Macrotrend-Based Impacts	Supply Chain Management Implications	Supply Chain Planning Considerations
Customer preference variation: Customer demand worldwide will diversify and rediversify in short-term bursts based on exposures to different consumption cultures, broader available offerings, human migration, and leveled ability to purchase.	Assortment divergence: Product bundles demanded will differ widely in similar or the same markets from period to period. Forecasting becomes difficult. The ability to divert finished inventory and produce new inventory quickly is highly valued.	Move to responsive systems for all but the most stable demand profiles. Stockpile work-in-process (WIP) inventory rather than finished goods, and postpone both form and place simultaneously. Engage social demographers and economic sociologists in forecasting processes.

Macrotrend-Based Impacts	Supply Chain Management Implications	Supply Chain Planning Considerations
Customer expectations leveling: Customer expectations for offering and delivering customization, build-to-order solutions, and quality will level out globally.	Quality management integration: Quality and service will become important and more difficult to assess. Quality management within supply chain processes will become a strategic differentiator in markets around the globe.	Develop competencies in quality management and assessment worldwide, and partner with known local suppliers where possible. Expand supplier certification programs widely. Establish local customer service in and near important global markets.
Demand/supply market diffusion: More demand centers will exist, both within nations and globally, each with greater heterogeneity of values and preferences within demand centers.	Network proliferation: Optimal networks are broadened in scope worldwide to include greater volumes and more products. More nodes and their support links are added, many via outsourcing.	The supply base will necessarily expand worldwide but should be rightsized for noncritical and leveraged products. Look to outsource groups of components and logistics services based on geography and importance. Seek outsource partners that can consolidate many supplies to minimize relationship management costs. Seek flexible contracts with local suppliers.
Viable market emergence: New demand centers will emerge in previously unserved locations. These may be distant from current network nodes. Some lead times will be very long for a significant amount of time until networks catch up with demand.	Network extension: Optimal networks are lengthened worldwide to include previously ignored markets. More links and their support nodes are added, many via outsourcing.	Establishing regional supply chain cooperatives for transportation and storage will be critical (in noncompeting industry sectors and/ or with competitors if necessary). Use geographic postponement and flexible manufacturing/labor as much as possible for highly volatile goods.

Macrotrend-Based Impacts	Supply Chain Management Implications	Supply Chain Planning Considerations
Product convolution: The products needed to meet a vast array of demands will be more complex to build and will contain more different materials. The quality of both materials and finished products will be harder to assess.	Strategic sourcing penetration: Supply bases will expand in scope and be more globalized. Supplier selection and scoring will require much standardization across geographies.	Seek to establish early supplier involvement in product development processes, and uncover economies across products. Use objective metrics for supplier scoring and development as much as practical. Perpetually seek to standardize product designs.

First, based on our earlier discussions of anticipated world changes, we predict that demand for goods and services will become increasingly volatile, while at the same time leveling somewhat across world regions. We see demand becoming increasingly unstable for all but the staples. Shopping tastes, channels, and frequency will increase, particularly in the resource-rich regions as those nations develop consumer classes. The proliferation of the Internet as both a promotional avenue and a marketing channel will force companies to wait longer to commit goods to final form. It also will severely curtail the utility of forecasting for products serving all but the most basic needs.

In light of these predictions, we suggest that future supply chain planners will be greatly concerned with the proliferation of products that the growing and moving world consumer class will demand. We believe that the leading-edge supply chain companies will deploy responsive and postponement-based systems much more widely across the product mix, with manufacturing and stockpiling of partially finished goods a key strategy for minimizing pipeline inventory. The blended use of form and geographic postponement will become more standard. Outbound distribution centers will increasingly need semi-skilled manufacturing labor (painters, pressers, packagers) to complete the product before it is shipped to retail or directly to the customer. In cases where forecasting is necessary, we also find opportunity for the utilization of regional social scientists who understand where people are moving, how their wealth levels are changing, and where and how the next demand changes can be expected to appear.

Second, our studies of the economic leveling macrotrend lead us to believe that the "power of the customer" is quickly becoming a worldwide mantra. It will greatly affect how manufacturers and retailers of shopping and specialty goods operate their supply chains over the next two decades. We are already seeing evidence that consumer expectations for product availability, quality, and customization are accelerating in developing nations. For example, it is expected that by the end of 2015, emerging markets such as China, Brazil, and India should account for more than 50% of luxury-goods sales. In fact, China already accounts for approximately 10% of the luxury-goods market worldwide.[7]

However, even though quality and service standards are indeed growing worldwide, the supply chain processes that support these have often been secondary concerns in many world regions. For example, India still greatly lags behind China in luxury-goods sales despite its booming economy. In 2011, India only made up approximately 1% to 2% of the global luxury-goods market, primarily due to supply-side issues. Some of the supply chain problems in India include foreign investment regulations and high import duties.[8] However, a bigger problem may be the lack of retail space and locations to actually sell luxury items. Many luxury brands try to currently collocate with upscale hotels. Few have their own actual storefront locations in India. In addition, culture has been another impediment in India, where luxury brands have struggled to tailor their offerings to local tastes and tradition. Trying to do so has been no guarantee of success. In the future, it will become important for global manufacturers and retailers to develop competencies in quality management that are both clear and consistent with the local market cultures. The best way we know of to do this is to collaborate with locally headquartered or operational partners via joint ventures (as an entry strategy) or strategic alliances (for the purposes of leveraging an established partner's knowledge of the local/regional supply market). Where partners are unavailable, objective measures may provide the greatest benefit in terms of partner identification. Creating extensive and rigorous

---

[7] "Is FDI reform the answer to the India problem?" (26 January 2012). *The Business of Fashion*.

[8] Ibid.

supplier certification and development programs, paired with highly specified metrics for quality, probably is the best substitute. Additionally, as customer tastes advance in formerly more embryonic markets, establishing "localized" customer service functions will become vital to minimize returns costs (which will be substantial) and maximize customer value streams. Firms that are seeking to enter and compete in evolving markets can get a leg up by providing great service along with solid offerings. They may capture durable market share before their industry matures there.

Third, due to the forces we've described, we expect that more demand centers will emerge that will stretch the current supply chain network(s) of many companies out of relative equilibrium. The combination of growing population and resource imbalances will spawn new locations for both primary and secondary demand. The result will be that supply chains of the future will be much more complex. This will be true primarily because of the necessary addition of nodes and links to ever-lengthening chains, as well as the increased prevalence of both global and local outsourcing. Products demanded within these locations will be of greater assortment, and the current networks won't reach close enough to serve demand adequately. To close the gaps, companies will need to work on both the demand and supply angles of the problem. Supply bases for mission-critical commodities will globalize, and new nodes in the network (plants and distribution hubs) will need to be established. Firms with the best insight into nation-specific real estate and legal/contracting services will have key advantages, as will those that can secure third- or fourth-party logistical services dedicated to the regions of critical interest. Yet, this type of expansion could also be the source of supplier and SKU proliferation, which are expensive problems even today. Firms should seek flexible but comprehensive and legally tenable contracts with regional suppliers to fill the key gaps. If possible, they also should develop strategic relationships in geographically advantageous areas several years before they are forecasted as necessary.

An alternative to this collection of plans, if feasible, may be the development of the previously mentioned concept of "flexworks." These are flexible networks that adapt to an order's product, customer, environmental, and transportation availability aspects in real time. The primary problem we foresee with the networks of the future is that they will increase dramatically in scope while infrastructure links and nodes will lag in development, and/or the need for change will come quickly and often. Our vision for flexworks includes multi-industry sharing of transportation that would allow load-sharing opportunities to reveal themselves in real time based on the technological location of transportation assets, distribution dock space, and labor. Suppose participants could be induced financially via cost savings to engage with inventory and transportation visibility tools. Networks could be calibrated and recalibrated in real time to handle loads taking many different routes to the same destination. This could be done by acquiring and paying for available capacity as it is located using a global, multi-industry software application. If enough "members" could be solicited to share, buy, and sell excess capacity on live markets, extended reach and the capability to handle problems and mitigate disruptions could be minimized. Security would, of course, be a major issue. But we are confident that a set of uniform standards could be devised that would provide acceptable ranges of risk for most common goods firms and industries.

Fourth, we expect that the supply chain processes that connect the four supply chain operational areas within the business enterprise will increase in both time and distance. They will have greater lead times, and constant reengineering will be required to keep the supply chain functioning near its optimum levels. The new demand centers we expect to emerge will probably often do so in areas of the world where little advanced infrastructure exists and/or that are far from our fixed supply chain assets. Establishing cooperative transportation agreements with noncompeting (or competing!) partners may be critical if a region explodes in demand. Likewise, intergovernmental partnerships between the host and home nation for infrastructure development may ease the costs of resource extraction if cost- and gain-sharing agreements can be forged. If and until infrastructure linkages and supply chain pipelines can be developed, geographic postponement conducted in a nearby region may be the ticket to entry. This is true particularly if a strategically located facility can be used as a consolidation point for distribution throughout the region. To this end, building bridge locations with partners located near, but not in, potentially exploding demand markets may be the ticket.

Finally, we expect that differences in customer preferences, in combination with numerous raw-materials shortages, will greatly increase products' complexity and quality variation. However, raw-materials shortages, consumer preference diversity, and the perpetual need to innovate will spawn more, new, and increasingly complex offerings that will require equally new and different supply chain support to flourish. For example, in an attempt to increase the diversity of its menu, McDonald's Corp. considered adding a new shrimp salad offering. However, when the impact of the new product on the supply chain was analyzed, it quickly became evident that the demand generated by the large number of McDonald's locations would be so great that it might actually deplete the nation's supply of shrimp.[9] Global supply bases will have to expand greatly, and measuring and evaluating both current and potential suppliers will become an arduous and overwhelming task. We advise supply chain planners of the present and future to work closely with supply managers. Gain early supplier involvement in the development of new offerings that contain new, different, or rare raw materials. Also seek to uncover sources (and designs) that allow for maximum planning synergy across products. This may be anathema to some product design engineers, because it might cause slightly suboptimal performance in certain products in exchange for enhancing the profitability of the entire product portfolio. As a corollary, we suggest that great opportunity for best practice comes in integrating demand management with product development and commercialization. Companies of the future would seek to standardize designs across different lines and categories, keeping commodity leveraging in mind.

As supply chains transform to meet the threats posed by these issues, we expect that supply chain planners of the future will take a more proactive role in driving organizational successes. Of course, the ultimate outcomes will be tied closely to whether their plans can ultimately be executed. These are the issues we address next.

---

[9] Bissonette, Zac. (30 January 2007). "The New McDonald's." www.bloggingstocks.com.

7

Implications for Sourcing/Procurement: Natural Resource Scarcity

At the beginning of 2012, government officials in Regina, Saskatchewan, were already looking forward to the year's end, when construction on an important bridge spanning the Saskatchewan River would be finished. Their hopes were dashed shortly thereafter when, in late January, they announced the project would have to be delayed because of unexpected shortages in steel needed to craft the bridge's girders. In North America, where the raw materials were to be procured, only certain mills could supply the specific type of steel needed to make the girders. Thus, the company charged with buying the steel to make the girders was unable to purchase the necessary quantities of raw materials from its North American suppliers, pushing back the estimated completion date to late 2013.[1]

This Canadian bridge will eventually become the final piece of an important project designed to address increasingly heavy traffic. This traffic includes important product distribution vehicles whose routes run from the province's southern parts to its northern ones. On the surface, Saskatchewan needs the bridge for public safety reasons: Its predecessor was old, unsafe, and heavily traveled. However, from a broader economic perspective, its construction is part of the greatest infrastructure investment in the province's history, enacted in response to the region's significantly increasing population and

---

[1] "Steel shortage stalls Prince Albert-area bridge project." (20 January 2012). CBC Radio-Canada. http://www.cbc.ca/news/canada/saskatchewan/story/2012/01/20/sk-bridge-steel-delay-120120.html.

economy. Unfortunately for Saskatchewan, scarcity of raw materials will put the bridge and its larger infrastructure implications on hold.

Understanding Resource Scarcity Today and Tomorrow

Around the world, the macrotrends we've described have already begun driving up the demand for natural resources and commodities needed to build infrastructure or produce more consumer and business products. In instances similar to the Saskatchewan bridge example, companies often can't find the right quantities of raw materials needed to supply their manufacturing operations. We can cite many other worldwide steel and iron ore shortages similar to the ones in Canada. These include reports from South Africa and India, where several industries' production has slowed because companies cannot meet local demand for critical steel supplies.[2] Japan's most notable shortages came in 2004, when an important Nissan Motor Co., Ltd., steel supplier surprised the automaker with its inability to meet purchase requests. This shortage came as a result of increased Chinese demand and actually triggered two shutdowns at three different Nissan manufacturing plants.[3] One step upward in the steel supply chain, India's largest steelmaker, JSW Steel, almost had to halt its manufacturing processes in late 2011 because it did not have the iron ore quantities needed to run blast furnaces.[4] A shutdown would have had a significant effect on Indian steel prices. Yet steel isn't the only critical metal facing shortage risks. In early 2012, Barclays Capital forecasted that aluminum would be in short supply by 2014,[5]

---

[2] "SA battles reinforcing steel shortage." (17 April 2011). http://www.fin24.com/Companies/Mining/SA-battles-reinforcing-steel-shortage-20110417.

[3] "Steel shortage halts Nissan factories." (25 November 2004). United Press International. http://www.upi.com/Business_News/2004/11/25/Steel-shortage-halts-Nissan-factories/UPI-58161101373759/.

[4] "Iron ore shortage brings JSW Steel operations on verge of shutdown." (28 September 2011). *The Economic Times*.

[5] Carpenter, Claudia. (7 February 2012). "Barclays forecasts aluminum shortage, copper surplus in 2014." *Bloomberg News*.

and a number of other important metals are forecasted to deplete in the coming decades. As with the issue of demand uncertainty, we tie future natural resource scarcity issues back to the global macrotrends. More consumers in more places having more buying power create more demand and subsequent shortages for metals such as steel and aluminum, as well as many other commodities required in companies' production processes. Our examples of material shortages foreshadow that firms' current assumptions about available resource quantities may not always hold true.

In other instances, quantities might be sufficient to meet demand, but available materials could and will fail to meet the quality standards that certain industrial processes require. For example, many grades of coal exist in various geological deposits around the world. One grade, commonly known as "coking" coal, is used primarily to manufacture steel. This grade of coal is in high demand due to the need for steel in the emerging Chinese and Indian economies. As a result, during recent years several foreign companies have sought to purchase mining companies in Australia that mine coking coal to stockpile the valuable deposits that will enable them to meet future global demand.[6] However, the geopolitical risks of allowing sizable purchases of high-quality resources have led the Australian government to reconsider allowing foreign acquisitions of rare commodities for fear of compromising the national interests and forsaking future resource needs.

Resource quantity and quality issues are inextricably tied to geography. Lacking resource quantity or quality at a given location has, in many instances, forced companies to procure materials from remote locations and then transport them great distances to manufacturing sites. Business and economic history have seen many examples of common raw-materials transportation. Whether sourcing diamonds from Africa or salmon from Alaska, the global economy depends on unique combinations of supply chain tasks that link the successful acquisition and efficient transporting of raw materials from one location to another. Differences in resource availability, quality, and price have helped establish a thriving global trade network composed of

---

[6] Winning, David and Gavin Lower. (2 August 2011) "McArthur Bid Goes Hostile." *The Wall Street Journal*, B2.

multiple overlapping supply chains for natural resources and commodities. However, as critical commodities become more scarce, these problems will expand in scope, going from being more "local" to more "global" problems in the next 20 years. As fundamental as effective transportation and logistics methods may be, they will simply not be enough to overcome the constraints on procurement and sourcing that resource scarcity will enact on global supply chains in all instances.

In many cases, eternal hope springs from a resource's renewability. Natural resources that are renewable can be regenerated over (relatively) short time periods. Of course, these issues are also tied to a critical macrotrend—environmental deterioration. Agricultural crops and timber are examples of renewable resources that can be re-created to meet future demand, but they are not immune to the effects of population growth, demand increases, and progressively polluted environments. The renewable resources that businesses need depend on clean air, soil, and water in the environment. If population, demand, and pollution continue to strain the environment, renewable resources will become less renewable. By losing the ability to regenerate, renewable resources that economies depend on are also in jeopardy of becoming scarce.

Resource scarcity also stems from geopolitical risks in the form of increases in raw-materials prices. Consequently, this increases companies' economic risks. Price impacts on industrial supply chains are immediately evident if you examine the rare-earth metals market. Rare-earth metals are a group of 17 precious metals used to produce a variety of high-tech products. Two rare-earth metals currently affected by price pressures are europium and dysprosium, which are used today in solar cells, lasers, lighting, and magnets. From the early 2000s to 2011, these commodities' prices shot up by over 300% thanks to export restrictions enacted by China.[7] Emerging nations' growing populations and economies are further exacerbating these metals' scarcity and their corresponding prices. However, the price pressure

---

[7] Shapiro, Gary. "China's price gouging of rare earth minerals: A wake-up call to the world." (18 April 2012). *Forbes*. http://www.forbes.com/sites/garyshapiro/2012/04/18/chinas-price-gouging-of-rare-earth-minerals-a-wake-up-call-to-the-world/.

is not confined to nonrenewable metals. Other renewable resources, such as beef, are under permanently exacerbating price and quantity constraints because people in emerging economies are consuming more meat. More common materials have also seen price increases. For example, from 2004 to 2008, aluminum and copper prices rose by nearly 100%, natural gas and industrial electricity prices tripled, and oil prices quadrupled. Increases in demand can have a ripple effect on resource scarcity levels and the corresponding worldwide prices of resources.[8]

It is important for sourcing and procurement professionals of the future to understand that a resource's scarcity level changes continuously over time due to macrotrend-generated economic forces—in both positive and negative directions. Constant resource discoveries and technological advancements play a big role, as do changes in population, environment, geopolitics, and economic balance. For example, as described in Chapter 2, "Global Population Growth and Migration," the shale oil and natural gas booms in North Dakota and other Western U.S. states were largely unexpected. Many of those deposits of oil are now expected to bring in amounts that are many times *more* than the initial projected quantities, which could depress prices for a decade or more. Changing competition and resource substitutions in product designs, stemming from human consumption in new or growing world markets, also have an enormous impact on demand levels and resource scarcity. These are the crux of supply uncertainty. Therefore, supply chain managers must learn to continuously reassess how natural resource scarcity levels are changing to fully understand the potential for sparse availability and how to deal with it.

Natural resource scarcity is a complex issue. Several resource attributes and forces determine the current scarcity level of a particular resource. Therefore, we need to take a more theoretical look at what's driving this scarcity and how it affects supply chains. Why is scarcity a major issue for some resources and more easily overcome for others? Depending on your industry and your products' (and services') designs, companies and supply managers might find that their supply chains depend on multiple resources across a broad scarcity portfolio.

---

[8] Voeller, John G. (June 2010). "The era of insufficient plenty." *Mechanical Engineering*.

This probably already impacts your company's purchasing practices and logistics functions. However, increased scarcity could also create expensive product redesigns or increase the need for recycling in your own supply chain in the decades ahead. How can we explain what causes natural resource scarcities in the supply chain? And what can future sourcing, procurement, and supply managers do about it? The remainder of this chapter will try to answer these questions.

Natural Resource Attributes and Their Future Implications

Three primary attributes and a set of related forces that act on them can be used to describe a natural resource's current status.[9] We will focus on the three primary resource attributes: heterogeneity, renewability, and scarcity. Understanding a resource's current state and how external dynamic forces are working to change it are critical for knowing how to manage resources in a changing world. First, we will take a look at heterogeneity.

Firms can gain competitive advantage by exploiting their resources. However, the exact quality and quantity of these resources determines the advantages that can be gained. *Heterogeneity* is the distinctness between apparently similar resources—the traits they possess that allow us to distinguish them from one another in terms of their exact physical and chemical properties. For example, it is easy to say that a farmer has 100 bushels of apples to sell. However, there are over 7,500 types of apples in the world, with different characteristics. So even if a supplier has 100 bushels of perfectly consumable apples, they may not be the type, color, size, or weight required to meet the demands of a specific customer, such as Kroger or Walmart. Apples vary by species, color, size, and origin, among other aspects. Dividing these 100 bushels into more "heterogeneous" and distinct types of apples directly and inversely reduces the quantity of each type and size available to sell. Hence, if a customer demands 50 bushels of the

---

[9] Bell, J.E., C.W. Autry, D.A. Mollenkopf, and L.M. Thornton. "A Natural Resource Scarcity Typology: Theoretical Foundations and Strategic Implications for Supply Chain Management," *Journal of Business Logistics*, Vol. 33, No. 2, 158-166.

Golden Delicious variety, only 10 bushels may be of the proper variation. Even though the farmer has 100 bushels to sell, the maximum he can sell is 10, and the remaining 90 bushels may have to be sold elsewhere at a different price.

Consider a different, industrial example: Not all grades of diamonds are fit for use in making fine jewelry. Diamonds used to make wedding rings possess different qualities than those used in manufacturing cutting tools, despite their hardness and clarity similarities. Even if a company possesses "diamonds," they may not be of the right quality to make the aforementioned products. Consider this: diamonds typically are classified based on specific criteria, including cut, color, clarity, and carat weight. Each category has a scale associated with it. For a diamond to receive a grade (such as industrial-versus jewelry-quality), it must score appropriately on these scales. Diamonds that do not pass the "Four C's" test are more numerous, but they cannot be sold as jewelry. However, such quality diamonds are far from useless. Since diamonds are composed of some of the hardest substances on earth, they make excellent cutting tools in the manufacturing world. Disfigured or discolored diamonds often make their way to this industry after scoring poorly on the Four C's test. The rarest jewelry-grade diamonds can cost $60,000 and more.[10] Prices typically are lower for industrial-grade diamonds. A glance at commodity purchasing website Alibaba.com[11] showed "saw grade diamonds" for sale in 200g bulk at $.70 to $1.30 per gram when we logged in during late 2011.

Therefore, heterogeneity as a commodity attribute describes the degree of distinctly different natural resource types that are possible. From the supply manager's perspective, it contributes greatly to commodity scarcity. High levels of heterogeneity for a resource such as apples or diamonds also indicate that many different types of the resources are possible and currently available to be utilized. Since consumer and industrial products generally require a wide variety of heterogeneous resources with different attributes, worldwide demand depends on a sufficient supply of heterogeneous resources.

---

[10] http://www.thediamondbuyingguide.com/diamondpriceguide.html.

[11] http://www.alibaba.com/product-gs/286423735/SMD5130_Saw_grade_
industrial_synthetic_diamond.html.

Unfortunately, consumption over time has sometimes used up the highest-quality and most available nonrenewable resources. In fact, consumption has often created instances where some resource grades are no longer available, so levels of heterogeneity are lower. Additionally, pollution and resource degradation have caused many plant and animal species to go extinct. They also have led to lower levels of heterogeneity of renewable natural-resource supplies needed to meet the wide array of ever-increasing demands.

Understanding the exact specifications of the natural resources needed in products and their available supply quantities is critical to supply managers' understanding and management of heterogeneity in the future. More and more resources are becoming scarce and/or exhausted. Assuming that apparently plentiful resources exist within broad homogeneous groups (diamonds, apples, coal) that are globally available is a dangerous way for a supply manager to speculate. Such thinking can cause a firm to be blindsided by growing scarcity of a distinct heterogeneous resource type. Instead, supply managers need to understand a resource's level of heterogeneity and how it corresponds to specific resource demands.

Renewability is the second primary attribute affecting a resource's current status. This attribute describes a resource's ability to regenerate new quantities in the future. Some "renewable" resources can be regenerated over relatively short periods of time. Crops that supply the world's food chains are regenerated and harvested once or more in a single year. In the case of forests, it may take several years or decades for a resource to be restored and ready for a new cycle of consumption. For fisheries and other living systems, renewability may depend on the resource's reproduction versus harvest rates, as well as the underlying environment's health. As such, these renewable resources depend on the continued availability of accessibly clean amenities such as water, air, soil, and even ecological systems. For example, fruit crops depend on honeybees for pollination, and fisheries depend on plankton for food. Therefore, just as an isolated supply chain disruption such as a hurricane can affect a company's product supply chain, so can an environmental or ecosystem disturbance disrupt the supply chain for a renewable natural resource. Additionally, economists and ecologists have established that as population, consumption, and pollution increase, renewable resources can become less renewable. By losing the ability to regenerate, renewable resources that economies depend on are in jeopardy of becoming scarce.

Other natural resources are, for all practical purposes, "nonrenewable," such as the metals, minerals, and petroleum currently used in large quantities in industry around the world. These nonrenewable resources have very long natural creation periods. As humans consume more and more of them, they will steadily and increasingly become more rare. Although better technology helps us discover new deposits of nonrenewable resources, the planet contains a finite quantity of many resources to exploit. Although many of us may never live to see the complete "exhaustion" of a natural resource, economic activity continually decreases resource supplies and forces us to use quantities of lower-quality resources. This usage is more costly, requires improvements in technology, and can create more pollution, which then harms the environment and other natural resources.

The third attribute is *scarcity*—the primary focus of this chapter. Scarcity of a resource is the balance of physical supply and demand of the resource in a given location. Following scarcity research in several academic fields, natural resources can be described as scarce or available in a particular location depending on whether demand exceeds supply (scarcity) or supply exceeds demand (availability). Therefore, in a geographic context, scarcity can be either a global or local phenomenon. For example, metals such as gallium, indium, lead, platinum, and silver are becoming more *globally* scarce—they are predicted to be in short worldwide supply in the future. This fact has the potential to impact product designs for capacitors, solar cells, lasers, magnets, and the high-tech consumer products they help comprise.

Other resources may simply be *locally* scarce. Even though Australia is an extremely resource-abundant nation, it does not possess enough nickel deposits to meet all of its local demand. Consequently, it imports large quantities of nickel from the nearby island of New Caledonia (Fr.). Local scarcity is also prevalent with renewable resources like beef, salmon, and timber. These are not necessarily globally hard to find, but they are locally scarce. They must be transported long distances to meet local demand in places they cannot be found. Location is a key aspect of resource scarcity. Managers must determine the local and global aspects of scarcity for resources they possess and figure out how changes in scarcity might impact future operations. Additionally, it is important for managers to understand that the related attributes of renewability and heterogeneity also affect the measurement of scarcity (demand-versus-supply balance) for a resource and help determine an overall resource status.

Scarcity of resources like rare-earth metals, oil, and natural gas can bloat costs and prices for businesses in the coming decades. Although such increases show the power that scarcity can have over business, supply managers must not overreact to short-term changes that could be due to simple market fluctuations. Instead, we need to understand the long-term forces that constantly affect a natural resource's availability and price. By analyzing the three attributes of a resource now, managers can assess how that resource's current status might change and can take action to ensure that their organization is not crippled by future scarcity.

The Seven Forces Driving Resource Scarcity

Researchers across several sciences have identified seven macro-level forces that change a specific heterogeneous resource's scarcity level: discovery, substitution, recovery, resource base reclamation, consumption, resource base degradation, and competition.

As shown in Figure 7.1, four of these forces make resources more abundant, and the other three deplete them. Balancing these forces helps us ensure a specific resource's global availability and keeps it from losing economic value due to exceedingly high prices. However, this balance may not always be possible. As has happened so often in the past, supply managers may make false assumptions about a resource's homogeneity and availability, thereby failing to understand how scarce a particular resource really is. That is why we, as business managers, must understand how the seven forces act upon the world's natural resources.

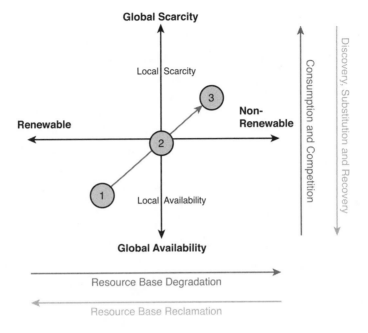

Figure 7.1 Resource scarcity dynamics[12]

Discovery of new resources has always been paramount to countering resource scarcity. As resource prices increase, so do the incentives to explore the Earth and create new technologies to find either additional volumes or new, less-scarce replacements. In 2011, over 300 activities were related to exploring the planet for rare-earth metals. This includes major efforts in California to reopen the United States' only rare-earth mine, which at the time was owned by Molycorp Inc.[13]

---

[12] Based on Bell, J.E., D.A. Mollenkopf, and H.J. Stolze. (2013). "Natural Resource Scarcity and the Closed-Loop Supply Chain." *International Journal of Physical Distribution & Logistics Management*. Forthcoming.

[13] Areddy, J.T. (17 August 2011). "A timeline for eroding China's rare earth chokehold." *The Wall Street Journal*. http://blogs.wsj.com/chinarealtime/2011/08/17/a-timeline-for-eroding-china's-rare-earth-chokehold/.

A major part of new-resource discovery is the related technological improvements developed to extract nonrenewable materials or harvest renewable ones. Recent efforts by major oil companies to find new resources depend on cutting-edge technologies to exploit shale gas and oil sand deposits. These deposits were previously believed to be far too expensive to extract. But with horizontal drilling and hydraulic fracturing technologies (fracking, described in Chapter 2), the northern and western areas of the United States, as well as significant portions of Australia and Canada, are at the forefront of a new natural gas and oil boom. Critics argue that the increased impact of these discoveries comes at a much higher ecological price and that the companies using these new technologies may not have fully considered the long-term environmental and social costs. But even as the debate over fracking rages, its use is becoming more widespread.

When a resource's availability erodes and price increases, the economic force known as *substitution* may take over. Business history offers many classic substitution examples. When whalers made their prey an endangered animal in the 1850s, whale oil prices soared. With whale oil no longer an economic possibility, kerosene soon became the standard for lantern fuel. Similarly, the lack of timber and wood for industrial purposes has often resulted in companies using substitute materials such as iron, steel, glass, or plastics to build their products. When engineers design new products, they search for substitute materials with similar physical characteristics that are not quite as expensive.[14]

Substitution has its limits, though. For example, the "tin whiskers" anomaly has made it difficult to replace lead solders with tin in electronics. The tin functions as a solder, eliminating the need for lead, but it creates electrical malfunctions as microscopic "whiskers" disrupt the robust way in which microelectronic designs operate. Few periodic table elements might serve as viable substitutes. Even if scientists could find a suitable replacement, each element comes with its own unique problems and benefits. As in a game of chess, design engineers find themselves strategically moving from one element to

---

[14] Lahart, J., P. Barta, and A. Batson. (24 March 2008). "New limits to growth revive Malthusian fears." *The Wall Street Journal*. http://online.wsj.com/article/SB120613138379155707.html.

another to avoid resource scarcity and achieve desired product characteristics, but they can make only so many substitutions. Therefore, like discovery, substitution often depends on improved technology, where potential risks and limitations almost always come with the territory.

Next, *recovering*, or recycling, natural resources can increase their supply and hence lessen their scarcity at local or even global levels. In the United States, a large portion of aluminum (30%), lead (63%), and titanium (50%) needed by their respective industries are supplied by recycled sources each year.[15] Products often are recycled for purposes other than just countering scarcity. For example, environmentally conscious policies in states like California and Oregon have compelled citizens to recycle. Some companies have started recycling efforts that focus on packaging materials (containers, cans, boxes) that can easily be reused. Others help consumers dispose of products that are obsolete or at the end of their life cycle so that they can be reused or recycled.

In some instances, these efforts are not always successful. In 2011 some cities fell far short of California's recycling goals, and some major companies were reported as not fully utilizing their recycling facilities. Given the increasing pressures of macrotrends on both the world and its supply chains, we expect this to change in the future. Scarcity, pollution concerns, and increased discovery/technology costs will make recycling natural resources more of a necessity than a marketing function. Managers must be on the lookout for ways to build closed loop supply chains to both recover value from obsolete products and design new ones so that they are easily recycled. When scarcity starts to take its toll, recovering reusable materials will be extremely important.

Similar to resource recovery, *reclaiming* the environment's air, water, and soil can mitigate, and possibly even reverse, the way in which resources are losing their renewability. Mining companies like Rio Tinto PLC have worked to reclaim and clean their mining locations by returning soil and groundwater to its original state, where it can be used for agricultural purposes. Much to the horror of many activists, governments, and a growing number of the world's population,

---

[15] Wagner, L.A. (2002). "Materials in the economy: Material flows, scarcity, and the environment." US Geological Survey Circular 1221.

pollution continues to spread in some regions of the world. Business still has a long way to go in terms of harnessing resource reclamation without also polluting the environment. This is probably due to the short-term inability to build profitable justification for such environmentally friendly activities, which do not always please shareholders.

As resource scarcity intensifies, supply managers should try to find ways to work with industry groups and government to reclaim damaged air, soil, and water to regain the renewability of resources. This concept should be obvious for companies like Georgia Pacific and ConAgra, which depend on timber and crops. They cannot afford to pollute the soil and water and expect their renewable resource supplies to remain sustainable. All industries should start to look into resource reclamation as a means to reduce the scarcity sure to strike them in the future.

The forces just described counter scarcity, but other forces amplify it. Increased *consumption* (as driven by our focal macrotrends) is a major worldwide concern and one of the most stressful forces acting upon natural resources. In economic and industrial activity, humans typically extract the highest-quality and most abundant resources first. Therefore, over time the highest-quality and easiest-to-access resources have disappeared due to past consumption. This helps explain why discovering new resources gets more difficult and more expensive and why products using those resources see continuous price increases. Some economists and environmental scientists are beginning to argue that we will probably never truly exhaust all of the world's oil. This is because global societies would be unable to afford the environmental impact or technological cost necessary to do so. Some economists believe that because the earth's environmental sinks are starting to fill up with air, water, and soil pollution, that trying to extract quantities of a resource (such as oil) to the point of exhaustion will create levels of pollution that the planet cannot bear.[16]

As we pointed out earlier, the planet's population will probably stabilize, and may even begin to contract, between the years 2030 and 2050. Until then, many of Earth's new citizens will seek more and more industrial and commercial products that will consume our natural resources. Consumption has the potential to change and disrupt

---

[16] Verbruggen, A. and M.A. Marchohi. (2010). "Views on peak oil and its relation to climate change policy," *Energy Policy*, Vol. 38, 5572-5581.

the balance of resource scarcity, as shown in Figure 7.1, in a truly daunting way. Without long-term approaches and strategies to counter consumption's growing effects, many companies will face a serious scarcity of resources that today are assumed to be globally available.

The *degradation* of underlying resource "bases" is making some renewable resources nonrenewable and some common ones more scarce. Economists and ecologists have observed this trend for many years. It is highly correlated with greater levels of consumption. For instance, environmental damage is threatening resource renewability around the globe. In China, some major rivers have become so polluted that even livestock cannot drink from them.[17] Similarly, overfishing and pollution threaten seafood sources, and overharvesting and ground pollution increase the scarcity levels of agricultural resources. Even though people and companies have started reclamation efforts, degradation rates are far exceeding reclamation rates. Degradation is hundreds of years in the making, and much of the damage has already been done thanks to previous industrial and commercial activity.

Although *competition* among firms is generally best for the consumer because it reduces prices in the short term, it also augments scarcity, which exacerbates prices in the longer term. With limited materials to go around, there is no guarantee that your firm will have access to them. If a direct competitor or a firm in another industry needs a natural resource and has secured large quantities of it for future use, it may be more difficult for your firm to gain access to it. Firms from countries all around the world are already "buying up," or hedging, numerous scarce resources because of anticipated future shortages. These hedging expenditures have been estimated at over $1 billion *per day*. Some companies are also hedging by vertical integration: They are buying up mining companies. Speculators are acquiring waste-collection companies to gain access to waste streams that will someday become reclamation sources.

Companies and managers need to understand that long-term availability of natural resources may be limited because firms and individuals are competitively buying up resources. Business competition

---

[17] Liu, B. and R. Speed. (2009) "Water resources management in the People's Republic of China," *Water Resources Development*, Vol. 25, No. 2, 193-208.

is generally viewed as a downstream, market-side phenomenon in commercial supply chains. However, growing competition among major firms upstream in the supply chain is expected to increase as firms seek to secure scarce resources needed to meet future demand. We are entering a business phase in which Demand-Supply Integration (DSI) will be not only important to world-class companies, but also a trait needed for any business's long-term corporate survival.

Resource scarcity has three primary attributes and seven primary forces that change its level over time. It is evident that prevailing economic macrotrends, such as population growth and economic leveling in emerging parts of the world (Asia and Africa), will tip the DSI balance for many resources toward higher levels of local, and even global, scarcity. This translates into much higher costs and may even mean an insufficient supply of natural resources to meet rapidly growing, industrial product demand.

Scarcity Strategies for the Future Procurement/Supply Manager

As supply managers start to make strategic choices about how to match demand with supply in the coming decades, they need to be careful not to make incorrect assumptions about a resource's scarcity status. Companies may make an assumption about the status of a resource that doesn't match its actual state (see states 1 and 2 in Figure 7.1). For example, a person may assume that the demand for a resource such as coal is very homogeneous and can be met with any type of supply. However, he may later find that only a specific grade of coal can be used and that the actual state of scarcity is much worse than he thought. Additionally, supply managers who do not analyze how forces are changing the actual state may not realize that they are headed toward a potential scarcity situation in the future (see state 3 in Figure 7.1). As you read in the preface, Coca-Cola may have made bad assumptions about freshwater availability for its bottling plant in India.

Similarly, designing a product such that a scarce natural resource is needed in its production, and then later finding out that there isn't enough of it to go around, could dramatically impact the product's (or company's) viability. Throwing money at the problem is not always the solution. A company may stockpile a resource in anticipation of growing scarcity and then have its investment undercut by the future discovery of a new major deposit. It is important to understand that it is possible to move in any direction shown in Figure 7.1, depending on how the seven forces are attempting to counteract and balance each other. Therefore, to prevent mistakes like this and to mitigate scarcity risks, firms need to collect better information on potential scarcity for their resources and build better processes for strategic decisions concerning resource scarcity.

Improved technology, resource discovery, and resource substitution may have the potential to temporarily mitigate short-term price fluctuations caused by scarcity. However, economists and energy scientists alike admit that there may be environmental, geological, and technological limits on alleviating scarcity in the long run. Many firms are already starting to feel the growing problem of scarcity and are bracing for tougher times ahead. Consulting firm Pricewaterhouse-Coopers surveyed over 60 industrial firms in December 2011. It found that over 50% of companies are struggling with scarcity of their key metal sources and that 75% of them anticipate the problems will get worse in just the next five years.[18] Additionally, many design engineers are beginning to document the difficulties associated with designing and manufacturing new products with scarce availability of important metals. Some metals are projected to have a 10-to-20-year global supply at current consumption rates. But this supply could be cut to fewer than 10 years if the rest of the world increases its consumption to even half of what the United States is consuming. With an insufficient supply of metals, how will we continue making the batteries, magnets, lasers, solar cells, and other components needed in future products? Or, more importantly, how much will these important subcomponents cost your company—and the world as a whole?

---

[18] Schoolderman, H. and R. Mathlener. 2011. "Minerals and metals scarcity in manufacturing: The ticking time-bomb." *Sustainable Materials Management*. The Netherlands: PriceWaterhouseCoopers.

Sourcing and Procurement Responses to Resource Scarcity Through 2030

This chapter has described the general problem of resource scarcity, mapped the playing field (by articulating resource attributes and forces), and described some of the growing risks anticipated in the next 25 years. Now we offer three general recommendations for managing future supply in a world of resource scarcity:

- Supply managers need to understand what resources (in terms of quality and quantity) are used in their key products' designs and how scarce those resources are. We suggest that managers must map these products' supply chains all the way back to the raw-material level to uncover hidden supply risks. Resource scarcity can affect the key GSCF supply chain processes of product development, supplier relationship management, and manufacturing flow management. Therefore, companies should work with supply chain partners in these processes to collect information and uncover hidden risks.

- Because scarcity is a dynamic issue, the sourcing functions of current and future businesses should consider investing in research activities to monitor scarcity changes caused by the seven forces. This includes monitoring changes and forecasts for consumption and competition for key resource supply. Global awareness and anticipating changing resource statuses will help supply managers identify demand and supply threats and also help them create opportunities for their companies. Instead of being caught off-guard by unanticipated scarcity crises, supply chain managers in proactive companies can differentiate themselves and create competitive advantage by getting ahead of scarcity trends.

- As soon as supply managers fully understand the resource scarcity dynamics that affect their firms, they should capitalize on opportunities by building comprehensive supply strategies that capture and leverage the described forces to get ahead of the competition. Firms should work with their supply chain partners to build long-term strategies for responding to growing scarcity levels by designing products and basing their technology changes on resources that will be available. Additionally, managers should leverage supply chain designs and build logistics approaches to ensure that products remain sustainable throughout their life cycle.

These three ideas are not new to world-class companies like GE, Unilever, and Kimberly-Clark. They have already faced challenges created by resource scarcity and have taken significant steps to do something about it. They have joined global groups, such as the World Business Council for Sustainable Development, to monitor issues like water scarcity and learn how these can affect their products. They are building long-term and multifaceted strategies to mitigate resource scarcity in the future. They understand what's coming, and they're doing something about it.

Let's look at GE's method for identifying scarcity risks as an example. In the production of its major aircraft engines, GE has recognized that many important metals are becoming scarce. This scarcity has affected GE's costs and is having a significant impact on how the company designs future engines. To make the best decisions about using scarce metals and to mitigate the impacts of scarcity on current engine product lines, GE has developed a multifaceted risk management approach.[19] GE uses approximately 70 of the first 82 elements in the periodic table in its manufacturing operations. However, since detailed analysis of all 70 of these elements seemed infeasible, the company ranked the annual purchase value of the elements from highest to lowest in a Pareto ranking. Doing so helped GE identify where the biggest scarcity impacts could occur. Using this approach, GE narrowed the list to 24 elements with a large-enough footprint in the company to have a significant impact on operations if supply became restricted. Next, it narrowed this field to 11 metals that were subject to recent price variability and instability. Then it conducted detailed research on the 11 elements and ranked them in a criticality matrix. On one axis of this matrix, elements were ranked from very high risk to very low risk based on the potential impact to the company. This impact was measured with four subfactors: the ability to substitute the element, the percentage of world supply used by the company, the revenue that would be lost if the element became unavailable, and the ability to pass on price increases to final customers. On the second axis of the matrix, GE ranked the 11 elements from very high risk to very low risk based on the potential supply and price risks.

---

[19] Duclos, S.J., J.P. Otto, and D.G. Konitzer. (September 2010). "Design in an era of constrained resources." *Mechanical Engineering*.

Subcategories in this category included abundance of the element in the Earth's crust, political risk, demand increase risk, whether the element is a by-product of another element, price volatility, and the ability to substitute. Overall risk scores for each of the two axes were determined by summing the risk rankings in each subcategory, and then the final position of each element was plotted on an x,y matrix. The results helped identify which elements were at greatest risk of being impacted by scarcity, and also how that would translate into an impact on GE. Overall, GE identified that the metal rhenium, used in its aircraft engines, was not suffering from scarcity but had the potential to have a major impact on the company. This allowed the company to take detailed actions, which we will describe in Chapter 11, "Mitigating Demand-Driven Imbalance." Unlike our opening example of the steel shortage in Canada, GE has built a formal and proactive process for identifying natural resource scarcity risks in its products and for doing something about it before it impacts the company. Managers should consider whether they have similar processes in place, or whether they will find out about the impacts of scarcity after it is too late and major disruptions affect their operations.

So what's the bottom line? Growing resource scarcity will play a major role in business over the next 25 years. In response, supply managers will have to avoid short-term thinking and invest more time and money in more proactive and long-term risk management strategies to avoid the scarcity pitfalls.

8

Implications for Production: Disrupted Process Flows

Filmmaker Stanley Kubrick warned us what a future might look like where humans and their computing machines find themselves in conflict, as the mission-fixated HAL conspired against his mortal crewmates in *2001: A Space Odyssey*. But computer processing power and the performance capabilities of computer-driven automation are exciting considerations today. A tour of a modern manufacturing facility equipped with robotic automation and guided vehicles can astound and amaze the casual observer. Following such a visit, you might think that humans' role in the production process is being marginalized as advanced technology takes over. However, humans and machines more often than not work hand-in-hand. When competition between humans and machines does ensue, the victor is not always so obvious at the outset. Consider, for instance, when the world's top national soccer teams descended on London for the 2012 Summer Olympics. There they played using an Adidas ball known as the Albert. Was it produced in the same highly automated factory as the notoriously unpredictable Jabulani ball used at the 2010 World Cup in South Africa? No. The company called on its supplier in Sialkot, Pakistan, a remote city in the Kashmir foothills, to make the Albert for the London games. In Sialkot, workers hand-stitch balls for the top competitions, which require the highest levels of quality and craftsmanship. Not long ago, Sialkot produced 75% of the world's soccer balls. But in recent years, its global share has dropped to around 40% as more balls are produced via automation elsewhere. Yet as the global appetite for soccer balls grows each year, companies like Adidas, Nike, and Puma continue to seek out the craftspeople of Sialkot to meet the demand for their premium-quality balls. In fact, the volume of high-quality

soccer balls produced in the rural region motivated the installation of
a private world-class airstrip that can support large cargo aircraft to
ship balls wherever the biggest games are played.[1] The repetitive jux-
taposition of technology and people is but one major production-
related theme impacted by the macrotrends we study in this book.
This chapter explores the various ways in which the macrotrends
affect the manufacturing function, as well as strategies for enacting
value-added production in rapidly transforming supply chains.

Manufacturing and the Larger Economy

Traditionally, no activity has signaled vibrancy in an economy like
manufacturing. For centuries, the ability to "make stuff" has been
among the most influential forces in a nation's economic vitality. Particularly throughout the past three centuries or so, the premise of
being a "world power" has been closely tied to the ability to compete globally in the creation of valued products. Hungarian economist
Nicholas Kaldor's work on the relationship between manufacturing
output and a society's quality of life is cited as a classic treatise in
support of domestic production. "Kaldor's First Law," conceived in
the late 1960s, conclusively demonstrated that GDP growth occurs
fastest when the share of manufacturing-to-nonmanufacturing work
in a nation is higher. It also showed that consumers' quality of life
grows roughly in parallel with the GDP.[2] However, being the world's
best "consumption society" is hardly a game plan for manufacturing
competence and economic prominence. Rather, consumption is the
reward for gaining economic prowess. There is reason to worry that
less production is occurring in many developed nations, including

---

[1] Soccer ball production in Sialkot is not without controversy, with rampant concerns about child labor used to produce the goods. During the 1970s and 1980s,
it was estimated that more than 7,000 children between the ages of 7 and 14
were employed full-time in home-based workshops to produce soccer balls. A
collection of interested stakeholders, including UNICEF, the United Nations'
International Labour Organization, industry trade groups, and the brand marketers, signed the Atlanta Agreement in 1997, which has helped curb the practice of
child labor and has improved the monitoring of middlemen and producers.

[2] Kaldor, N. (1967). *Strategic Factors in Economic Development*. New York:
Ithaca Publishing.

the U.S. Much concern is being voiced in the U.S. over manufacturing's shrinking share of the GDP.[3] It is feared that outsourcing considerable production activity to distant locations guts manufacturing capacity and causes a loss of critical skills needed to produce goods.

Additionally, for the last decade or so, we have seen the relative impact of manufacturing on overall domestic production wane. A countervailing argument can be made that Kaldor was wrong because he never anticipated that knowledge could generate more value than production. Critics say that a knowledge economy leads to more prosperous outcomes, and the immediate data seems to support their views. U.S.-based Apple nets 30% profits on iPads produced in China, where the final assembler Foxconn claims merely 2% of the product's revenues.[4] In fact, South Korean component suppliers claim a substantially higher share (7%) than Foxconn's stake earned for the final assembly process.[5] Consider also the macroeconomic data point illustrated by Thailand, where the nation leads world production in dollars per capita but is ranked only in the 70s in GDP. This flies somewhat in the face of traditional wisdom on the value of manufacturing within domestic borders. We see the issue as a matter of control: The societies that will be able to drive manufacturing in other locations as a result of their aggregate knowledge development will prosper the most.[6] Regardless of its location, production continues to serve as the engine for the world economy, and it will continue to do so for as long as value to consumers is embedded in physical goods.

---

[3] Manufacturing represented 13% of the United States' GDP in 2010, compared with 79% for services. The balance was in government spending. This represents a consistent decline from 16% in 2000 and 18% in 1990.

[4] We acknowledge that the example of an electronics product of the nature of Apple's iPad is an extreme one given the "healthy" margins and seemingly boundless demand it enjoys.

[5] Kraemer, Kenneth, Greg Linden, and Jason Dedrick. (July 2011). *Capturing Value in Global Networks: Apple's iPad and iPhone.*

[6] A countering argument to this line of reasoning stands in the replacement of high-paying manufacturing jobs for lower-paying service jobs. The jury is still out as to whether knowledge capital or manufacturing capital exerts greater influence on economic vitality in the long term. Another corollary to the argument is that the knowledge capital associated with knowing how to make products (R&D and engineering skills) is sometimes lost in the transfer of production activity. Hence, not only is the manufacturing expertise lost, but also key aspects of knowledge.

Simply performing—or controlling—value-added work is insufficient to generate economic outcomes, because a viable marketplace must be willing to consume the output. The matter of enticing demand for one's output makes for an interesting history lesson. Consider the British Industrial Revolution, which is widely regarded as the most significant societal transformation since the domestication of plants and animals. England's ability to transform textile industries from manual to machine-driven processes that were highly efficient, precise, and replicable helped the country move from an agrarian economy to the world's first truly industrialized nation. Innovations such as the use of interchangeable parts within products and machinery led costs of production to decrease markedly, while opportunities for manufacturing employment simultaneously exploded. A second revolution was triggered by developments in power-generation technologies such as steam engines and, ultimately, the internal combustion engine and electric power generation. These inventions dramatically boosted production speed and efficiency. The combination of lower costs for goods and rising incomes led to the greatest, most sustained rise in living standards the world had ever known. The paradigm spread virally from England to Western Europe, North America, and Japan throughout the balance of the second millennium. Manufacturing skill touched every aspect of daily life for the citizens of these societies, but it has sometimes resulted in conflict among nations (such as the two world wars of the 20th century).

The production of steel serves as a proxy for comparing nations' productivity, given steel's integral role in both consumer and business goods. Steel production represents a bellwether measure primarily due to its position as a critical input for staple industries, such as construction and heavy manufacturing. Table 8.1 lists the top ten nations in crude steel production in five-year increments from 1991 to 2011. These numbers are effective proxies for the combination of material resource wealth, processing capability, relative economics, and regulatory environment that mark leading-edge industrialized nations. The table points out the dominance of Chinese steel producers over the past decade, with China providing nearly 46% of the world's supply of steel, up from less than 10% in 1991. While global supply has more than doubled over this 20-year time frame, China's capacity has increased nearly tenfold, outpacing its nearest rival (Japan) by 635%.

International competitors make claims of undue government support in the form of an undervalued currency; export rebates; generous financing arrangements; and lax regulations in the areas of environment, labor, and safety. Yet the rise of China is not the only compelling story to be found in the data. Also noteworthy is the rise of nations like India, Brazil, and Turkey as major players in the global steel industry. These nations can support their own growing appetite for steel and also provide export volumes for global production.

Table 8.1 Top Ten Nations in Crude Steel Production, 1991–2011

		Volume (in Millions of Metric Tons)				
Rank	**Nation**	**1991**	**1996**	**2001**	**2006**	**2011**
1	China	71.0	101.2	150.9	422.7	683.3
2	Japan	109.6	98.8	102.9	116.2	107.6
3	United States	79.7	95.5	90.1	98.6	86.2
4	India	17.1	23.8	27.3	49.5	72.2
5	Russia	67.0	49.3	59.0	70.8	68.7
6	South Korea	26.0	38.9	43.9	48.5	68.5
7	Germany	42.2	39.8	44.8	47.2	44.3
8	Ukraine	41.8	22.3	33.1	40.9	35.5
9	Brazil	22.6	25.2	28.7	30.9	35.2
10	Turkey	9.4	13.6	15.0	23.3	34.1
	World Totals	**733.6**	**750.0**	**850.3**	**1,250.0**	**1,490.1**

Source: World Steel Association

Yet crude steel production is only part of the story. Table 8.2 shows the export volumes of semifinished and finished steel products during roughly the same 20-year period. (Note that we must look at the top 11 exporting nations in order to include the United States in this analysis.) Examining these processed steel products indicates how nations move up the industrial food chain, by not only producing raw materials but also adding value to them. Meanwhile, examining exports indicates that the supply exceeds the demands of the home nation and that the supply of steel is competitive in the world markets. Several stories emerge from this analysis. Starting at the top, we see that Japan regained its leadership in the most recent reading, edging out China. Japan enjoyed substantial growth in exports during the 1996–2001 period, surpassing Germany and Russia for the global lead at the time. However, it's hard to find the words to describe China's rise in the 2001–2006 time period, because it increased 710%! Global demand for steel increased markedly in the boom years of the early 2000s. This led many to accuse China of unfairly (and illegally) dumping steel supplies on the world market, saturating supply, and putting international competitors in peril due to falling prices. The problem was worsened during the "Great Recession" that choked demand in the United States and Europe beginning in 2008. Although China reduced export volumes in the most recent reading, the nation continues to feed its own demand. This demand is greater than the world has ever seen, with substantial volumes available to supply more than 10% of the global export volume.[7]

Table 8.2 Top Exporters of Semifinished and Finished Steel Products, 1991–2010[8]

		Volume (in Millions of Metric Tons)				
Rank	Nation	1991	1996	2001	2006	2010
1	Japan	17.916	19.262	29.494	34.557	42.735
2	China	4.378	7.131	7.276	51.706	41.646
3	Russia	—[9]	26.994	25.575	31.462	27.382
4	Germany	19.531	20.437	23.890	29.219	25.352
5	Ukraine	—	12.142	24.380	30.600	25.201
6	South Korea	8.062	10.438	14.078	18.016	24.628
7	Turkey	4.330	6.697	10.587	9.180	16.223
8	Italy	8.954	10.922	11.804	17.052	15.316
9	Belgium	14.368	14.673	20.531	20.098	15.153
10	France	12.071	13.124	16.897	18.795	14.141
11	United States	5.905	4.641	5.823	9.565	11.082
	World Totals	**177.045**	**247.044**	**300.385**	**418.285**	**386.839**

Source: World Steel Association

[7] In 2012, the World Trade Organization ruled that China unfairly imposed duties on imports of U.S. electrical steel. In that same year, however, China filed a dispute claiming that the United States was unfairly dumping supplies in China. The World Trade Organization dismissed the suit, but it underscores the tensions found among these trade powers.

[8] 2011 data were unavailable at the time of this writing.

[9] Data are unreliable for the former Soviet states of Russia and Ukraine prior to 1992.

We again ask: Does such manufacturing dominance yield wealth for a nation and its people? Let's look at one common measure of national wealth, per-capita GDP (the nation's GDP divided by the population). Based on 2011 data, the United States ranks 13th ($48,442), and China ranks well below, with a per-capita GDP of merely $5,430 (but an amazing increase of 1,650% over the past 20 years). So do the oil-rich nations of Qatar, Kuwait, the UAE, and Saudi Arabia top the rankings? They are near the top, but tiny Luxembourg stands tall among its wealthy neighbors of Western Europe. With a per-capita GDP of $115,038, it earns 17% more (on a per-capita basis) than #2 Norway, and it is ahead of the oil states of the Middle East. How did it get there? The nation is something of a financial center in Europe,[10] but it exports large volumes of steel and is home to ArcelorMittal, the world's largest steel company. The company earned 2011 revenues of almost $94 billion and ranked #70 on *Fortune*'s Global 500 list. It is the nation's largest employer and its largest contributor to exports. Housing this manufacturing powerhouse is instrumental in the nation's wealth creation. Yet if ArcelorMittal is to maintain its position in an intensifying marketplace, it must successfully navigate the churning waters of global competition. To explore the strategies of individual companies in the face of these massive shifts, we look to the manufacturing-driven supply chain strategies employed by firms today.

Manufacturing-Driven Supply Chain Strategies

Given the central role that manufacturing plays in the supply chain, the strategies employed by manufacturers set the tone for supply chain execution throughout the network of companies. This suggestion is largely based on two driving factors:

- Manufacturing is often the most capital-intensive and value-inducing process in the supply chain.

---

[10] Luxembourg's secretive banking environment makes it a tax haven and financial hotspot internationally.

- Manufacturing represents a common bottleneck in supply chain operations.

Taken together, these observations imply that manufacturing capabilities can be a key competitive differentiator, separating the most capable providers from the pack.

A common way to define the strategy for an entire supply chain is to identify the *strategic decoupling point*. This is the point up to which product is *pushed* through the supply chain based on sales forecasts and beyond which it is *pulled* based on actual end-user demand. Where manufacturing lead times prove long and insufficient to meet customers' needs in a timely manner, the various entities of the supply chain will be forced to generate forecasts (usually independent of one another) and place orders in advance of end-user demand. This stockpiling of inventory at the various tiers of the supply chain is characteristic of a "pure push" strategy of anticipatory supply chains described in Chapter 6, "Implications for Supply Chain Planning: Demand and Supply Uncertainty." The strategic decoupling point in this case is located at the store shelf, where consumers are greeted by waiting inventory. Great faith is placed in the forecast. It drives not only production, but also the procurement of raw materials through the materials requirements plan (MRP) and the allocation of finished-goods (FG) inventory through the distribution resource plan (DRP). Such strategies are best used when demand is relatively "known" or when speculation is relatively safe and inventory carrying costs are low. Holding too much inventory is of minimal concern under these circumstances, compared to the risks of stocking out.

However, the pure push strategy is usually quite inflexible and blind to market changes. With execution throughout the supply chain based on forecasts, the pure push strategy is susceptible to bad planning. As a result, it is prone to the ills of excess inventory when demand drops and extended stockouts when demand surges unexpectedly. Despite these concerns, marketers of grocery and household goods deploy the pure push in stocking stores in advance of demand. Given that the traditional supermarket stocks, on average, 38,718 different items,[11] the challenge of achieving forecast accuracy across this range

---

[11] According to a 2010 estimate from the Food Marketing Institute.

is obvious. By some estimates, grocery stores average only 80% in-stock performance at the item level. Out-of-stocks are often covered up by ready substitutes, in which a different flavor, count, or pack size can be chosen. The big fear of the manufacturer is that the consumer will switch to a competitor's offering. Meanwhile, the fear of the retailer is that the consumer will take issue with the stockout and switch stores.

One way that companies in the supply chain seek to counter the uncertainties of demand in a pure push system is to abandon independent planning efforts and collaborate on the forecast. Such efforts help bolster confidence in the forecast by virtue of making it a team effort while providing supply chain partners with an opportunity to identify and remedy supply issues. However, this does nothing to shift the strategic decoupling point further upstream from the retail store shelf. Furthermore, it raises the ante on the shared forecast by generating one "best guess" that all parties buy into. To boot, it does not necessarily improve the accuracy of the forecast. For these reasons, the synchronized push strategy remains the domain of products either believed to have stable demand or for which the costs of stockout are so great that companies are willing to invest in sizeable inventories and position them throughout the supply chain.

Such a supply chain system is more aware of changes in demand. However, the make-to-stock provision employed by manufacturers in this arrangement often remains too inflexible to change the speed and direction of operations. Besides, it does nothing to shift the strategic decoupling point any further upstream in the supply chain, keeping it firmly entrenched at the retail location, with inventory waiting patiently for buyers. Historically, this has been the case with U.S. automotive manufacturers. They operated highly integrated supply chains with dedicated suppliers and company-owned and -franchised dealers, and point-of-sale data flowed freely. Yet the long lead times and inflexibility in operations prevented more pull-based orientations to provide the in-stock performance that auto buyers had come to expect. Although it's less common around the world, traditional U.S. auto buyers want to kick the tires and test-drive the very automobile they will subsequently take home. This requires the dealer to stock a seemingly endless assortment and quantity of vehicles to achieve a match between their supply and the customer's demand. Given the countless options available on vehicles today, you can readily recognize that it would be almost impossible to achieve a perfect match between the customer's expectations and a nearly infinite assortment of automobiles. Despite those odds, it is not uncommon for automakers and dealers in the United States to hold more than 100 days' supply, totaling more than 3 million vehicles nationwide sitting idle in anticipation of demand. Inventory has been known to balloon so much among the Big Three U.S. automakers that dealers and regional distributors cannot accommodate the deluge. The massive parking lots at the Michigan State Fairgrounds are used to house the excess.

To address this imbalance, many companies today are embracing the philosophy and principles of Lean Manufacturing. Inspired by the Toyota Production System and made famous by authors James Womack and Daniel Jones,[12] Lean Manufacturing seeks to reduce various forms of waste, or *muda*, that are created by poorly defined or ill performing processes. In their influential book *Lean Thinking*, Womack and Jones succinctly state that lean-ness is achieved by the following:

- Specifying value by product
- Identifying the value stream for the product
- Making the product flow
- Pulling from the customer
- Pursuing perfection in operations

The persuasion of the "Lean" argument has been considerable and it is widely embraced, with nearly 70% of U.S. manufacturers claiming to pursue Lean as of 2007.[13] This number is likely to exceed 90% today. Also, application of Lean principles has spread widely into every walk of life. Devotees can be found among manufacturers of virtually every product category; providers of industrial and consumer services; and even government, schools, and charitable organizations, with resounding success. Yet the fourth principle in Womack and Jones' list often leads to confusion and keeps Lean's fullest potential

---

[12] Womack, James P., Daniel T. Jones, and Daniel Roos. (1991). *The Machine That Changed the World.* New York: Harper Perennial; Womack, James P. and Daniel T. Jones. (2003). *Lean Thinking.* New York: Free Press.

[13] This data point comes from the last installment of *IndustryWeek*'s "Census of U.S. Manufacturers" in 2007.

from being realized. When suggesting that companies "pull" (demand) from the customer, the question that often arises is, "Who is the customer?" Is it the firm's immediate customer, the end user, or even an internal customer (the person who receives your work)?

Manufacturers often seek to pull demand from their immediate customer, which is typically a distributor or retailer. This equates to using a forecast to preposition inventory at the distribution point that serves the manufacturer's customer(s). When inventory is depleted at the distribution location, these supplies are replenished in kind. This presents the appearance of a "pull" system, but the replenishing supply is still speculative. In other words, it is produced before actual orders, making this provision nothing more than a glorified make-to-stock system. The strategic decoupling point for this "Lean-push" supply chain does shift one tier upstream, however, from the retail shelf to the distribution location that serves the retailer. You need look no further than Toyota's operations in North America to see this kind of system in action. Even though Toyota is the benchmark in the industry, with the most flexible mass production system in the market, it still relies on forecasts to determine the initial supply of vehicles to be allocated to distributors and dealers. This so-called "supermarket supply" is then replenished based on actual consumer sales and the market reads provided by Toyota Motor Sales, the distribution company serving the Toyota Motor Corporation in North America.[14] But if you visit a Toyota dealer, you will find more than a day's supply at the lot. In fact, currently Toyota keeps 49 days of supply on hand. This is below the industry average but still is a very large and valuable supply.[15] Some of this supply comes from domestic production locations. The rest (namely, cars sporting the Lexus brand) originates outside the United States—particularly Japan, Canada, and Mexico. The longer lead times associated with imported vehicles generally result in greater supplies of these vehicles.

Toyota has experimented in recent years with a variation of its conventional manufacturing and distribution arrangement. Arguably,

---

[14] This arrangement of replenishing supermarket supplies based on sold quantities is the general replenishment logic employed in vendor-managed inventory (VMI) relationships found in several different product industries.

[15] According to WardsAuto "U.S. Light Vehicle Inventory by Company," July 2012.

this arrangement is considerably more "lean" than the primary method Toyota employs in making and selling cars in the United States. Beginning in 2002, Toyota launched the Scion brand in the U.S. market. This brand was designed to appeal to the younger market segment of individualism-minded Generation Y consumers. They were believed to be willing to wait a few days to receive a "custom-built" automobile based on a menu of options and standard pricing. Initially, three models (the xA, xB, and tC) were offered in a limited number of colors and options, ranging from the substantive (sport shocks and struts) to the cosmetic (an adhesive Scion logo to adorn the hood). Shoppers were encouraged to go online to "Build your own" automobile. What surprised many a prospective buyer was that the "custom-built" vehicle that was promised to arrive in 2 to 14 days was not produced, for the most part, in the United States. Rather, generic versions of the cars were built in Toyota City, Japan, and shipped to major distributors located in the U.S. (Tacoma, Washington, for customers in the western U.S. and Jacksonville, Florida, for eastern U.S. customers). Consumer orders were then placed against the supply of generic vehicles stocked at major distributors located at these two port cities. The distributor customized the vehicle in this provision of "forward-positioned postponement," delaying the final form of the product until a firm customer order was in hand. Aside from the make, model, and color, other aspects of the car could take shape close to the consumer, allowing for precise accommodation of demand within a few short days. This strategy has come to be known as configure-to-order (CTO) manufacturing, or mass customization. Postponing the product's final form until a firm customer commitment is in hand reduces the risks faced by the manufacturer in serving diverse customer needs.

Configure-to-order is a common practice in the consumer electronics industry. Consider the often-cited case of Hewlett-Packard serving customers in Western Europe. Customers of the company's printers could be quite varied depending on their location, given the different languages spoken in the region as well as the different electrical voltages used in each nation. The printer itself, however, was uniform in its engineering and function, whether used in England, France, or Germany. To accommodate the diverse needs in the most economical fashion, the company elected to perform the packaging operations close to the market. Once printers arrived in Rotterdam via ship from the Asian supply location, they were maintained in a generic state until customer orders were placed. With the aid of a capable third-party logistics provider, HP bundled the proper power pack, software, and instruction manual to support the customer. This provision still relies on a forecast for production of the base configuration and the supplies for customization. Yet the level of speculation and the economic risks of a poor forecast are lower when the company is holding generic work-in-process (WIP) inventory rather than finished goods. Though the strategic decoupling point in supply chains for mass-customized products remains at the distribution center, the provision of generic WIP reduces the risk of costly forecast errors. The forecast is aggregated at the platform level (across several different varieties that customers might seek) and involves a lower-cost generic item that has yet to see its final value-added processes and associated costs. Granted, the cost of production is often higher in these arrangements, because assembly occurs in two locations. (The factory produces the generic item, and the forward-positioned distribution location performs the customization.)

Many supply chain experts advocate the application of Lean principles in the provision of generic items and the rapid, or agile, support of customization as soon as the customer order is received. This blending of Lean and Agile strategies results in "Leagile" supply chains. Revisiting our Scion example, Toyota is Lean in the production of the generic Scion car. When the car arrives at the U.S.-based distributor, the company reacts agilely to accommodate the specific configuration that suits the customer. Configure-to-order postponement may also occur at the factory, rather than at the downstream distribution location. When this is the case, the manufacturer is off-setting the risk of misallocating inventory (inventory located in the wrong location) by adding lead time to the delivery service. The goods will have to be transported from a central manufacturing facility, as opposed to the region's distribution point.

Centralized postponement extends the strategic decoupling point upstream one tier in the supply chain, allowing the pull of the end customer to reach the factory. In fact, the role of the distribution facility might be diminished to the point of dismissing it from the logistics network and delivering directly to customers from the factory. Conducting all value-added processing in one location can reduce costs, yet transportation economies may be lost when products are shipped directly to customers from a central location. This represents another version of the Leagile strategy and, like forward-positioned postponement, it is employed by several prominent companies. Foremost among them are Dell and its successful direct-to-consumer model, which was described in Chapter 6. Golf equipment manufacturers, like TaylorMade and Calloway, custom-build golf clubs to their customers' specifications, including club head angle, loft, shaft length, and grips at their manufacturing facilities. Package-to-order services also belong in this class of manufacturing strategy. In these instances, the customization occurs in the bundling and/or packaging of the goods, with the core product remaining unchanged. Delaying the commitment of the product's final packaging can help mitigate the proliferation of stock-keeping units (SKUs) that differ only in their packaging.

The final strategy to find common usage among modern manufacturers is the make-to-order (MTO) provision. MTO is the least speculative of all strategies presented here, because the manufacturer does not commit to work-in-process or finished goods until the customer order is placed. The manufacturer may still generate a forecast, however, to allow for the procurement of raw materials and to plan capacities. Both would help reduce the extensive lead times associated with MTO operations. Note, however, that despite recognizing that more operational steps must be performed from the time of order receipt until delivery (such as building product and delivering it from a central plant location), customers sometimes lack this understanding. They expect service that competes with other companies' speculation-based models, which have inventory prepositioned in the supply chain. With this in mind, MTO companies emphasize agile response to orders. When a manufacturer stops short of committing to the raw materials on hand for the impending orders, the company is employing a buy-to-order (BTO) strategy that is even less speculative than MTO, where inventory of raw materials is on hand. MTO and BTO strategies essentially extend the pull of the end customer all the way back to the manufacturer's first-tier suppliers. This strategy ordinarily is reserved for products that are described as "impossible to forecast" or for which the risk of inventory obsolescence is too great for the company to bear. Aircraft, missiles, industrial and home construction projects, and custom-built automobiles fall into this category.

Table 8.3 and Figure 8.1 summarize these manufacturing-driven supply chain strategies and note their key distinctions. The strategic decoupling point distinguishes the push/pull boundaries of each supply chain strategy and the drivers of action. These strategies accommodate the range of products and diverse customer demands found in modern supply chains. Though they have served us well in the early phases of globalization, they will undergo considerable adaptation with the advent of the macrotrends we feature in this book. We continue by reviewing the influences of the macrotrends on the production function in general and the strategies companies will employ to address the transformative changes that lie ahead.

	Pure Push	Synch Push	Lean-Push	Leagile 1	Leagile 2	Lean-Pull (Agile)
Description	Multiple forecasts throughout supply chain	A single forecast for mfg. and distribution	Forecast pre-positioned inventory and replenish	Decentralized postponement at DC's	Centralized postponement at factory	No WIP or FG inventory
Strategic Decoupling Point	Push to customers	Coordinated push to customers	Push to DC and pull from DC	Push WIP to DC and pull FG from DC	Push WIP to factory and pull FG from factory	Pull from material supply
Manufacturing Strategy	MTS (pure speculation)	MTS (coordinated guess)	MTS (guess at start, then replenish)	CTO (guess base, customize rest)	CTO (guess base, customize rest)	MTO (customize from beginning)
Driver of Action	Respective forecasts	Shared forecast with supply	Shared forecast with supply and DC's	Forecast for base, order for FG	Forecast for base and WIP allocation	Customer order
Best for	"Known" demand	Very stable demand	Consistent, stable demand	Consistent base demand	High variation; inconsistent	Impossible-to-forecast items

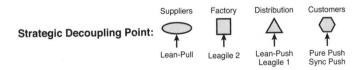

Figure 8.1 Manufacturing-driven supply chain strategies

Table 8.3 Summary of Manufacturing-Driven Supply Chain Strategies

	Pure Push	Synchronized Push	Lean Push	Leagile 1	Leagile 2	Lean Pull (Agile)
Description	Multiple forecasts throughout the supply chain	A single forecast for manufacturing and distribution	Forecast pre-positioned inventory and replenish	Decentralized postponement at DCs	Centralized postponement at the factory	No WIP or FG inventory
Strategic Decoupling Point	Push to customers	Coordinated push to customers	Push to DC and pull from DC	Push WIP to DC and pull FG from DC	Push WIP to factory and pull FG from factory	Pull from material supply
Manufacturing Strategy	Make to stock (MTS) (pure speculation)	MTS (coordinated guess)	MTS (guess at the start, and then replenish)	CTO (guess the base, customize the rest)	CTO (guess the base, customize the rest)	MTO (customize from the beginning)
Driver of Action	Respective forecasts	Shared forecast with supply	Shared forecast with supply and DCs	Forecast for base, order for FG	Forecast for base and WIP allocation	Customer order
What It's Best For	"Known" demand	Very stable demand	Consistent, stable demand	Consistent base demand	High variation, inconsistent	Impossible-to-forecast items

Manufacturing Strategies for the Future Production Manager

Like planning and procurement strategies, manufacturing will undergo immense stresses resulting from the macrotrends. Manufacturing strategies must accommodate the rising demand and heterogeneous needs resulting from global population growth and migration. Companies will seek to capture less-developed markets that heretofore were regarded as unattractive, marginal, or unviable. Our examples of soft drink manufacturers entering India and automakers investing in the Chinese market spell out this realization. Global connectivity and socioeconomic leveling underscore the growth potential in less-developed markets as the consuming classes grow exponentially in these regions and gain greater awareness of and interest in a broader array of products and services. The stresses on manufacturing and supply chains are elevated in contending with natural resource scarcity and constraints of the physical environment. Geopolitical and social systems that are at odds with one another add to the challenge. The macrotrends hold major implications for demand and supply that will force transformation among manufacturing strategies. Table 8.4 outlines how specific forces have given rise to change, the implications for supply chain management, and the ensuing production considerations.

Table 8.4 Macrotrend Impacts, Supply Chain Implications, and Production Function Responses

Macrotrend-Based Impacts	Supply Chain Management Implications	Supply Chain Production Considerations
Customer preference variation: Customer demand worldwide will diversify and rediversify in short-term bursts, based on exposures to different consumption cultures, broader available offerings, human migration, and leveled ability to purchase.	Assortment divergence: Product bundles demanded will differ widely in similar or the same markets from period to period. Forecasting becomes difficult. The ability to divert finished inventory and produce new inventory quickly is highly valued.	Manufacturing will balance the ability to reconfigure with the assistance of contract manufacturers and the ability to control operations with internal capabilities. Logistics service providers will assume an increasing role in the value-added processing of goods as well as in their distribution.

Macrotrend-Based Impacts	Supply Chain Management Implications	Supply Chain Production Considerations
Customer expectations leveling: Customer expectations for delivering customization, build-to-order solutions, and quality will level out globally.	Quality management integration: Quality and service will become important and more difficult to assess. Quality management within supply chain processes will become a strategic differentiator.	The pursuit of a single-market standard for product quality will remain elusive. Customers in different regions with divergent values will possess differing expectations and measures of quality. Manufacturing must adapt to the preferences of distinct segments.
Demand/supply market diffusion: More demand centers will exist, both within nations and globally, each with greater heterogeneity of values and preferences within demand centers.	Network proliferation: Optimal networks are broadened in scope worldwide to include greater volumes and more products. More nodes and their support links are added, many via outsourcing.	Manufacturing capacity will become centralized, where possible, to serve high concentrations in large, developed markets and become decentralized in the form of smaller, leaner, more agile manufacturing facilities to accommodate growing pockets of demand. Contract manufacturers and logistics service providers expand their roles.
Viable market emergence: New demand centers will emerge in previously unserved locations, and these may be distant from current network nodes. Some lead times will be very long for significant time periods until networks catch up with demand.	Network extension: Optimal networks are lengthened worldwide to include previously ignored markets. More links and their support nodes are added, many via outsourcing.	Manufacturers will seek regionalization of manufacturing capacity where markets are growing in close proximity. In the absence of close proximity, the provision of "mini mills" and shared capacity will find application such that a foothold is established in promising markets. Contract manufacturers will specialize in emerging markets. Efficiency and the assortment of product offerings will increase with growing sales volumes.

Macrotrend-Based Impacts	Supply Chain Management Implications	Supply Chain Production Considerations
Product convolution: Products will be more complex to build and will contain a greater variety of materials. The quality of both materials and finished products will be harder to assess.	Strategic sourcing penetration: Supply bases will expand in scope and be more globalized. Supplier selection and scoring will require much standardization across geographies.	Manufacturers' desires to standardize for efficiencies will give way to customers' desire for tailored goods and services. Greater modularity will be built into products such that postponement strategies can adapt a common product platform into several variations.
Physical environment restrictions: Markets and governments will expect greater care in resource use, reductions in emissions/pollution/contamination, and responsibility for full life-cycle stewardship of products and services.	Sustainability reporting and visibility: Standard methods for measuring the environmental impacts of products and processes will define the viability of companies and the competitiveness of their products. Companies regarded as deficient in environmental and societal dimensions of performance will be marginalized.	Assume full responsibility for the environmental performance of products and the processes that generate them. Understand the processes performed by suppliers and customers in the end-to-end supply chain, as well as the end-of-life prospects for products, packaging, and associated services. There will be no shielding of these responsibilities or acceptance of excuses for not knowing how products reach the market, are used, and subsequently are disposed of or reused.

Depending on how a company regards the macrotrend forces described in Table 8.4, the future could be laden with fears and challenges or robust in opportunity. What becomes clear is that the role of production in the transformation will be central. The means by which goods and services achieve their function and form utility have been and will continue to be a focal point in supply chains for all companies. Not to be lost in the conversation is the fact that the transformation in production will affect manufacturers and nonmanufacturers alike. Upstream parties to manufacturers, like commodity suppliers (agricultural, mining, fishing), will face a whole new set of challenges when their customers (the manufacturers) impart new demands. Consider a food processor that seeks to sell its products in Europe, where consumers fear the use of genetically modified organisms (GMOs) in the foods they consume. Can the farmer verify that the seeds used to grow the grains contained no GMOs? Can the farmer produce evidence that the grains' integrity was maintained throughout the storage and distribution activities on the farm and beyond? Most farmers in the Americas today do not manage the genetic identity of grains independently or ensure that the handling and transportation of GMO and non-GMO grains are carried out in wholly separate supply chains. Similarly, vendors are not held fully accountable for the environmental and sustainability aspects of their materials and processes—yet. When sustainability reporting becomes mandated by governments and expected by consumers, manufacturers will require transparency in their vendors, and the definition of "quality" will expand to include these broader aspects.

Downstream of the conventional manufacturer, parties will expand their roles in the production process as well. Retailers that "own" the touch with the final consumer will continue to market private-label goods. But the more exciting developments will be found in other means of generating form utility as the roles of these downstream parties evolve. Logistics service providers have taken great strides in recent years to expand beyond storing and transporting goods. Large global providers like UPS, Exel/DHL, and Ryder, along with specialized providers like Kane Is Able and LeanCor, are gladly assuming the roles of final assemblers and packaging specialists. By performing postponed product customizations close to the customer market, these service providers can engender Leagile strategies to support the manufacturer's diverse market needs. In one interesting development, steamship line companies are developing a service provision that would allow light assembly and packaging to occur while goods are being transported over the long ocean routes. In this way, the three weeks of transit time, during which merchandise is sitting idle, awaiting delivery to the import port location, could be put to better use. As many experts point out, however, the long and sometimes uncertain transits do not aid in lean and agile response. As Lean gurus

Womack and Jones pointed out, "Lean thinkers don't like large, slow ships. They like small, fast trucks."[16]

Postponement and customization will proceed even further downstream in the supply chain, however. Retail locations also will increasingly be looked to as locations for postponement. Perhaps most exciting, though, is the prospect of consumers themselves performing postponement activities at home. In this way, brand marketers are de-industrializing product processing through at-home customization. Arguably, this personalizing of products was established by Apple with the applications (apps) that consumers can download to their iPhones and iPads. Apple provides the basic product platform, and the individual user customizes it at home to meet his or her unique needs. This may seem like a subtle shift in roles, but it marks a great departure in the conventional wisdom around value-added processing in the supply chain. Mass customization provides a limited assortment of product variety, and ultimate control over the product's form and function rests with the manufacturer. But consumers are exhibiting greater interest and even are demanding to take control. Consumers in emerging markets will be quick to embrace this notion and exert their own influence on the products they buy and adapt.

These developments lead to one conclusion: Creating form utility is no longer the sole domain of "manufacturers." Other supply chain members, including consumers, are creating form utility. To go further, informed and empowered consumers are seeking control over the form and functionality of the products they buy. Taken to an extreme, traditional manufacturers could be disintermediated, or bypassed, in favor of creating customized goods in the home. One small indication of this tendency might be found in the growing number of homebrewers, or people who craft their own beers and wines. The American Homebrewers Association boasts 30,000 members and claims that there are one million homebrewers in the United States. The trend could expand greatly with the advent of disruptive technologies, like 3-D printing. Such technologies could be

---

[16] As quoted in Kleiner, Art. (Summer 2005). "Leaning Toward Utopia." *strategy + business*.

game-changers—not only as they relate to the development of proto-types and engineering mock-ups for global corporations, but perhaps also as micro-assembly machines used in small shops and even homes in the future. This is among the many technology developments the world will watch closely in the next two decades as the evolution of humans and machines advances and the supply chains are called on to adjust to and accommodate the macrotrends.

9

Implications for Transportation/Logistics: Congestion and Infrastructure Decay

Stop, go. Stop, go. Stop, go.

Sound familiar? This is how many of us begin and end our workdays. Though traffic jams allow us to catch up on the latest news and sports scores while gaining "bumper sticker enlightenment," they aren't exactly the most enjoyable or productive part of the day. According to the 2011 Urban Mobility Report, produced by the Texas Transportation Institute (TTI) at Texas A&M University, the average annual rush-hour delay that commuters experienced in the United States was 34 hours, up from 14 in 1982. The TTI expects this average to rise another 3 hours by 2015 and 7 more by 2020. Washington, D.C. ranked as the worst commuter environment in the country, with delays that averaged 74 hours per year. In a not-too-distant second place, Los Angeles commuters endured 64 hours of lost time. Even smaller cities, like Columbus, Ohio, and Knoxville, Tennessee, see delays of 18 and 21 hours, respectively. The TTI estimates that annual congestion costs in the U.S. exceed a staggering $100 billion.

The U.S. is not alone when it comes to transportation congestion; this is a worldwide problem. Stuttgart, Germany, home to Porsche and some of the world's fastest production automobiles, sees its cars stuck in neutral much of the time, with drivers there wasting 56 hours per year in traffic. The toll is 54 hours in London, 65 in Brussels, and 70 in Paris. Asia, with its increasing appetite for automobiles, is catching the driving bug. Guangzhou, China, sees more than 200 new personal vehicle registrations every day. Delhi, India, is adding about 1,000 new vehicles per day! This dynamic addition of vehicles to a static infrastructure is compounding the ailments of the driving bug in cities around the world, resulting in overcrowding, delays, and frustration. In one particularly famous 2010 incident, traffic was so backed up in Beijing that it took *ten days* to clear it out. But these instances pale in comparison to the 165-mile backup in the world's most congested city, Sao Paulo, Brazil, in 2008. According to some estimates, congestion costs consume about 10% of Brazil's GDP per year. If you think these statistics are eye-popping, imagine what they will look like when the city adds millions of tourists and other visitors into the mix. That's exactly what will happen when Sao Paulo hosts the 2014 FIFA World Cup and the 2016 Summer Olympic Games.

Just as we waste time in traffic, so does freight. Congestion slows our goods' transit times in our supply chains. Slower and less reliable transit times force many companies to hold more inventory because so many delays make it hard to guarantee on-time delivery. A 2004 Federal Highway Administration study estimated that U.S. shipper inventory costs associated solely with congestion exceeded $7 billion. The problem is exacerbated on a global scale when you consider that congestion is found not only on the roadways, but also at our ports, canals, intermodal shipping yards, railroads, and even on airplane tarmacs and in the friendly skies. According to one estimate, a runway incursion happens every day somewhere in the world.[1]

The macrotrend of urbanization, described in Chapter 2, "Global Population Growth and Migration," will greatly exacerbate the congestion problem as more people and businesses cram into our largest cities. Freight too must make its way into these bustling urban areas to serve the growing populations. People's relocation patterns and the goods needed to serve these highly clustered populations are sure to be challenged, and certain key questions will emerge. Can we maintain or improve our quality of life under constrained mobility? Can we "build our way out" of the problem through enhanced infrastructure? Is society willing to make tough decisions about transportation access and funding? How might our own behaviors change to embrace bold new opportunities? How will our supply chains adapt to the worsening congestion problem? Chapter 8 explores these critical issues and how they will affect the way we manage tomorrow's supply chains.

---

[1] Allett, Tom. (2011). "Easing Congestion in Europe's Busy Skies." Airports International. www.airportsinternational.com/2011/11/easing-congestion-in-europes-busy-skies/.

Friction of Distance

Economic geographers often speak of a concept called the "friction of distance," a measure of how easy or difficult it is to cover a certain distance, as measured by time, money, and/or energy. Historically we have found that distance friction decreases over time thanks to the advent of things like wheels, roads, and propulsion technologies. This is seen in the evolution of transportation methods, such as going from horse-drawn carriages to steam engines to internal combustion engines. Reducing distance friction allowed people to live remotely from the workplace and hence gave birth to the suburb. Suburban living represents independence, a certain isolation that separates one's personal space from the world of work and big-city problems. U.S. suburbs experienced a boom following World War II, with cities throughout the country hosting abundant smaller cities on the outer fringe of the metropolitan area. The suburbs have come to represent the American Dream. This view of "ideal living" is gaining traction around the world as the burgeoning middle class in emerging nations seeks its own piece of the dream. Yet despite the advantages of this kind of living, congested roadways are putting the brakes on suburban sprawl, and many people are again seeking the conveniences and amenities of city living. According to 2010 U.S. Census data, urban populations grew by 12.1% since 2000.[2] In California, the country's most populous state, an astonishing 95% of people live in urban areas. In China, cities represent the exciting promise of prosperity for a youthful population looking for a life away from family farming in the rural regions. China now boasts more than 120 metropolitan statistical areas (MSAs) with populations exceeding 1 million inhabitants, compared to 51 such MSAs in the United States.

Distance friction is a significant factor in the World Bank's Logistics Performance Index (LPI), which rates nations' supply chain operations on their overall efficiency and ease of use. The United States, typically regarded as a worldwide trade and commerce focal

---

[2] Lambert, Lisa. (26 March 2012). "More Americans Move to Cities in Past Decade." Reuters. www.reuters.com/article/2012/03/26/usa-cities-population-idUSL2E8EQ5AJ20120326.

point, ranked number 9 in the 2012 LPI ratings.[3] Even though the United States' performance in customs and international shipments weighed it down in the rankings, its fourth-ranked infrastructure was regarded as one of its strengths. However, some would argue that the infrastructure's slipping capacity and performance are hobbling the economy—that distance friction is actually impairing the movement of people and goods across the country.

Table 9.1 describes the United States' transportation infrastructure as of 2012. The numbers are impressive: The U.S. has enough roads to circle the globe 157 times! With almost 20,000 airports, virtually every 25,000-person town enjoys relatively easy access to an airport. But the complete story on the state of the infrastructure invites a closer look. For instance, the rail network isn't quite what it used to be. In 1916, more than 254,000 miles of rails covered the nation and served as the most critical mode of transportation for intercity passengers and freight in the days before highways. Since then, rail coverage has declined steadily, and markedly so since 1980. In that year industry deregulation allowed carriers to more freely abandon unprofitable rail lines, leaving many shippers either captive to a single rail operator or unserved in rural areas. Despite its reduced coverage, rail still accounts for 35% of the freight ton-miles moved in the U.S. each year. This is slightly greater than trucking, even though trucks are involved in the transit of virtually all goods at some point during distribution. Motor transportation accounts for about 80% of all transportation revenues, which is why shippers consider it the most dominant method.

Given the burden placed on the United States' highways and roads, its declining health is of great concern. Despite the seemingly endless orange barrels marking construction along our streets, roadway systems are aging faster than they can be repaired. In one tragic 2007 incident, the main span of the I-35 Bridge in Minneapolis, Minnesota, collapsed and fell into the Mississippi River. Even though it had been declared "structurally deficient" in 2005, the bridge remained in operation, and it was not scheduled for replacement for another 15 years. Throughout the U.S., more than one in ten bridges receive the same "structurally deficient" rating as the I-35 Bridge.

---

[3] Singapore narrowly outperformed Hong Kong for the top ranking in 2012.

Another 13% are rated "functionally obsolete," meaning that they are too narrow, prone to flooding, or force drivers to slow down. That's

Table 9.1 U.S. Transportation Infrastructure Inventory

Mode	Inventory
Highway	Total miles: 4,059,330
	47,002 miles of interstate highway
	117,084 miles of other National Highway System roads
	3,895,244 miles of other roads
Air	Total airports: 19,802
	5,175 public airports
	14,353 private airports
	274 military airports
Rail	Total miles: 140,791
	95,700 miles operated by Class 1 (major) railroads
	12,000 miles operated by regional railroads
	32,456 miles operated by local freight railroads
	21,178 miles for passenger service (though only 3% of this network is dedicated to passengers)
Water	Navigable channels: 25,320 miles
	Commercial waterway facilities:
	647 Great Lakes miles (origin-destination miles)
	1,949 inland channel miles
	5,588 ocean channel miles
	238 lock chambers
Pipeline	Miles of oil pipeline: 176,271
	Miles of gas pipe:
	324,984 transmission miles
	1,220,999 distribution miles

Source: *The Pocket Guide to Transportation* (2012), Bureau of Transportation Statistics, U.S. Department of Transportation

nearly a quarter of the country's bridges that need almost immediate repair.

In a lesser-seen mode, the U.S. river network's aging lock-and-dam system has limited the growth of an otherwise environmentally friendly mode of transportation. Since a single river barge has the capacity equivalent of 15 railcars or 60 large trucks, we should start to take a more serious look at our rivers as a way to alleviate congestion. In addition to offering superior carrying capacity, traveling by river can be far more fuel-efficient than doing so by rail or truck. Barge transportation averages 514 ton-miles per gallon of fuel, compared to 202 for rail and 59 for truck. Engineers constructed the majority of the locks and dams along the main barge corridors of the Mississippi River and Ohio River some 80 years ago, effectively outlasting their intended 50-year useful life. Investments in industrial river navigation pale in comparison to the urgency with which potholes are viewed. To meet the needs of a river system in desperate need of repair, as of 2012 the U.S. Congress authorized $8 billion for projects that will rehabilitate the dilapidated waterway mechanisms, but it chose to fund them in a piecemeal fashion.

The "fix when fail" approach to maintaining the lock system is characteristic of the short-term horizon that pervades many transportation-related infrastructure policies. An infrastructure that fails to keep pace with the needs of commerce creates distance friction that impairs quality of life and impedes growth. This holds true for all economies, but according to the World Bank, it represents the biggest gap between the highest performers and everybody else on the Logistics Performance Index.

It would appear that the best solution is to embrace a long-term vision and invest in the infrastructure. However, many hurdles must be overcome before such progress is seen. In most settings, a country's infrastructure is both owned and maintained at federal, state/provincial, and local levels. Larger projects like those connecting major cities tend to be the federal government's responsibility. Unfortunately, political gridlock is rampant across many of the world's developed regions, including the United States, which prevents aggressive development of the infrastructure—especially during times of economic recession or flagging growth. Only in a national emergency or in the interests of national defense are large projects expediently addressed and subsequently funded. At the juncture of tenuous political circumstances and necessary infrastructure overhaul, a new solution must come forth.

Public-Private Partnerships and Other Solutions

One emerging trend offering promise is public-private partnerships (P3s), in which private-sector entities assume responsibility for maintaining—and, in some cases, building—transportation infrastructure. In return, they reserve the right to collect fees for their services. P3s have garnered significant interest because they afford the opportunity to improve infrastructure while bypassing political stalemates, generating revenues for the contracting government and private-sector operator. Partnership activities typically target toll roads, bridges, and tunnels but also include large-scale projects like outsourcing International Space Station supply missions ever since NASA halted its space shuttle program.

The United States employs P3s selectively, but China has relied on P3s to aggressively finance its extraordinary infrastructure development over the past two decades. China's blossoming transportation infrastructure projects, ranging from expressways to subways, numbers well into the hundreds. Similarly, neighboring Kazakhstan is looking to a P3 to improve the transit link between China and Europe by implementing the "New Silk Way." This promises to double freight flows by 2020 by providing a land route instead of a roundabout water route through the Suez Canal in northeastern Africa. One comparable United States P3 megaproject was the Trans-Texas Corridor. The proposed venture would develop roads, rails, and utilities that would crisscross the massive state. At the time, it was expected to take 50 years to complete and cost an estimated $184 billion. Although the plug was pulled on the overly ambitious project in 2011, these kinds of P3 initiatives will blaze the trail for future infrastructure upgrades.

Although P3s are gaining traction, critics condemn private operators for holding citizens captive to their profit motives. Others criticize governments for pinning high risks and minimal rewards on interested investors, thereby making P3s unattractive to savvy developers. Counterarguments suggest that the greatest benefit of P3s is that they aggregate the best minds—not just the government-appointed ones—when collecting proposals. These types of for-profit entity proposals flounder too often when only the government oversees them. For these reasons, P3s are viewed as a viable method for accelerating future transportation developments, despite the opposition to them.

Though P3s offer a significant infrastructure development alternative, the question remains as to how much new and rehabilitated infrastructure countries will require to keep pace with demand. Unfortunately, improving roadway capacity by 30% does not yield a 30% productivity enhancement. Such a relationship is perhaps best explained by the law of diminishing returns. This law embraces the idea that total output does not see as great a gain with only marginal improvements. Applying this idea to highway infrastructure, each successive lane added to the highway will be less productive than the lane added before it. One economic assessment suggests that every $1 invested in highway spending produced just $.08 in annual congestion cost savings![4] The precise number could be disputed, but nearly all experts' opinions suggest similar, disappointing levels of return.

What solutions remain if adding capacity is not the best answer? Many suggest that the most effective method to solve transportation congestion is found not in improving supply, but in tempering demand. Some of the world's major cities have found success in doing so by charging high tolls to enter the central business district during peak hours. Singapore pioneered the idea in 1975, with a handful of European cities (London, Milan, and Stockholm) following suit. New York City and the state of New York are among the most staunch advocates of congestion pricing in the United States. The state charges tolls amounting to $88 on freight traveling from Buffalo to New York City.[5] The strategy is based on a fundamental economic principle—asking users of a resource to compensate others for the incursion of negative social effects (namely, congestion and pollution). However, some criticize the practice for introducing inequities to those who can

[4] Shirley, Chad and Clifford Winston. (March 2004). "Firm inventory behavior and the returns from highway infrastructure investments," *Journal of Urban Economics*, Vol. 55, No. 2, 398-415.

[5] In May 2012, the New York State Thruway Authority sought to increase tolls by 45%, raising this figure from $88 to $127.

and cannot afford to pay such fees. Opponents disapprove of charging trucking companies high tolls when they already face narrow operating margins. Others argue that the practice is unfair to city retailers, where congestion restricts consumers' access.

Most of the evidence suggests, though, that this kind of congestion pricing is effective in reducing traffic while also reducing greenhouse gas emissions, energy consumption, and noise pollution. Among cities implementing such policies, reduction estimates range from 10% to 30%. This fact has generated considerable interest among many policymakers, but paying for something that has forever been free may prove unsavory to many.

Responding to Congestion, Distance Friction, and an Overwhelmed Infrastructure

To this point, our discussion has focused mostly on traffic congestion's macroeconomic causes and effects. This is because individual companies or managers can do little to reduce congestion on their own. Instead, it requires a collaborative supply chain effort, where decision makers rely on microeconomic variables that lead to product supply matching customer demand. Not surprisingly, achieving this basic equilibrium proves extremely challenging when our infrastructure is choked with traffic and other congestion-related issues. Holding large inventories is neither attractive nor feasible when space is at a premium in crowded, congested areas. Therefore, supply chain managers must devise creative solutions that allow them to meet customer needs without relying on fallback inventories. Large urban retailers are already implementing practices likely to become common in the future, such as making optimal use of overnight hours, when traffic is not at its peak, to receive shipments and replenish store shelves. This often means hiring a third shift dedicated to receiving merchandise. Incurring labor costs while the store is closed can be hard for a retailer to accept, yet it allows for greater reliability in receiving and more expeditious restocking.

To make use of off-peak hours, the customer relationship management (CRM) and supplier relationship management (SRM) processes must devise product-service agreements that reflect suppliers' and customers' requirements. These contracts need to consider the delivery costs during peak hours and provide guidelines as to who should bear the burden of applicable tolls and fees. In turn, order fulfillment would be affected, because companies would have to operate more on a "just-in-time" basis. Suppliers could replenish more numerous and smaller distribution points with greater frequency. Starbucks delivers this way every night to its hundreds of stores in U.S. urban areas.

Shared distribution models may also become more common, a process where competitors share transportation capacity. Defined as "horizontal collaborations," these arrangements are gaining traction among fast-moving goods companies in Europe. They are driven, in part, by the continent's relatively expensive energy costs. It depends on imported energy inputs more than any other developed region. If vendors are serving the same customers, couldn't we solve some congestion issues by filling half-empty trucks that permeate the industry, even if it means doubling up with competitors? Through close collaboration, companies could allow the freight to ride-share for the vendor's and retailer's mutual benefit. With shared transportation comes the prospect of shared storage. Though competitive advantage is lessened when companies share services, parity is preferable to being left out and facing the disadvantages presented by operating on your own.

Consolidating shipments might evoke a vision of using larger transportation vehicles to accommodate increased volume, but a more practical answer might be to increase delivery frequency with smaller vehicles. Lean logistics principles suggest that aggregating diverse assortments of small shipments frequently can result in better "in-stock" performance across a wide product portfolio *and* reduce logistics costs. Some savings can be found in lower inventory and warehousing costs, but more surprisingly, transportation costs can be reduced as well through these "milk run" deliveries. By virtue of achieving consolidated volumes, companies can improve how they use vehicles. With fewer half-empty trucks and less transshipment due to misallocated inventory, transportation costs would not increase with higher frequency. It is even possible that shippers might actually lose their infatuation with using 53-foot trailers in the United States should they be banned in the city. The city would become the domain of small (20-foot) "pup" trailers or, better yet, straight trucks and vans.

One area where heavy vehicles will gain traction is in truck-rail-truck intermodal transportation. Intermodal transportation could help lighten congestion by taking trucks off the road. Using inter-modal modes for moves of 750 miles or more is giving way to shorter moves, such as 500 miles, as the following events occur:

- Trucks and drivers become harder to find
- Trucking companies develop aggressive intermodal strategies
- Intermodal service improves thanks to investments made by rail carriers
- Investments in transloading facilities improve how quickly trucks transition to railroads and back to the roads again

RoadRailer technology is an ongoing experiment offering faster transloading. If you have ever seen a train consisting of what looks like conventional road vans rolling down the railways, you have seen Road-Railer in action. RoadRailer allows modified van trailers to hook up to rail bogey carriages without the aid of the lifts and cranes required of conventional trailer on flatcar (TOFC, or "piggyback") intermodal transportation. Trains of RoadRailer vans can more quickly assemble and disassemble than TOFC trains that rely on lift equipment. Though this experiment has existed in several forms for more than 50 years and its use was discontinued in the United Kingdom, Australia, and New Zealand for various reasons, it remains alive in the United States. This is particularly true with the support of the railroads in the eastern U.S., where congestion is greatest.

Beyond RoadRailer, there are also opportunities for railroads to deliver goods into cities. Rail has become the preferred mode for coal shipments from rural points to the electricity generation plants near the cities, and for shipments of grains (again, in rural areas) to food processors near cities. The question is whether rail might regain favor as a delivery mechanism into the core of cities, where it has established rail links in place. These links, which date back to the formation of the cities, will prove invaluable as corridors for heavy freight and commuter passenger service. They might also carry twilight freight and replenish the cities overnight. Companies like BNSF are already taking the initiative to mix commuter rail lines with freight lines along one of their most important freight routes into and out of Chicago.[6] Someday soon we may see roads used specifically to transport goods in places where railroads do not exist.

Overseas shipments, meanwhile, continue to be hampered with extensive congestion at port locations. Despite significant investments in port facilities, like those on the U.S. eastern seaboard, Sao Joao da Barra, Brazil, and India, shipping is plagued by slow and variable transits over the deep blue seas as well as delays at export and import locations. As indicated in Chapter 8, "Implications for Production: Disrupted Process Flows," it is difficult—if not impossible—to be lean and agile when crossing oceans to bridge supply and demand. Some companies are electing to produce in the markets in which they sell those goods in spite of higher labor costs as a way to avoid the long and variable transits altogether. In a fascinating development, athletic footwear manufacturer Nike designed a running shoe that requires very little stitching and labor to produce. The upper of the Flyknit Racer is made from a single piece of durable woven fabric to provide a sock-like fit with 35 fewer pieces than a conventional running shoe. This reduction in the number of materials reduces waste, but also the complexity and labor associated with assembly, essentially negating the labor cost differential between high- and low-cost countries.[7] Until 3-D printing gets perfected, locating innovative production methods closer to consumption points might represent the next best way to reduce the stresses and costs associated with transporting goods over long distances and dealing with the congestion found on the roadways and water that separate disparate locations.

The future is laden with these challenges, each presenting an opportunity for advantage for the business that can navigate more effectively and expediently. Transportation will be instrumental in addressing the macrotrends. Table 9.2 illustrates several congestion-related impacts, supply chain implications, and considerations for transportation and logistics.

---

[6] Robl, Ernest. (25 April 2008). "Mixed-use rail." *Mass Transit*.

[7] Townsend, Matt. (15 March 2012). "Is Nike's Flyknit the Swoosh of the Future?" Businessweek.com. www.businessweek.com/articles/2012-03-15/is-nikes-flyknit-the-swoosh-of-the-future.

Table 9.2 Macrotrend Impacts, Supply Chain Implications, and Transportation/Logistics Responses

Macrotrend-Based Impacts	Supply Chain Management Implications	Supply Chain Transportation/Logistics Considerations
Congestion worsens: More cities will be affected by congestion as urbanization increases and municipalities find themselves unable to keep up with the growing demand.	Growing transportation delays: Congestion is adding time and uncertainty to service performance and increasing costs to supply chain operations. The operational processes of manufacturing flow management and order fulfillment are particularly susceptible to delays.	Network analyses will determine ways to serve customers without requiring trucks to enter cities. Shippers will seek to provide deliveries during off-peak hours. Consolidate shipments, explore alternative modes, and leverage intermodal transportation.
Congestion pricing: Cities will leverage tolls on passenger vehicles as well as trucks entering central business districts. Tolls will be charged on more intercity routes. Limits will be placed on deliveries in overnight hours under noise ordinances.	Smarter delivery schedules: Roadway tolls will challenge conventional methods shipping and delivery, especially in metropolitan areas with greatest congestion problems. Order fulfillment and delivery must adjust to accommodate pressures.	Build congestion and toll rates into pricing models. Develop strategies with shippers and carriers to consolidate loads within and across companies. Use quieter hybrid and electric vehicles to deliver in the cities during the overnight hours.
Failing infrastructure: Investments in infrastructure rehabilitation fail to keep up with the rates of use and deterioration.	Unexpected hazards and delays: An aging transportation infrastructure will increasingly fail and disrupt normal operations.	Integrate transportation-related disruption into risk modeling. Develop alternatives in modes, routes, and carriers. Support consortia and public-private partnerships (P3s) that can develop or enhance critical infrastructure for your business.

Macrotrend-Based Impacts	Supply Chain Management Implications	Supply Chain Transportation/Logistics Considerations
Energy and carbon reduction: Transportation remains the most energy-intensive and carbon-generating economic activity.	Spurred to act: Economics and customer concerns will spur motivations to reduce energy usage and carbon emissions on inbound and outbound transportation.	Look for ways to reduce energy usage and carbon emissions. Assume hedge positions on energy inflation. Explore alternative energy sources. Do not hold onto technology that is in decline.
Labor shortages: Turnover among long-haul truck drivers exceeds 100% for many carriers. Recruiting, hiring, and training costs will continue to rise as carriers seek qualified drivers with high safety ratings.	Drivers as a strategic resource: Carrier capacity is constrained and service is impacted when qualified drivers are in short supply. Those carriers and private fleet operators that maintain a loyal driver pool will have a distinct advantage.	Better utilize drivers' time. Develop discipline in shipping and receiving schedules to reduce driver frustration and fatigue. Charge and collect for detention of drivers and equipment beyond agreed time allotments. Reduce turnover among the best drivers.
Capacity shortages: Transportation capacity across the modes tends to lag the market—with undercapacity in times of surge and overcapacity in slow periods.	Finding balance: Customers will have little tolerance for suppliers that fail to ensure their capacity needs. Many companies will consider investing in private fleet operations or devising dedicated contract carriage to ensure capacity.	Employ hedge strategies and forward contracts to deal with surges in volumes. Become the "customer of choice" to the best carriers to ensure availability when capacity gets tight.
Natural disasters: Natural disasters and weather-related events imperil transportation operations with greater frequency and severity.	No tolerance for excuses: Customers will demonstrate less understanding for suppliers that fail as a result of natural disasters. Resilient supply chains will demonstrate that disruption due to natural disasters can be minimized.	Incorporate disaster planning into network design and risk management analyses. Devise alternatives in the event of losing nodes and links in the supply chain configuration. Reduce dependence on single sources and locations.

Diffusing Congestion with Advanced Technologies

Thanks to advances in information and communication technology, we are changing our work patterns and our household purchasing and consumption. These changes could affect the matter of congestion in some interesting ways. The Internet is one technology that continues to escalate and evolve. Though home grocery delivery has a checkered past in the United States, Internet retailers that sell books, electronics, fashion apparel, and so on suggest that the model *can* work if properly executed. Online business-to-consumer sales represented almost 8% of all 2010 U.S. retail sales, with a 14.8% average annual growth rate.[8] Increasingly, confidence is growing such that many consumers in developed markets no longer think of starting their shopping process in conventional bricks-and-mortar stores. Most never venture there for the purchase, either. Is it possible that we might see consolidated deliveries to the household? Imagine individual households hiring third-party logistics providers (3PLs) for all their errands, shopping, and delivery needs. Webvan is regarded by some as the biggest flop of the dot-com boom of the early 2000s. But Peapod, another online grocery delivery service operated by Royal Ahold, has outlasted its competitors and is soon expected to turn a profit in major U.S. cities.

How might the economics change, though, when a more diverse array of household items is introduced with bundled delivery? If this sounds familiar, the trajectory of Amazon might come to mind. What started out as an online purveyor of books and music has expanded to apparel, food, jewelry, and much more. The company is quickly adding distribution centers to its network to provide same-day delivery in several major metro areas of the United States. Further, Amazon has established self-service pickup stations at 7-Eleven stores and other neighborhood locations in select cities to add a new element of security and convenience for its customers.[9] Take the concept of home delivery to another level, however. Consider the prospect of entire

---

[8] Internet Retailer Top 500 Guide, 2011.

[9] Bensinger, Greg. (7 August 2012). "Amazon's New Secret Weapon: Delivery Lockers." *The Wall Street Journal*.

housing communities and neighborhoods contracting with 3PLs to provide service to the many households that compose them. Waste collection is handled on this basis. Might the forward deployment of inventory go this way, too? Might the likes of UPS, FedEx, DHL, or Amazon seek to be the delivery agent for your community?

If we are willing to hand over our household shopping and errands to third parties, what other activities might we be willing to liberate? Suppose we let computers drive our cars for us. That's the premise of intelligent vehicle highway system (IVHS) technology, which claims that doing so would be both safer and more efficient than relying on our imperfect judgment and driving skills. Many of us already put ourselves at the mercy of GPS systems to navigate for us, but are we willing to take the next step and let the computer actually *drive* us down the road? Studies indicate that, yes, many people are willing to do so. They also imply that we might be safer and reduce infrastructure congestion if intelligent vehicles make decisions instead of humans.[10]

Recall this chapter's opening paragraphs, detailing the monotony of the daily commute. Consider what happens when a driver taps his brakes. The car behind him slows down at least as much, which leads the driver two cars back to slow down even further, until traffic reaches a point where everyone must stop—all because the first driver tapped his brakes! Intelligent, self-driving vehicles would not tap the brakes in the first place thanks to advanced risk calculation and collision avoidance detectors. They also would better calculate speed changes for all following vehicles. In essence, cars could become personal transit pods programmed to take us to our destinations without causing congestion backups. Autopiloted vehicles would then group to form train-like bands, removing the imperfect whims of driver inconsistency from the routine. Cars would enjoy racecar-like drafting techniques, which is far more energy-efficient than traveling at varied speeds.

These IVHS technologies allow us to better utilize our existing roadways by all but eliminating the empty spaces, thereby fully

---

[10] "Self Driving Cars will take over by 2040," Forbes.com. Retrieved September 20, 2012.

utilizing capacity without moving at a snail's pace. Imagine texting to your heart's content while rolling down the road! Or if texting isn't your forte, you could also read, write, talk, or conduct a meeting on the go. What will it take to make such a vision reality? At a minimum, more R&D to perfect the technology and devise a supporting infrastructure, drivers willing to give up control, and automakers willing to embrace it. Such automation might then transfer to commercial trucking, bringing even greater benefits to trucking operations that struggle to achieve efficient movement.

Congestion is a pressing problem facing our businesses and personal lives today. It has such a great effect on us that sometimes it even determines how we plan and spend our days. Distance friction is increasing, reversing a decades-long trend, making it more difficult to close the gaps in time and space. Moving forward, we need to take steps to lessen its impact. This issue surrounds our supply chains. Inability or unwillingness to act at both macro and micro levels is sure to invite the return of incidents like Carmageddon, described in Chapter 1, "Supply Chain Management in the 21st Century."

Part III
Macrotrend Risk-Mitigation Strategies

10 —————————————————————

Mitigating Supply-Driven Imbalance

Gold.

Just the sound of the word is enough to captivate us with grandiose fantasies of power and wealth. Gold's rare and unique properties have made it one of mankind's most desired treasures throughout our history. People have hoarded it, traded it, killed for it—and some scientists even found an efficient way to capture more of it. In late 1890s Colorado Springs, a fledgling city nestled in the western Rocky Mountains near the Cripple Creek gold fields, a shrewd businessman named Spencer Penrose formed a partnership with an innovative metallurgist named Charles M. MacNeill. The problem faced by these partners was how to extract a higher percentage of gold from the very hard Cripple Creek ore. Bankrolled by Penrose, MacNeill pioneered new milling methods to extract gold and copper from low-grade ores and, in so doing, paved a path to greater personal wealth and riches. Together with their partner, Charles L. Tutt Sr., they became three of Colorado's leading industrialists (and among its first millionaires), eventually forming the Utah Copper Company. This company later became Kennecott Utah Copper LLC, one of the 20th century's largest mining companies, which is now a part of Rio Tinto.[1] Besides fame and fortune, why should this type of partnership, and subsequent innovation, pique our interest? If you listen carefully, you will find that Penrose, MacNeill, and Tutt tell the story of how natural resource scarcity can be triumphantly mitigated with the right kind of innovative thinking.[2]

---

[1] Rio Tinto, "Our History," 2012. www.kennecott.com/our-history.

[2] Sprague, Marshall. (1953). *Money Mountain: The Story of Cripple Creek Gold.* Lincoln, Nebraska: University of Nebraska Press.

Business history books are full of stories like this, and they often contain similar instances of science and technology put to perfect use in the right business environment, thereby creating a dominant competitive advantage. Today, businesses are confronting similar metal scarcity challenges yet leveraging innovation in addressing them such that competitive advantage is gained. Honda Motors recently announced that it would partner with Japanese Metals & Chemicals, a firm that developed an improved metal extraction method. Doing so will help Honda recycle and reuse rare-earth metals in its automobile battery supply chain.[3] Such a process is dramatically different from the one-way production course Honda followed before. Much like the Penrose, MacNeill, and Tutt example, this story illustrates another successful combination of essential business leadership and scientific innovation.

To understand Honda's motivation and what it means for the automobile industry, we need to look at how rare-earth metals are used in hybrid automobiles. Experts estimate that by 2008 over 2 million nickel-metal hydride batteries were operating in these vehicles. The total worldwide sales of hybrid vehicles for fiscal 2010 were estimated at just over 900,000, of which 154,000 vehicles were from Honda's leading models.[4] As of 2012, Honda had sold over 800,000 hybrids alone; the Fit Hybrid, Freed Hybrid, and Insight Exclusive among them. These cars' nickel-metal hydride batteries use an alloy of the rare-earth metals lanthanum, cerium, neodymium, and praseodymium. These metals have also been used for many years in certain kinds of lighting and flint igniters. Together they bring unique physical traits to a battery's design, such as maintaining magnetism at high temperature, but unfortunately they are not very easy to extract from the Earth's geological deposits. Some geologists admit that rare-earth metals are not actually as "rare" as their name suggests, because they are found in many common ore deposits around the world. However, of those deposits, rare-earth metals are seldom found in ore concentrations higher than 2% to 3%, and they are not always in mineable

---

[3] "Honda to reuse rare earth metals contained in used parts," Honda News Releases. 17 April, 2012.

[4] Schreffler, Roger. (2011). "Hybrid, EV Sales Lag Forecasts, But Plenty More Models on Way." http://wardsauto.com/ar/hybrid_ev_lag_111129.

form. According to a 2010 Reuters article that details the process that a rare-earth metal undergoes from its reserve to its final product (in this case, wind turbines), it can take anywhere from 6 to 86 tons of ore to extract 1 ton of rare-earth metal.[5]

Because of the toll taken on their host minerals' geological deposits, these battery metals are prime recycling candidates. During the early hybrid production phases, the technology needed to implement a mass recycling effort had not been available. However, in April 2012, Honda announced that its partner had successfully come up with a way to extract the metals from returned batteries. The process extracts up to 80% of them, all the while keeping them as pure as their newly mined and refined counterparts. Honda has seen so much early success with the extraction process that it has decided to capitalize on the breakthrough. It will extend the process to other parts that flow through its returns supply chain to recover additional rare-earth metals.

In many ways, the 17 rare-earth metals are today's gold and silver comparable to their focus in Colorado and the western United States over a hundred years ago. Many of the 21st century's most technologically advanced products require some quantity of these increasingly scarce metals. Selecting an approach to mitigate such scarcity and create opportunities for competitive advantage is the focus of the remainder of this chapter. Honda capitalized on a strategic partnership yielding innovation to successfully "recover" a scarce material. But recovery isn't the only option. We also will look at other firm-level employment and conservation approaches and the need to combine them into strategies that allay the supply-driven imbalances described in Chapter 7, "Implications for Sourcing/Procurement: Natural Resource Scarcity." In doing so, we will look for ways to both identify and take advantage of the dynamic changes in the status of macro-level natural resource scarcity. The goal is to prepare your firm by suggesting timely strategies that, if implemented now, will put your firm in a much better position to succeed in the future.

---

[5] Gordon, Julie. (14 November 2010). "From Mine to Wind Turbine: The Rare Earth Cycle." Reuters. http://in.reuters.com/article/2010/11/14/idINIndia-52767220101114.

Employment Approaches

A firm can choose different "employment" approaches for how it manages the occurrence of scarce resources in its products. Doing so successfully helps mitigate the impact of scarcity levels on operations by balancing a resource's supply and demand. Academics classify some common employment approaches as avoidance, logistics, allocation, or sustainment.[6] Let's take a look at each approach by breaking down when and how a firm might use it when faced with resource scarcity.

Avoidance techniques describe the strategic decision to prevent engineers from using a scarce natural resource when designing products, services, or processes. This is especially critical for globally scarce materials as they become more difficult to secure and then utilize in production and manufacturing operations. As scarce supplies' availability shrinks and costs increase, the firm will realize that the advantages of using a particular raw material have vanished. The materials' quality, quantity, and cost variability have increased the uncertainty in a firm's operations, making it difficult to derive value and thereby provide valuable outputs for customers. Therefore, to eliminate excessive cost and variability, forward-thinking companies must attempt to reduce the number of these resources they use in their operations, or even remove the resource from a product's design. Often the ability to avoid using a scarce material depends on how quickly new technologies develop that can produce identical product functionality with less resource consumption, or how feasible it is to substitute a more common, or less expensive, raw material for the resource.

A recent avoidance approach is illustrated in 3M Corporation's strategic decision to avoid using oil-based materials in many of its products. According to its 2011 sustainability report, 3M is removing petroleum-based films and fibers from its materials to counter

---

[6] Bell, J.E., C.W. Autry, D.A. Mollenkopf, and L.M. Thornton. "A Natural Resource Scarcity Typology: Theoretical Foundations and Strategic Implications for Supply Chain Management," *Journal of Business Logistics*, Vol. 33, No. 2, 158-166.

unstable petroleum supply.[7] In 2012, General Motors and Toyota made a similar decision to avoid using rare-earth-based magnets in many of their automobile battery designs. Instead, they chose to use a specific type of induction motor that does not incorporate rare-earth metals into its design. General Electric is taking similar avoidance approaches with its wind turbines and generators by redesigning them to avoid the use of scarce resources.[8]

Though these decisions seem like the most obvious response to scarcity circumstances, they are not always easy to pull off, and they do have their limitations (for now). According to a 2010 study conducted by Dutch industrial design engineers, the engineering field lacks the necessary scarcity information to make proper design choices.[9] Design engineers do not always know an intended-for-use material's current scarcity status. Nor are they always informed of how selecting a particular resource will impact supply chain functions, especially with items that will be produced for many years to come. This study goes on to state that we need to improve our engineering information databases and educate our industrial design engineers so that they can do a better job of employing avoidance and substitution approaches specifically intended to counter resource scarcity. Proactive firms with proper information systems and engineers skilled enough to know how to use them will create a significant competitive advantage as they implement innovative avoidance approaches into their supply chains.

A *logistics* approach to resource scarcity describes purchasing, storing, and transporting resources to a location where they are locally scarce. Chapter 7 mentioned the logistics approach of moving fresh salmon from distant Alaskan supply sources to markets around the world, or of purchasing diamonds from places in Africa and then

---

[7] "2011 Sustainability Report." 3M Corporation. St Paul, MN, 25 June 2011.

[8] Elmquist, Sonja. (28 September 2011). "Rare earths fall as Toyota develops alternatives: Commodities." *Bloomberg.* www.bloomberg.com/news/2011-09-28/rare-earths-fall-as-toyota-develops-alternatives-commodities.html.

[9] Kohler, A.R., C. Bakker, and D. Peck. (2010). "Materials Scarcity: A New Agenda For Industrial Engineering." *Knowledge.* Collaboration & Learning for Sustainable Innovation ERSCP-EMSU Conference, Delft, The Netherlands, October 25-29, 2010.

transporting them to industrial centers in Europe, Asia, and the United States. Logistics approaches to countering scarcity depend on available and economically viable transportation systems.

An example of transportation capability dependence can be seen in the fresh tuna market, where some of the fish is sold to sushi restaurants in Japan. Tuna companies struggled to supply the market in the years prior to 1972 because they lacked the ability to quickly and efficiently transport fresh tuna to the Japanese markets. Their hopes were renewed in that year, when Pan Am airliners brought Tokyo the first Atlantic tuna by air. The supply for Atlantic tuna exploded as Atlantic suppliers rushed to feed the "sushi economy."[10] Today, nitrogen freezing and frozen-container ships have greatly increased the tuna quantities and have improved the transportation costs involved with shipping to Japanese sushi markets. Worldwide sushi demand has also exploded; it has actually been correlated with an emerging new economy. As countries like Brazil, China, and India have strengthened their respective economies and achieved higher levels of discretionary income, their demand for fatty foods, sushi included, has also risen. Not only does this drive up global demand for a precious supply of tuna, but it also places a bigger burden on firms and global transportation systems to implement logistics approaches that will help transport the tuna to places where it is locally scarce.

We must always keep in mind that logistics approaches depend on the most efficient and cost-effective energy sources. Today, approximately 96% of the U.S. transportation sector uses some form of fossil fuel for energy.[11] As pointed out in Chapters 8 and 9, world populations are demanding more and more of these nonrenewable, organic natural resources, each of which is subject to its own volatility levels in scarcity and pricing. This means that logistics approaches in the future may be limited. Therefore, managers must consider how much of an energy source they need to move available resources from one location to another.

---

[10] Isenberg, Sasha. (2007). *The Sushi Economy: Globalization and the Making of a Modern Delicacy*. New York: Gotham.

[11] The Institute for Energy Research. (2010). www.instituteforenergyresearch.org/wp-content/uploads/2008/05/fossil-transportation-sector.jpg.

A third resource employment approach managers can take is *allocation*. When a firm realizes that it possesses locally abundant resources that may not necessarily be globally available, it must consider how to use its valuable heterogeneous resources to maximum advantage. Firms can do this by determining how, and when, to ration their available quantities and thereby maximize their long-term profits and competitive advantage. For many decades, economists such as Hotelling[12] have found that the prices and usage rates of today's finite resources depend on marginal opportunity costs of not having the resource quantities available in the future. It may be unwise for a firm to use up all its scarce resources without considering what those resources will be worth in the future.

Commodity and futures markets hedging strategies can lead a firm to obtain this kind of competitive supply advantage. Southwest Airlines has done this for many years by purchasing future fuel and oil quantities at a lower cost in advance of rising oil prices. Starting in 1999, analysts at Southwest have locked in as much as 70% to 80% of their fuel costs each year using a hedging strategy.[13] In doing so, the airline earned huge profits throughout the last decade when other airlines suffered from volatile oil markets. This strategy gave Southwest an advantage as it was able to properly ration its low-cost fuel resources, stabilize operational costs, and keep tickets prices down. In doing so, Southwest created value for its customers and paved the way for profits that its competitors simply could not match.

Firms often use an allocation approach by speculating which resources will become scarce in the future and "buying up" those resources in anticipation of future demand. Chapter 7 gave examples of waste management and coking coal companies to illustrate resource stockpiling. Toyota provides a more recent example: The Japanese automaker is trying to secure a solid supply of lithium to meet projected future demand. Toyota is one of several companies that use lithium in their hybrid car batteries. Toyota believes this approach represents a more palatable alternative in comparison to the expensive

---

[12] Krautkraemer, Jeffery A. (1998). "Non-Renewable Resource Scarcity," *Journal of Economic Literature*, Vol. 36, 2065–2107.

[13] Pae, Peter. (30 May 2008). "Hedge on Fuel Prices Pays Off." *Los Angeles Times*.

rare-earth metals currently used in many batteries. However, lithium is also a relatively scarce metal and is not readily available in all locations around the world. Since South America has the majority of the world's lithium reserves, the company has partnered with international exploration companies to secure some of the lithium reserves there. Toyota also has made significant investments in developing Argentinean lithium deposits and hopes that these investments will secure its future needs. Lithium prices have tripled over the past ten years, and the lithium demand percentage from auto manufacturing has risen from 25% to 40% or more.[14] Therefore, by virtue of such allocation strategies, Toyota (like Southwest) could soon find itself in a significantly better financial position than its competitors.

Sustainment is the fourth and final employment approach for scarce natural resources. Sustainment recognizes that firms should practice sustainability even if their resources are not yet scarce. Using this kind of wise stewardship is a good way of recognizing the dynamic nature of a resource's status. As European colonists settled North America in the 15th to 19th centuries, the passenger pigeon was one of the healthiest and most widely populated bird species on the continent. It was an abundant food source for pioneers and explorers conquering the new world. In fact, ecologists believe the passenger pigeon was once one of the most populous bird species on the *planet*. Historical accounts describe how flocks in Ontario and Michigan were actually measured by the number of miles they stretched across the sky!

Unfortunately, settlers needed food, and passenger pigeons were an easy source. Hunters overharvested the birds, and with commercial exploitation of passenger pigeon meat in the 1800s, the once-abundant natural resource was exhausted without regard for the consequences. With no plan to sustain the species' existence, the passenger pigeon was decimated by the 1890s and officially declared extinct in 1914, when the last captive bird died in the Cincinnati Zoo.[15]

---

[14] Kumar, Aswin. (2011). "The Lithium Battery Recycling Challenge." *Waste Management World*. www.waste-management-world.com.

[15] "The Passenger Pigeon." (2012). *Smithsonian*. www.si.edu/encyclopedia_Si/nmnh/passpig.htm.

Passenger pigeons show us that just because a resource is currently available does not mean it will exist forever, especially if the resource is excluded from firms' sustainable planning actions. Firms such as International Paper are taking sustainable approaches by replanting more trees each year than they harvest. Metals and mining companies like Alcoa are trying to balance extraction with new discovery methods and more efficient extraction technologies to ensure that the resources they have available today are not gone tomorrow. With responsible sustainment approaches, companies can ensure current access to critical resources without putting future supply in peril.

Conservation Approaches

Aside from the employment approaches described above, a firm also can use conservation approaches to help mitigate the impacts of resource scarcity on its operations. These approaches include resource base protection initiatives, or those aimed at securing and improving renewable resources, and resource recovery initiatives, such as recycling and closed-loop supply chain management for non-renewable resources. Let's examine each approach and identify what kinds of situations call for their respective use.

First, a *protection* approach is used when we want to conserve environmental amenities that support resource renewability. Companies have a long-term incentive to ensure that they protect air, water, and ground resource bases to guarantee that they are available for future supply chain uses. As mentioned in Chapter 7, brewing and bottling companies like MillerCoors, Coca-Cola, and Pepsico have partnered with firms around the world to track water availability in their supply chains. Additionally, food growers like ConAgra Foods and timber/paper companies like Georgia Pacific—are companies that derive value from the land—and have boundless incentives to keep erosion, global warming, and ground pollution from undermining the ability to regrow grain and timber.

Some leading companies have even gone so far as to take a "zero waste" approach to ensure that ground and soil renewability is not threatened. Burt's Bees implemented such a policy by sending absolutely no waste to its landfills at all of its operating locations. The company has goals to, by 2020, drastically reduce how much electricity it uses, eliminate all shrink-wrap packaging from its products, and implement waste-to-energy initiatives. Its parent enterprise, the Clorox Company, has adopted similar goals to achieve zero-waste status for some of its major manufacturing facilities.[16] In California, global mining company Rio Tinto PLC rehabilitated its boron mining sites. There it has renewed over 50 mining acres each year, reduced fuel and hazardous-materials usage, and reintroduced native plant species it may have disrupted.[17]

In an effort to ensure continuous access to high-quality water sources, 3M worked during 2001 to 2010 to massively reduce how much water it uses in operations. The company also has started water reduction programs in geographic areas classified as "water-stressed" to make more water available for crops, forests, and fisheries. A company already mentioned for its tree-planting program, International Paper, also has set up aggressive goals to protect air quality. In 2011, the EPA awarded International Paper for reducing greenhouse gas emissions by 40%. But IP has even greater goals: By 2020, the company wants to reduce its emissions by another 20% and shrink its pollutants by 10%.[18]

Though IP makes it look easy, protecting a resource base as precious as the air we breathe has been difficult for some companies. In 2010, Exxon Mobil actually saw a 3% emissions increase despite spending over $400 million that year on emissions-reducing technologies.[19] Exxon's efforts to invest in better technology are steps in the right direction, but they may not be enough to overcome the environmentally damaging impacts of the company's supply chain operations. For firms that depend on renewable resources, transitioning to

[16] "The Clorox Company." (2012). www.thecloroxcompany.com/corporate-responsibility/planet/our-progress/operations/solid-waste/.

[17] "Mining reclamation success." Mineral Information Institute. http://www.mii.org/Rec/RioTinto/RioTBorax.html.

[18] "What Matters Most: 2011 Sustainability Report." International Paper (2012). www.internationalpaper.com/documents/EN/Sustainability/IP_Sustainability_Re.pdf.

[19] "Mitigating greenhouse gas emissions in our operations." (2012). ExxonMobil. www.exxonmobil.com/Corporate/safety_climate_action.aspx.

protection approaches is a logical decision and may result in a more immediate return on investment, because their bottom lines rely on the environment. Other companies in the nonrenewable sectors may find it more difficult to produce a direct and immediate return from a protection approach.

The second conservation approach is *recovering* resources from products at the end of their life cycle or from the waste streams where they have accumulated. Many firms recycle packaging and other raw materials to improve efficiency and reduce short-term costs by avoiding the use of new materials. However, there is also a longer-term operational incentive for companies to recover, recycle, and reuse products and resources—especially nonrenewable ones—since global scarcity of some important materials appears to be growing. The Earth has a limited quantity of metals such as iridium, palladium, and indium. As we deplete the most accessible geologic deposits, these materials' primary sources may soon transition from mining to the returns-management portion of the supply chain. Other minerals, such as gallium (used in solar cells, diodes, and window coatings), are "hitchhiker" or "companion" metals obtained only as by-products when zinc or aluminum is extracted from the parent ore. This means that no commercial mining activity primarily obtains hitchhiker metals. Because mining for the primary metals may not produce enough supply to meet the growing demand for hitchhiker metals like gallium, recovery and recycling may be the only way to balance supply with growing demand.

Governments around the world are beginning to recognize the need to improve and increase recovery efforts. In 2009, the Japanese government published its "Strategy for Ensuring Stable Supplies of Rare Metals." This plan asked companies to recycle scarce metals from their supply chains' scrap and called for an improved national recycling system. This was followed by $1.2 billion of research and development funding for firms to develop new recycling technologies that mitigate scarcity. The United States and European Union have created similar rare-earth metals strategies. In 2011, the U.S Congress asked the Department of Defense to identify and implement solutions to improve rare-earth metal availability. In April 2012, the United Kingdom issued a "Resource Security Action Plan" to directly confront the rising threat of resource scarcity. According to the plan's survey, over 80% of UK manufacturing firms' chief executives believed resource scarcity would impact their 2012 operations. To counter the threat, the government challenged firms to improve product designs and optimize recycling practices. The UK report also lauded the GE approach for assessing scarcity risks and impacts (described at the end of Chapter 7). Finally, the report stated that the government planned to offer greater incentives for companies to extract and recycle more scarce resources.

In addition to the Honda example, other companies, like Hitachi, Ltd., have started using recovery approaches in their supply chains. Hitachi has invested Japanese government funds toward developing a process to recycle rare-earth metals from discarded computer hard drives, an effort termed "urban mining." Hitachi separates rare-earth magnets from obsolete hard drives using an automated shaking process and then uses a dry heating process to separate metals, such as neodymium, from the magnets. Hitachi plans to implement this recycling capability in 2013.[20]

However, recapturing and recycling precious, nonrenewable metals from products at the end of their lives is not always easy. One problem is that many of the metals are widely dispersed in small quantities, making it difficult to build mass production recycling processes. Experts estimate that hundreds of millions of obsolete cell phones that exist in the returns supply chain could be recycled. But each cell phone contains only minute quantities of the metals (a phone typically has .034 grams of gold).[21] Although this might not amount to much in one phone, when 250 million obsolete cell phones contain a total of 9.37 tons of gold worth over $531 million (based on September 2012 prices), the incentive to recycle builds quickly. The problem arises of how to build a logistics recovery approach that can physically extract small quantities and combine them into economically valuable lots.

[20] Messenger, Ben. (2011). "Recycling: Rarely so critical." *Waste Management World.* PennWell Corporation.

[21] Bishop, C.A. (2009). "Dwindling Resources, a Molehill Out of a Mountain." *Vacuum Technology & Coating,* Vol. 10, No. 12, 49–52.

Technological difficulties also complicate recovery efforts. For example, future battery and energy storage capabilities for hybrid cars and wind turbines will depend on lithium supply. However, technologies to recycle lithium are still in their infancy, and prices for recycled lithium still greatly exceed the price of newly mined quantities. Producers expect the demand for lithium to increase greatly by 2015 and beyond, and so will the need to recycle this metal, because its reserves will not last forever (as discussed in the earlier Toyota example).[22]

Another complication arises with recycling rare-earth metals: They exist in products as alloys or as ingredients of other metals. For example, magnets may consist of one-third rare earth and two-thirds iron. In this type of mixture, the rare-earth metal neodymium gives the magnet stronger magnetic forces, and the metal dysprosium helps make it heat-resistant. But when the magnet becomes useless, separating and then recovering these two metals is hazardous and inefficient. The current process uses chemicals and boiling acids and takes far too much time, resulting in safety concerns, environmental hazards, and increased costs.

Recovery is an important approach for mitigating the scarcity of nonrenewable metals. It may be our only option when new metal deposits are exhausted, or when energy and pollution costs are too high to extract virgin materials. This presents a bevy of opportunities for companies to get ahead of their competitors, like Honda and Hitachi did, by developing processes and technologies that will recover scarce resources in their closed-loop supply chains. Proactively designing a supply chain that leverages scarce-resource recovery will make firms more competitive in comparison to slower-moving competitors as scarcity levels grow and competition for raw materials increases. Though developing recycling technologies still has risks, the rewards of doing so are great. Proactively building both recovery and protection approaches will help position a company for success in the coming decades.

[22] Kumar, Aswin. (2011).

Resource Scarcity Mitigation Strategies for the Supply Chain

The best way to use these differing resource mitigation approaches is to combine them into a strategy that best fits a firm's resources. As pointed out in Chapter 7, resource statuses differ because of demand and supply imbalances. Because the Demand-Supply Integration model has two components, resource mitigation solutions can act on either side. Firms need to work with their supply chain partners to integrate scarce resource supply with the market demand for the products containing those resources. Figure 10.1 overlays what we believe are the best approaches for mitigating a heterogeneous resource's current and declining resource availability conditions. Avoidance approaches are appropriate for global scarcity's highest levels, logistics approaches for securing a locally scarce resource, allocation approaches for rationing locally available resources, and sustainment approaches for maintaining global availability. The most effective approaches to managing a resource's scarcity status will also depend on the renewability of a resource. In Figure 10.1, resource base protection approaches are used for renewable resources and recovery approaches for nonrenewable ones. This is not to say that recovery and recycling should not be used for a renewable resource. In fact, some companies, like Georgia Pacific, are leaders in recycling wood fibers. However, approaches that sustain timber-growing resource bases are considered to be more important to long-term scarcity mitigation.

	Renewability	
	[Conservation Approach]	
Scarcity [Employment Approach]	**Renewable** [Resource Base Protection Approach]	**Non-Renewable** [Resource Recovery Approach]
Globally Scarce [Avoidance Approach]	Global Degeneration Mitigation Strategy: Fortification	Global Depletion Mitigation Strategy: Discretion
Locally Scarce [Logistics Approach]	Local Degeneration Mitigation Strategy: Mobilization	Local Depletion Mitigation Strategy: Compilation
Locally Available [Allocation Approach]	Local Munificence Mitigation Strategy: Cultivation	Local Abundance Mitigation Strategy: Utilization
Globally Available [Sustainment Approach]	Global Munificence Mitigation Strategy: Perpetuation	Global Abundance Mitigation Strategy: Preservation

Figure 10.1 Resource scarcity mitigation approaches[23]

Combining different approaches for a resource's scarcity and renewability attributes implies that different mitigation strategies are available to a firm, depending on the resource's current and future availability. For example, when a resource is locally scarce but still renewable, a firm should concentrate on a *mobilization* strategy, which uses logistics and conservation actions. Firms using this approach should transport quantities of the renewable resource from locations where it is available to those where it is scarce. All the while, they should actively conserve the air, water, and soil quality needed to maintain the resource's renewability.

One example of this type of strategy is in the U.S. fruit-growing industry. Local producers work hard to maintain their orchards'

---

[23] Bell, J.E., C.W. Autry, D.A. Mollenkopf, and L.M. Thornton. (2012). "A Natural Resource Scarcity Typology: Theoretical Foundations and Strategic Implications for Supply Chain Management," *Journal of Business Logistics*, Vol. 33, No. 2, 158–166.

growth and renewability but are forced to import fruit supplies from other locations when their crop output decreases. It is not surprising to find South Carolinian or even Chilean peaches on Georgia growers' fruit stands after all of their own crops have been harvested and sold.

In contrast, for nonrenewable resources that are locally available, firms should concentrate more on a *utilization* strategy, where they wisely allocate local supply for future use and implement recovery actions to recycle as much local supply as possible. An example of this type of strategy comes from Japanese firms that use rare-earth metals. Since 90% of the global rare-earth metal supply originates in China, firms in Japan must wisely ration and allocate how they use their locally available supply sources. These companies simultaneously concentrate on recovery and recycling strategies since many of their locally available resources exist in the product returns supply chain.

Perpetuation strategies for globally abundant renewable resources advise firms that grow crops to simultaneously protect their resource bases with a sustainment approach to manage their supply. For example, International Paper might try to avoid using chemicals that could damage the land, water, and air it needs to grow future timber crops while also replanting trees and training workers how not to damage saplings.

Figure 10.1 shows similar combinations of mitigation approaches. Although this figure provides the best way to combine two approaches for different resource statuses, this does not mean that a strategy cannot include three or more approaches aimed at mitigating scarcity. A firm suffering from global depletion may allocate scarce resource quantities by transporting them to locations where they are needed while also concentrating on its primary avoidance and recovery approaches.

As resource statuses fluctuate, we need to recognize that our current strategies regarding them may have to change as well. For instance, if a firm is using a *cultivation* strategy for a locally renewable resource, but macro-level forces make the resource nonrenewable and, in turn, locally scarce, this strategy may have to change to *compilation*. As shown in Figure 10.2, consumption over the next several decades may increase a resource's global demand while depleting its supply. Additionally, pollution and environmental damage can create resource degradation that has the potential to destroy renewability.

Such an occurrence is a perfect storm for creating an imbalance among the seven forces described in Chapter 7 and could put a firm's resources in a state of local depletion. If that happens, a firm that recognizes the change early and adopts a *compilation* strategy before its competitors do will have a couple of distinct advantages.

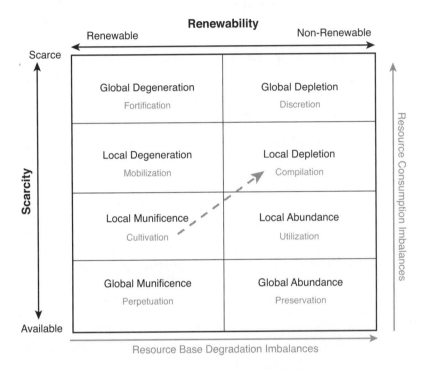

Figure 10.2 Resource degradation and consumption imbalances

First, *compilation* strategies will allow the firm to secure top-of-the-line transportation agreements that give it the best way to get resources to where they are not locally available (logistics). It will also give the firm the distinct advantage of being the first to develop improved recycling capabilities (recovery approach). Building intangible supply chain capabilities that are difficult to replicate will help put a firm in the best position to succeed, relative to its competitors, in terms of how it secures and uses scarce tangible resources.[24]

---

[24] Bell, J.E., D.A. Mollenkopf, and H.J. Stolze. (2013). "Natural Resource Scarcity and the Closed-Loop Supply Chain." *International Journal of Physical Distribution & Logistics Management.* Forthcoming.

Mitigating Supply-Driven Imbalances

This chapter has covered approaches for mitigating future supply-driven imbalances. It also has discussed how to combine these approaches into strategies applicable in dynamic environments. Finally, it has provided examples of how a handful of innovative companies have applied such strategies to their operations. Taking all of this into account, we have three overarching recommendations for companies that want to take steps toward mitigating future resource scarcity in their supply chains:

- Build appropriate mitigation approaches that match your supply chain's important natural resources' scarcity and renewability levels. Identifying risk is only the first step toward managing it. To be truly successful, companies need to collaborate with their supply chain partners to implement the best approaches to managing resource scarcity levels. This gives the firm the opportunity to build internal business policies that control how, and when, to use scarce resources.

- Combine employment and conservation approaches into multi-faceted strategies that effectively mitigate a particular resource's growing scarcity. Firms should consider building closed-loop supply chain capabilities that recover scarce resources and protect renewable resource bases. They should combine conservation approaches with well-designed avoidance, logistics, allocation, and sustainment methods to balance scarce resource demand and supply.

- Implement forward-thinking strategies by anticipating growing scarcity levels to build capabilities and secure advantageous positions. Firms should understand that the world is transforming and that future resource scarcity challenges are transforming with it. As population growth, urbanization, global connectivity, economic leveling, and geopolitical conflict change how we meet demand, the resulting consumption levels and resource degradation can only become more pronounced. Designing supply chain networks and products around these anticipated challenges will best position a company for sustained future success.

These are not revolutionary concepts for the companies described in this chapter. They have already taken action to manage resource scarcity in their supply chains. They are striving to meet their governments' challenges by developing metal recovery technologies and securing long-term access to future important supplies of global resources. They have even started to build multifaceted strategies to augment their efforts. They understand what's coming, and they're doing something about it.

As this chapter comes to a close, we would like to take a look at one more critical example of a company that has devoted time, energy, and capital to its scarcity mitigation efforts. General Electric uses a *discretion* strategy for rhenium, a metal used in its aircraft engines.

Rhenium is used in steel to maintain its hardness under higher pressures and temperatures, such as those seen in aircraft engine designs at GE. Rhenium is the by-product of molybdenum, which itself is a by-product of copper production. Because rhenium is a hitchhiker of another hitchhiker metal, there are not primary mining operations for the extraction of rhenium around the world. This makes the supply of rhenium very inelastic in response to changes in demand (supply scarcity and short-term prices rise in response to increasing demand levels).

In the past, GE might not have seen how much rhenium, or the lack of it, would adversely affect its operations. However, in 2006, increased global demand sent rhenium prices shooting up tenfold (a single pound cost over \$6,000).[25] This gave GE a major incentive to figure out ways to cut back rhenium use in its aircraft manufacturing operations.

When GE woke up and started its risk identification method, it targeted rhenium as a high-impact scarcity risk and set out to build a strategy that allowed it to adjust to inflated prices and resource scarcity. First, from 2006 to 2011, GE scientists and engineers were able to avoid using two-thirds of the amount of rhenium they had used previously through design and process changes. But avoiding using rhenium did not completely solve GE's problem, so it had to come up with another method to create a multi-approach strategy. Thus,

[25] Shumsky, T. (12 September 2011). "Testing their metals." *The Wall Street Journal*.

GE helped start a worldwide aircraft-manufacturing group that urged member companies to do a better job of recycling this scarce metal. Thanks to GE's efforts, parts containing rhenium are now removed from steel scrap piles, and the recycling partners recapture the metal in a closed-loop system that returns the metal to partner organizations. In doing so, the rhenium supply for GE has stabilized, driving down its demand for newly mined resources.

GE has learned from its success with rhenium and now actively looks for ways to recycle, reduce, and substitute many of the other critical metals it uses in its product designs. This includes developing nanotechnologies to reduce neodymium use in wind turbine magnet manufacturing. Such a proactive style has led GE to adopt multi-approach strategies to manage scarcity in its current products. These technologies and strategies will help the company be successful well into the future and also will prepare it to operate its supply chain in a transforming world.

GE and the Colorado gold tycoons from our opening example should make us ask the following: "When resource scarcity strikes us in the future, whenever that may be, will we be ready?" By taking to heart the strategies presented in this chapter, your company should be able to answer that question with a resounding and assured "yes."

11

Mitigating Demand-Driven Imbalance

Today's great achievements do not guarantee tomorrow's successes. Similarly, a business built strictly to address our current realities may be poorly prepared for the challenges presented by our transforming world years down the road. Perhaps the greatest challenge for future supply chain managers, which we have saved for our final discussion, will be to build the flexible and adaptable supply chains that companies can use to detect, combat, and even manipulate demand-driven imbalances. Failure to aggressively manage demand spikes or change directions can lead to future companies' demise, especially in light of the uncertainties brought about by the world macrotrends. You only need to consider the failure of former consumer electronics giant Circuit City to see how the inability to proactively recognize and manage customer demand problems can wipe out a major player.

About a decade ago, Circuit City was the second-largest consumer electronics retailer in the U.S., with over 700 retail outlets. But it filed for bankruptcy on November 10, 2008. The question is, why? According to *Time* magazine's Anita Hamilton, the primary reason Circuit City perished was "good old-fashioned bad management." Unlike rival firm Best Buy, Hamilton suggests, Circuit City did not make the necessary moves to understand and react to dynamic demand patterns in the volatile and highly competitive consumer electronics market.[1] According to the *Time* story, Circuit City's first blunder was failing to secure prime real estate for its stores, which were often located in out-of-the-way spots that inconvenienced ever-hurried retail customers. Rival Walmart, on the other hand, is regarded as a

---

[1] Hamilton, Anita. (11 November 2008). "Why Circuit City Busted, While Best Buy Boomed." *Time* magazine online.

maven of real estate wheeling and dealing, acquiring properties and devising developments that draw other businesses and consumers, alike. Circuit City also made some serious blunders related to consumer trends in the retail electronics market. For instance, it stopped selling kitchen appliances during the late 1990s, just as one of the largest housing booms in U.S. history took flight. This resulted in a drop in revenue of almost 14% where much was available to be gained.[2] The company neglected to establish a serious Internet presence, instead attempting to use the Web merely to drive sales for its brick-and-mortar locations. Customers knew these stores were staffed by aggressive salespeople that online shoppers could avoid. During its death spiral, Circuit City's customer service standards virtually fell apart. Although the company strategy was to compete as a specialized or differentiated provider, it fired over 3,400 of its most experienced service representatives and replaced them with lower-wage workers. Ironically, this 2007 cost-saving move essentially ensured the retailer's demise.[3]

What went so very wrong? Overall, Circuit City became complacent and failed to evolve when consumer preferences underwent wholesale change.[4] But how does a company that once ranked #160 on the Forbes 500 end up in liquidation only two years after having sold over $10 billion worth of consumer electronics? During its postmortem, *Forbes* authors Benton et al. outlined five demand-side lessons that can be learned from Circuit City's path to destruction:

- **Recognize your consumer base.** Circuit City failed to overhaul its selling methods. It was slow to move into the Internet retail space, never fully leveraged the power of electronic retailing, and kept its pushy salespeople. Customers became savvy, relied on online product reviews, and avoided salespeople by buying online.

---

[2] Benton, Dan, Dave Davidson, Kyle Larsen, Dan Oliver, and Long Chul Park. (18 January 2011). "When Innovation Disappears: Five Lessons from Circuit City." *Forbes India*.

[3] Spolsky, Joel. (1 May 2009). "Why Circuit City Failed, and Why B&H Thrives." *Inc.*

[4] Benton, Dan et al. (2011).

- **Appreciate the competition.** Walmart and Target moved into the retail-electronics market and stole business from Circuit City. They used their existing supply chains, locations, and websites to capture market share, and Circuit City did little to respond.

- **Maintain strategy implementation consistency.** Circuit City claimed to have a differentiation and specialty strategy, but actually it implemented cost efficiency practices. It also suffered from a poor cash-to-cash cycle and too much inventory. In the end, it couldn't compete with Walmart and Amazon on cost efficiency, and it lagged behind Best Buy's differentiation and innovation approaches.

- **Pay attention to demand trends, and forecast accurately.** Circuit City not only quit selling appliances during the U.S. housing boom, but it also spun off CarMax, which went on to be a huge success. The retailer also built a large number of stores right before the 2008 financial crisis hit.

- **Don't apply a bandage to a gaping wound.** The company's response to its demand and supply problems was too little and too late. Circuit City was overconfident in a model that no longer matched demand trends, and it made operational changes only to copy BestBuy. Major strategic changes were needed for its supply chain to succeed.

Because it failed to recognize and address these problems, Circuit City closed its doors and liquidated its inventory in 2009, just as its competitor CompUSA had done two years before. Today, experts wonder if the days of the giant electronics retailer are completely over, noting that BestBuy (which posted a $1.7 billion loss in the fourth quarter of 2011) might be the next to collapse.[5] As of this writing, BestBuy is trying to carve out its space with wily competitors Walmart and Amazon skillfully encroaching. Regardless, the above noted companies failed (or are struggling) because they were unable to adjust to changing demand, did not fully understand the implications of future trends, and were left in the dust by a market that rapidly was redefined by new paradigms.

---

[5] Crothers, Brooke. (29 March 2011). "Is Best Buy following CompUSA, Circuit City to certain doom?" CNET News.

The lesson to be taken from the Circuit City story within the specialty retail electronics market is that business in the changing world will require demand-focused and demand-shaping supply chain strategies that influence and redirect demand to match supportable supply levels. Chapter 10, "Mitigating Supply-Driven Imbalance," focused on potential disruptions and mitigation strategies for moving upstream or supply-side activities into alignment with known demand. This chapter looks at strategies that move demand into alignment with the firm's known supply functions. These activities are designed to preempt or mitigate problems created by an imbalance between demand and supply by moving the company's demand levers. Our focus is primarily on micro-level or firm-based strategies to integrate supply and demand via demand-side balancing. Nevertheless, it is important to also recognize that the macro-level environment in which firms operate is also changing based on both social and geopolitical forces that attempt to "shape" demand. In the transforming world, we expect forces at the micro and macro levels to exert pressure on the future demand for products and services, and thereby on companies' supply chains as a whole.

Demand Shaping in the Transforming World: Macro and Micro Issues

This book's primary contribution to knowledge has been integrating macro-level forces that will impact the world greatly in the future with leading-edge supply chain thought from the present. Moving forward, the demand implications of these forces will have great bearing on how end users consume products, and therefore how supply chains must be designed to satisfy their increasingly differentiated and potentially chaotic demand. We see the macrotrends as impacting future consumer demand patterns in a number of ways. First, societies might want to consciously curb demand of some products in recognition of the planet's limited supply and capacity of natural resources. For example, "green" and "sustainability" initiatives are often aimed at protecting the planet and its resource base, including activities such as shifting demand to environmentally friendly products and packaging. Additionally, initiatives designed to reclaim land

and grow crops closer to consumption locales are aimed at reducing transportation distances and expenses. In one recent essay, three preeminent marketing academics call for the "mindful consumption" of goods and resources in the future to keep from overwhelming the supply and to allow for the building of a more sustainable demand stream in the future.[6] However, while such ideas may be feasible in developed nations and regions, on a global level such societal initiatives often fall short of limiting demand to match current levels of supply due to more pressing consumer needs. In some cases, political and governmental activity may determine the rules under which supply chains of the future operate. For instance, although several European countries have mandated recycling of certain packaging wastes, it seems unlikely that similar laws will take hold in less-developed nations. There the costs of collecting and processing recyclables could be viewed as impractical and infeasible.

Governments also sometimes create regulations and policies to change the playing field under which businesses and society operate. China's well-known initiative to limit family sizes is aimed at controlling population growth and, therefore, the resulting consumption levels of its citizenry. In fact, some economists believe that controlling population growth and accelerating wider demographic transition to lower fertility levels will be the primary method of achieving sustainable economic growth in the future.[7] Regardless of whether governments initiate further radical changes to limit populations, the trend toward increased geopolitical activity is increasing, as described in Chapter 5, "Geopolitical and Social Systems Disruptions." Governments have instituted and will continue to devise laws and policies that limit demand for sensitive renewable resources. These include limits on timber cutting, fishing regulations, and export quotas that limit the amount of demand that can be filled for key strategic materials such as rare-earth metals. Future lack of resources, combined with backlash against regulatory activities, may create increased conflict

---

[6] Sheth, J.N., N.K. Sethia, and S. Srinivas. (2011). "Mindful Consumption: A Customer-Centric Approach to Sustainability," *Journal of the Academy of Marketing Science*, Vol. 39, 21–39.

[7] Brander, J.A. (2007). "Viewpoint: Sustainability: Malthus Revisited?" *Canadian Journal of Economics*, Vol. 40, No. 1, 1–38.

among sovereign nations, regional trade groups, and international organizations such as the World Trade Organization (WTO). These conflicts, if not managed proactively, can lead to war when societies with unfulfilled demands employ more drastic means to find a suitable resource supply. Within the macro-level limits placed by government and society, firms themselves will need to actively manage the demand side of their supply chain.

However, at the micro/organizational level, the problems are more situation-specific and pronounced. From a practical standpoint, these macro-level issues mean that, fundamentally, firms will more frequently find themselves unable to match demand with current supply levels. Thus, they will seek economic solutions to more closely shape (i.e., "right-size") demand. The idea of right-sizing demand seems anathema in capitalistic societies, where generating infinitely more revenues is often viewed as the path to success. But in fact, we consider these sorts of imbalances just as damaging as rote supply shortages. To see why, it is first important to understand that the business activities of individual firms can influence the size and direction of demand in the marketplace. For example, market leaders and other innovative niche firms often seek to revolutionize the marketplace by looking for new ways to provide utility to customers. When such innovations succeed, they effectively destroy the demand for older products. Taken to the extreme, they can create entirely new industries and market segments that allow the most innovative firms to realize a sustainable (or at least semipermanent) competitive advantage. These types of transformations have been dubbed "creative destruction." Examples include the rise and success of e-commerce and the subsequent birth of Information Age firms such as Apple, Dell, Amazon, and Google.[8] Though such transformations typically add great value to customers' lives, they also play havoc with the systems designed to provide supply and can generate suboptimal profits even while increasing revenues dramatically. Barnes & Noble's Nook e-reader is a prime example. As of July 2012, the Nook occupied a solid position in the growing product segment with a 27% share, second only to

---

[8] Hart, S.L. and M.B. Milstein. (1999). "Global Sustainability and the Creative Destruction of Industries," *Sloan Management Review*, Vol. 41, No. 1, 23–33.

Amazon's Kindle.[9] Expert and consumer reviews were quite positive, yet the Nook division reported a $286 million loss in 2012, following a $230 million loss the previous year. On the heels of this news, the company announced a 10% price cut to remain competitive in the increasingly crowded marketplace. Clearly, the supply chain must innovate and adapt to sustain this sort of business strategy in hopes of achieving any margins under such competitive pressures.

We strongly suggest revisiting (and, if necessary, revising) company strategies such that both demand and supply are key considerations when pursuing customers. This is based on the idea that shortages of supply and surpluses of demand are equally suboptimal situations. Though many companies have traditionally been concerned with the former, with the latter regarded as a "pleasant problem" that the supply chain operations will just have to figure out how to handle. We argue that the right-sizing of demand is a key consideration for companies of the future, because the pursuit of extraneous demand in the face of limited supply inevitably creates inefficiencies. These inefficiencies will actually reduce overall enterprise profitability as orders and revenues grow past a critical point. In effect, we are describing the notion of *demand shaping*: the migration of demand to customers who are the most profitable to serve, and for the products that are most appropriate and available for serving them. Theoretically speaking, demand is often reshaped by the substitution of products/goods/services that deliver similar but distinct bundles of consumer utility. Chapters 7 and 10 briefly discussed the use of *supply substitution*—using a different raw material to make the same finished good. But the opposite strategy can also be effective when conscientiously devised and employed. Finding alterative end products that provide the same utility can afford the same benefits by shaping demand to match limited available supply sources. This competency will become even more important in the business environment of the future. Furthermore, short of substitution, there are also other intermediate ways to influence and shape demand to more closely match available supply. Chapter 1 described this demand-shaping strategy as Demand-Supply Integration (DSI). We explore this critical concept further.

---

[9] Gottfried, M. (14 August 2012). "B&N's Nook Getting Pushed into a Corner." *Wall Street Journal*, C8.

The Case for Demand/Supply Integration

As a business approach, DSI provides a theoretical but practical means of supporting organizational strategy with structure. DSI also integrates the voice of the customer with the constraints placed on supply chain operations within the organization. Overall, DSI includes the coordination of processes that reflect the firm's customer focus with the operational supply-side activities that make demand fulfillment attainable. By employing DSI as an operational philosophy, firms can maximize relevant revenue streams from "customers of choice"—customer segments whose value best aligns with the actual organizational capabilities that will generate the most profit for them.[10] For example, consider Dell Computer. Dell has initiated rules within its customer service management process to redirect customers to products that are in stock rather than taking an order for a product that is not in stock and that will result in an immediate lost sale or stockout. The rules are predetermined. Dell's call center staff is empowered, when necessary, to offer-higher quality products that are currently in stock as substitutions for those that are in short supply or stocked out. Demand-shaping activities such as these are also prevalent in companies such as Lowe's, which works with key suppliers such as Whirlpool to reshape demand. Lowe's and Whirlpool use face-to-face meetings to stimulate demand for products the supply chain can more readily fulfill. They also promote products that are in greater supply in the short run and adjust the pipeline of supply and transportation for fast-moving products in nearly real-time reaction to changes in demand.[11]

Recent research on DSI[12] illustrates how companies pursuing cost leadership strategies tend to focus on operational efficiency but

[10]   Esper, T.L., A.E. Ellinger, T.P. Stank, D.J. Flint, and M. Moon. (2010). "Demand and Supply Integration: A Conceptual Framework of Value Creation Through Knowledge Management," *Journal of the Academy of Marketing Science*, Vol. 38, No. 1, 5–18.

[11]   Stank, Theodore P. and John T. Mentzer. (17 December 2007). "Demand and Supply Integration: A key to improved firm performance." *IndustryWeek*.

[12]   Stank, Theodore P., Terry L. Esper, T. Russell Crook, and Chad W. Autry. (2012). "Creating Relevant Value Through Demand and Supply Integration," *Journal of Business Logistics*, Vol. 33, No. 2, 167–172.

sometimes fail to hear the "voice of the customer." Alternatively, firms pursuing differentiation strategies tend to focus on the customer, but sometimes to the detriment of supply chain operational excellence. In other words, they fail to hear the "voice of the business." DSI addresses these imbalances by uniting and integrating demand-side and supply-side functions within the firm. They align the missions of product development, sales, marketing, and demand planning with procurement, logistics, production, and supply chain planning. This alignment allows companies to achieve higher levels of both efficiency and customer service.

As shown in Figure 11.1, only by using a DSI strategy can firms avoid being "stuck in the middle"[13] by balancing both sets of interests to maximize profits. Via the adoption of a DSI philosophy, companies can become more flexible and adaptive and thereby achieve high levels of customer service *and* high levels of operational efficiency. Toyota achieved such a milestone when it introduced a radically redesigned version of its popular Siena minivan in 2004. The new model was larger and more fuel-efficient and offered performance features and quality attributes that would set the standard for the minivan market. Although the conventional wisdom for such product launches is to release the new and improved item at a premium price point, Toyota offered the revamped vehicle at price that was 6% *below* the old model.[14] Such a feat could be attained only by achieving innovations in the supply chain that permitted healthy margins at such competitive prices. The company would later raise prices on the Sienna and other vehicles as a sort of "mercy" provision. In fiscal year 2004 the company racked up a record profit of $11 billion. Rival General Motors, on the other hand, would incur roughly this same sum in losses in 2005 despite generating record sales volume. GM's record losses on record sales were "achieved" with deep price discounting

---

[13] Porter, M. (1985). *Competitive Strategy*. New York: Free Press.

[14] Ulrich, Lawrence. (1 June 2003). "Outside the box bigger, faster, better: A new wave of minivans arrives to challenge SUVs." CNN Money.

in a desperate ploy to maintain market share.[15] Unfortunately, GM's supply chain was unable to operate on comparably discounted costs.

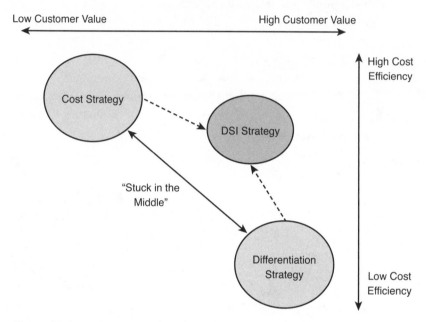

Figure 11.1 Using Demand-Supply Integration for strategic advantage

We believe that DSI will be especially important in a world defined by transportation congestion, geopolitical activity, environmental damage, and growing/migrating consumption. Firms will have to take a hard look at exactly what demand they are most capable of fulfilling and will have to make hard choices about where and in what capacity they try to please a limited set of "customers of choice." In the end, companies that employ a DSI approach will co-create value with supply chain partners through both goods and service capabilities. Sometimes this means sacrificing effectiveness for efficiency, and other times it means sacrificing efficiency for effectiveness. The choice depends on the demand articulated by customers

---

[15] General Motors offered deep discounts on automobiles throughout much of 2004 and 2005, even offering employee rebates to all U.S. buyers in an effort to clear out inventories in late 2005. www.msnbc.msn.com/id/10075026/#. UCsWKKOHFBk.

and the costs and assets required to deliver on those needs.[16] Thus, DSI strategies will be critical in a transforming world where adaptation and flexibility will be the key to survival. Such approaches may not be as cost-efficient in the short term as a rigid "lean" system, or as accommodating in customer service as an agile system. However, they will achieve levels of flexibility needed to mitigate the risks of an increasingly uncertain world and will ensure the long-term survival and sustainability of future firms.

As an aside, we should mention that in many industries, businesses have begun to look at supply chain strategy a little too ubiquitously. The "Go Lean" mantra has converted many—perhaps too many—businesses to a strategy that worships cost efficiency and implements mass customization of products across global markets. We caution that such a strategy assumes unlimited supplies, no-fault transportation, and relatively stable demand variation. It is important to remember that lean systems[17] were originally built for repetitive automotive manufacturing by Toyota and later were adapted to numerous other supply chain contexts. Although they have achieved monumental success within many settings, such strategies are not well suited to all future realities. We believe in the lean model when deployed in the right scenarios and suggest that its uses are many. But we also warn that it will be challenged by supply disruptions in future decades and will strain to meet high levels of consumption and respond to higher levels of variation in demand. Agile strategies that give up some cost efficiency to obtain high levels of customer service may better aid in demand shaping and fulfillment, but at the expense of higher transportation and fulfillment costs.

Let's return to the case of Circuit City. The company set out to be a specialty store with unique talents and a differentiation strategy. But in the end, it could not compete on differentiation with Best Buy. It also failed to beat the cost efficiency of Walmart, Target, and the other

---

[16] Stank, Theodore P. et al. (2012).

[17] Here, "lean systems" refers to those of the Lean-Push variety described in Chapter 8, "Implications for Production: Disrupted Process Flows." They employ the make-to-stock manufacturing strategy to replenish forecast-based supermarket supplies. This is the "Lean" philosophy that is practiced by Toyota in North America and employed by many companies seeking to implement Lean in different industries.

mass retail outlets that moved into the consumer electronics space.[18] Instead, Circuit City found itself stuck in the middle, between supply and demand-side focuses—a doomed situation that management guru Michael Porter famously points out will result in fewer customers and poor performance.[19]

Implementing DSI to Mitigate Demand-Side Imbalances

To deploy DSI for the purposes of eliminating demand-side imbalances, first you must distinguish between two seemingly similar—but behaviorally distinct—types of demand that occur in the supply chain. *Independent demand* comes directly from end-user preferences. It is traditionally concerned with the volumes and assortments of consumer products that are desired. As we have shown, this will vary more widely and frequently in the coming years. For example, the number of bicycles sold annually at a bike shop represents independent demand and can be readily forecasted using past data adjusted for future trends expectations. But the extent of those future changes will certainly factor in as costly error. Alternatively, *dependent demand* stems from independent demand by way of *supporting* end-user preferences. Traditionally, dependent demand reflects needs for parts, accessories, or components of finished goods whose independent demand levels have been determined. For example, only a subset of children buying a bicycle will purchase a helmet, and some helmet buyers will not purchase a bicycle. In this way, dependent demand is correlated with independent demand, but not perfectly. Typically, dependent demand is less flexible in how it is filled by a components supplier and is more variable or "lumpy" in nature.[20]

---

[18] Benton, Dan et al. (2011).

[19] Porter, M. (1985).

[20] Ballou, Ronald H. (2005). *Business Logistics/Supply Chain Management: Planning, Organizing and Controlling the Supply Chain*. New Jersey: Pearson Prentice Hall, 288.

However, independent demand generally is less variable than dependent demand, and there is more flexibility in how a company serves this demand.

These types of demand must be addressed very differently by organizations that want to engage a DSI philosophy across four different demand attributes that are susceptible to the macrotrends. As shown in Figure 11.2, both independent and dependent demand imbalances stem from, and are affected by, demand volume, demand variety, channel/location, and product form/functionality. Each of these factors is expected to be difficult to predict because of population, economic, environmental, and geopolitical effects. When considered together, the demand attributes and types converge to form eight unique demand imbalance statuses that will increasingly challenge companies as the macroenvironment continues to evolve.

Demand Type

Demand Attribute	Dependent	Independent
Volume	Component Imbalance	Finished Good Imbalance
Variety	Parts Line Imbalance	Product Line Imbalance
Location	Supply Chain Imbalance	Channel Imbalance
Form	Fit Imbalance	Utility Imbalance

Figure 11.2 Demand imbalance statuses

The eight scenarios call for unique approaches to DSI and will require different managerial resources and capabilities. We define the eight demand imbalance statuses as follows:

- **Finished-goods imbalances** reflect a situation in which the amount of finished-goods inventories available is either insufficient or extraneous when compared with actual demand. These imbalances reflect typical stockout or overage situations and generally can be predicted within a reasonable margin of error.

- **Component imbalances** are misalignments in which a dependent demand volume is available, but actual demand is unpredictable because the demand itself is derived at least somewhat from the sale of other products. As a result, this type of demand falls within a partially predictable range yet it is susceptible to more extreme deviations within that range. As an added complication, the demanded components often are laden with high variable costs. Consider, for example, computer chip makers, which must provide component supplies in anticipation of computer sales. If an ample supply of chips is not available, the shortage can substantially delay delivery of the computers. The advanced supply of chips, then, serves as an insurance policy against stockouts. Yet the risk of holding chips that are highly susceptible to obsolescence given the short life cycles of high-tech products makes inventory holdings particularly expensive. Chip suppliers, therefore, seek volume commitments and risk sharing provisions with computer makers as a way to offset the actual and prospective expenses.

- **Product line imbalances** reflect situations in which independent demand is difficult to predict—not because of sheer volume, but because the variety of available SKUs is large, and the SKUs cannot be converted to other types. For example, a department store may feel confident that it will sell a certain volume of men's hiking boots in a given period, but it may be unsure which brands and sizes will be specifically demanded.

- **Parts line imbalances** are found when (dependent) supplies are unavailable in the proper assortment to feed the necessary supply for finished goods. The likely scenario is that of a bottleneck, or one item in short supply that holds up production of the finished good. Also, given that products are often sold today in assorted bundles, shortage of any one item can keep the assortment from coming together. Lean guru Taiichi Ohno famously quipped, "The more inventory a company has, the less likely they are to have what they need." Ohno was suggesting that companies often become complacent when they have large supply stocks, yet those supplies are no guarantee that they are holding the right inventory types (the parts that are actually needed to build end products to serve customers). This observation proves both poignant and true.

- **Channel imbalance** indicates that goods and services are available, but not at the proper location(s) to meet demand. Planning-based systems that allocate the supply of finished goods in advance of demand, like distribution requirements plans, are prone to error. They can misallocate inventory when history fails to serve as an accurate predictor of future demand locations. In these instances, the goods must be transshipped from the available supply to the desired location, often using expedited transportation to achieve this balance.

- **Supply chain imbalance** refers to the imposition of inputs to meet the needs of independent goods/services as a result of being at the wrong location when demanded. As with the other forms of imbalance involving dependent supplies, having inputs in the wrong location delays or prevents the assembly of demanded finished goods from occurring at the time of demand. Rush parts shipments are often the costly remedy for such imbalances.

- **Utility imbalance** implies the mismatch between the desired attributes and realized performance of the goods and service offered. This imbalance is critical, because it reflects the prospect of disappointing customers when their expectations go unfulfilled. Customer dissatisfaction with realized performance is difficult for companies to overcome today since customers—both industrial customers and consumers—tend to be less tolerant and more unforgiving of suppliers that fail to live up to expectations. Global competition that provides customers with more alternatives and rising expectations, as well as income levels of global customers, raise the ante for companies seeking to retain loyal customers.

- **Fit imbalance** speaks to the misalignment of supply qualities to meet the needs of the finished goods for which they are inputs. Consider the supply of tires for an automobile. The provision of high-performance sports car tires for an economy car used as a city commuting vehicle represents a mismatch. There is little need for a V-speed-rated tire engineered for speeds of up to 149 miles per hour to be used on a car that will rarely exceed 35 miles per hour. This would represent a waste. Yet more disconcerting would be the use of an S-speed-rated family sedan tire on a Porsche racecar. Clearly, both circumstances impart their own risks.

Based on the eight demand imbalance statuses shown in Figure 11.2, we can derive generic approaches toward mitigating the imbalances. The mitigation approaches are arranged around the axes of Figure 11.3 and are described in the following sections.

| | **Demand Type** | |
Demand Attribute	Dependent [Function Approach]	Independent [Utility Approach]
Volume [Quantity Adjustment Approach]	Component Imbalance Mitigation Strategy: Customer Differentiation	Finished Good Imbalance Mitigation Strategy: Market Differentiation
Variety Variety Adjustment Approach	Parts Line Imbalance Mitigation Strategy: Part Mix	Product Line Imbalance Mitigation Strategy: Product Mix
Location [Network Adjustment Approach]	Supply Chain Imbalance Mitigation Strategy: Supply Chain Selection	Channel Imbalance Mitigation Strategy: Channel Selection
Form [Substitution Approach]	Fit Imbalance Mitigation Strategy: Part Substitution	Utility Imbalance Mitigation Strategy: Product Substitution

Figure 11.3 Demand-imbalance mitigation strategies by demand status

Quantity Adjustment Approach (for Volume)

Market differentiation and *customer differentiation* strategies distinguish the most valuable customers from the crowd. These customers are deemed most worthy of the highest priority when limited supply forces allocation decisions to be made. The GSCF process of customer relationship management (CRM) provides several different dimensions by which customers can be segmented and relative importance assigned. The profitability of the customers (profits that each customer generates for the focal company) should be among the primary bases for segmentation. Additional key factors might include the customer's competitive position, his or her influence in the marketplace, and the account's growth potential. Taken together, the focal company must assess the upside opportunities and the downside risks associated with providing elevated service to choice customers, particularly when nonselect customers conclude that they are cheated in the process. Demand management must be employed to minimize the likelihood and severity of shortages by seeking a match in supply and demand.

Variety Adjustment Approach (for Variety)

Product mix and *part mix* strategies seek to reduce undue variety that leads to confusion and the opportunity for imbalances in product lines and parts lines. The proliferation of goods and parts is among the most common ailments facing supply chain managers. Companies generally are much more eager to introduce new products than to "sunset" old ones. To some extent, getting rid of obsolete items implies an inability to maintain relevance and sustainment for that item as customers shift demand to alternatives. In another regard, companies, in their eagerness to keep innovation cycles running at full speed, incite the obsolescence of their own goods and services as a means of driving evolution in customers. When products become obsolete, their subcomponents often become obsolete as well. Hence, the relationship between independent and dependent demand is present in the part-product relationship. Product and part mix strategies impart reduction in undue variety and complexity that confound both the buyer and seller and force the seller to be burdened with risky inventory. Rather, firms are encouraged to counter the tendency to proliferate in products and parts and instead employ design for manufacturability (DFM) practices, which underscore part standardization, modularity, design simplification, and a reduction in the number of components. These considerations should factor into the product development and commercialization process that spans the functions of R&D, marketing, sales, purchasing, production, and logistics, among others, in the focal company while including select customers and suppliers when their inputs are merited. Demand management also factors significantly in the struggle to minimize complexity and enhance flexibility in operations.

Network Adjustment Approach (for Location)

Channel selection and supply chain selection strategies seek to ensure that the fundamental provision of "the right product at the right place at the right time" is delivered. Missing the mark on serving customers given a lack of presence is difficult for companies to accept in an age when physical distance seems to have shrunk as a result of enhanced connectivity. Yet, most products must still navigate the dimensions of time and space successfully to fulfill time and place utilities. Two ubiquitous companies approach this problem in distinct ways. Starbucks uses a saturation strategy by flooding the market with locations. Can you fathom that the company has over 140 stores in the Houston, Texas, area alone? Why? The merchant known primarily for coffee can meet demand pretty economically by operating small stores in a variety of formats (stand-alone stores, strip mall storefronts, kiosks). Furthermore, the stores carry a fairly limited assortment of inventory that presents relatively low costs and few risks. Walmart, on the other hand, while aggressive in the intensity of its physical network, cannot achieve the same intensity as Starbucks. The footprint and investment in a Walmart Supercenter store preclude the company from locating in small lots or vacant storefronts. This retailer holds an estimated $23.5 billion of real estate on its books. These expansive stores average close to 200,000 square feet and require something in the range of a 40-acre lot to accommodate the store, parking space, and shipping/receiving.

Network adjustment calls for the company to match the network, location, and channel structure with the right-sized logistics footprint. What works for Starbucks will not work for every company. In fact, the rationing of locations is sometimes the solution. In other words, the company reduces store locations and keeps only the most profitable ones. It reduces floor space and infrastructure at existing stores that are not sufficiently profitable. Furthermore, the company looks to alternative channels such as the Web or futuristic ways of meeting demand without a physical presence. As noted in Chapter 9, "Implications for Transportation/Logistics: Congestion and Infrastructure Decay," online retailers like Amazon are starting to leverage the physical locations of non-competing retailers, like 7-Eleven stores. Lockers are installed in the stores to provide consumers with a secure pickup point where they can collect their merchandise. An element of convergence is occurring among virtual and physical storefronts, with many companies looking to bypass the conventional physical channels. The order fulfillment process is at the forefront of these determinations.

Substitution Approach (for Form)

Product substitution and *part substitution* address the "form" imbalances for items that experience independent and dependent demand, respectively. A utility imbalance for independent goods is particularly "touchy" for companies since it represents a performance mismatch in the eyes of customers. Fault is not necessarily found in the product development and commercialization process for such a mismatch. An inability to understand customer expectations or to effectively communicate instructions for product use can sometimes be at fault with this imbalance. Therefore, you must look to customer relationship management to help understand customer needs and direct them to products and services that best fulfill those needs. Furthermore, customer service management fulfills the obligation of properly informing customers of instructions for use and anticipating issues that the customers might face with the focal company's products or services.

Part substitution is more functional in nature and can present some added challenges under dependent demand. Parts demand often experiences "lumpy" demand patterns since production typically is performed in batches. The methods of filling demand are relatively fixed because the end-product attributes typically are fixed. Therefore, the availability of methods to respond to dependent demand sometimes is more limited, making changes in how dependently demanded parts are fulfilled less flexible compared to finished-goods demands. Though the part may not be as visible to the end customer, you must determine whether the substitute part performs the same function as its predecessor. Manufacturing flow management and supplier relationship management are likely to be significant factors in these determinations.

Each demand imbalance status has two generic mitigation approaches. These combine to form a specific demand-side imbalance mitigation strategy for each status. Next we will briefly describe each of these strategies and how they might be applicable to a future world that is being transformed by population growth, geopolitical change, economic leveling, and communication connectivity.

Customer Differentiation

For the dependent demand for parts, a firm supplying parts or components will strategically adjust the volumes it supplies to a set of relatively fixed end-product makers. The firm will make certain decisions about the different volumes that go to different customers (manufacturers) in its downstream supply chain. Essentially, for customers of choice, firms will be able to maintain or even increase component volumes. It is assumed that these will be the most strategic and profitable firms. Other firms that do not provide enough value or profit will have volumes reduced and will not receive priority allocation of inventory volumes and/or shipments of key products. A firm's supply chain relationships with downstream manufacturers will dictate who gets preferred volumes and service. Other companies may receive only a limited or rationed share of the parts volumes that can be made. In a transforming world, it will be difficult to supply all the parts and components demanded by all customers. Therefore, firms will have to make strategic choices about who to serve with large quantities of parts and who will have their volume cut so as not to exceed the available supply.

Market Differentiation

Similarly, using a utility and quantity adjustment approach for independent customer demands, a firm employing a market differentiation strategy will not serve every end customer the same. Companies must determine a subset of customers of choice that can be served efficiently and effectively to make a profit within the social, political, and economic (scarcity) limits placed on them. Trying to create utility for all end customers may simply not be a profitable endeavor, so firms will have to make hard choices about whom they can serve in a profitable manner. Then finished goods volumes should be adjusted downward for nonpriority customers. Over the same period of time, select customers will receive higher fill rates and be authorized higher levels of available inventory. Such a strategy is aimed at selectively using available supply sources and serving the most profitable demand centers and end customers. We believe the world of the future will not allow a company to be everything to everyone, or to dominate an entire global market. Additionally, metrics such as "market share" to measure a company's strength will be replaced with more productivity-oriented measures, such as profit per strategic market segment served or profit per volume supplied.

Part Mix

This strategy combines a variety adjustment approach with a functional approach needed for dependent demand. As part of the manufacturing flow management process, firms should aim to adjust the variety in their parts lines to match the most important demands within available supply constraints. Supply levels simply may not allow for continued parts proliferation in the future that eats up key natural resources that will continue to become more scarce. Firms might start by eliminating nonessential traits that cause increased variety, such as color and fashion, which may be the first to go. Additionally, in the future, it will be important for firms to create process technologies for parts manufacturing that can accomplish more with less and reduce the aggregate demand for supplies. Additionally, firms using the parts-mix strategy should aim to create a limited set of available parts to serve the functional requirements of key supply chain customers (manufacturers). This limited parts mix should meet only the most important demand attributes (but not all of them) for the most profitable segments while staying within near-term and long-term supply constraints. The use of standard parts that can be used in multiple end products will also continue to be an important concept for matching demand to supply.

Product Mix

Combining a utility approach with a variety adjustment strategy results in a product mix strategy. For independent end customer demand, firms will actually have more flexibility in how they choose to meet customer utility in comparison to parts-demand scenarios. Therefore, firms can aim to build the smartest mix of products to satisfy customers within given supply constraints. This can include flexibly manufacturing single products that meet a variety of end customer demand requirements, thereby getting the most out of available supply levels. Additionally, initiatives such as standardization and design for manufacturability can be used to reduce product variety. This puts less strain on available supply sources while still meeting the most important requirements of "customers of choice." Using a product mix strategy, a firm's product design and commercialization process will have to focus on shaping demand for different product varieties and optimizing the right product mix to maximize profit for a select set of customers. For example, following the economic downturn of 2008, companies such as Kroger, Walmart, Procter & Gamble, and Walgreens greatly reduced the assortments offered in their retail stores to cut supply chain costs.[21] In the future, we believe that continued downward adjustments to the variety of products that a company offers will be critical to staying within the growing constraints and limits of a transforming world. Implementing a product mix strategy that shapes demand to match supply will help firms build a more sustainable and long-term ability to meet end customer demand.

Supply Chain Selection

As demand-shaping activities based on just volume and variety reduction fail to achieve the right balance between supply and demand, firms may choose to use a locational approach to determine where and how to serve parts and component demand. For these dependent demand items, firms need to select which supply chains

---

[21] Brat, Ilan, Ellen Byron, and Ann Zimmerman. (26 June 2009). "Retailers cut back on variety, once the spice of marketing." *Wall Street Journal*.

and industries they will choose to take part in. Not all industries or geographic locations will provide the right levels of profit to justify serving the market, especially considering the limits on supply and resources that are expected in future decades. Firms will have to carefully select the supply chains they enter, keeping an eye on the focal firm in the supply chain that controls the actual end customer demand. This firm often has the most power in that supply chain. Firms that supply parts and components in the dependent demand arena may choose "supply chains of choice" and elect to leave other markets where they cannot make a profit. For example, in the computer industry in the late 1990s, Intel made a strategic decision to leave some military aircraft computer markets. This was primarily due to the low volumes and profits Intel could achieve in comparison to the booming commercial PC market. In the future, firms may have to make similar decisions about what supply chains to leave when low profits and volumes do not justify the use of limited supply resources.

Channel Selection

For serving end customer demand, firms may choose to use a channel-selection strategy that combines a location adjustment approach with the utility approach used for independent demand. In doing so, firms must make critical decisions about what target markets and end customers to serve and, more importantly, how to serve them. As seen in the Circuit City example, holding onto a large number of physical brick-and-mortar locations with large inventories may not be smart in a transforming world defined by information, computers, and quickly changing demand. Firms will have to find the optimal mix of physical locations, virtual and electronic sales channels, and outsourced licensees to sell their products and services. Similar to selecting customers of choice, firms will have to find "locations of choice" where they will aim to sell a limited supply of goods and services. They cannot attempt to serve every location in the same manner and will often have to make downward adjustments to the number and size of locations in their network. For example, during the economic crisis of 2008, firms such as outdoor retailer Cabela's Inc. had to delay store openings and downsize new stores that were already being built to account for the new economic realities.[22] Similarly, firms may have to look for flexible ways to adjust the size and location of their networks and the demand they aim to serve. Additionally, in the future, the sale of knowledge by firms may replace the manufacture of goods and services that are currently transported over long distances. Firms of the future may use the global communications networks to sell and transfer information about how to make a product to local, on-site production facilities. Here the product will be made on demand, with limited need for speculative finished goods inventory. Technologies such as three-dimensional (3-D) printing may redefine channels for serving demand and help shift the economy to more regionalized and local manufacturing. Such changes would help account for the expected transportation congestion and supply constraints of the future.

Part Substitution

When volume, variety, and locational changes do not accomplish the needed demand-shaping effects, parts suppliers may have to initiate parts substitutions to meet demand from manufacturers. Firms will have to find part substitutes that meet the same form, fit, and function needed in the end product being manufactured. This will be especially important because some current end products may become unsupportable in the future due to limited resources, unavailable parts, and the related increasing costs. Therefore, technologies that create cheaper part and component substitutes out of available resources will be necessary. Firms may be encouraged to shape parts demand by changing configurations and substituting parts that are more easily manufactured with given supply. In addition, firms may choose to adapt to local supply sources and find substitutions that will decrease costs and risks associated with increasing supply and transportation constraints. Additionally, supplier relationship management processes will need to encourage suppliers to find newer, more sustainable ways to support parts demand for customers of choice by finding substitutes that rely less on global transportation and therefore reduce the energy footprint.

---

[22] "Cabela's says new Billings, Montana store will now open in 2009." (4 February 2008). Montana Associated Technology Roundtables.

Product Substitution

In the most extreme and well known of these strategies, firms may aim to achieve full end product substitution. This strategy aims to provide utility to end customers in a different way. In a transforming world, this may include substituting products made locally that meet 95% of customer service requirements and do so within supply, transportation, and customer service limits. Such a DSI strategy includes the trade-offs discussed earlier between efficiency and effectiveness. For example, firms may implement product substitutions that are not as effective at meeting utility but that maintain supply-side efficiency and viability. Additionally, in the transforming world, this may mean using the returns management process to reclaim, reuse, and recycle more products. These efforts should be aimed more at balancing demand and supply and responding to natural resource scarcity, where current efforts have been more about short-term efficiency improvements and marketing a green supply chain.[23] In shaping demand, customers of choice may still receive virgin or preferred products. Others may have to take substitutions that include refurbished or used products that have been reclaimed from the reverse supply chain. In doing so, demand will be shaped to meet supply.

Finally, as alluded to in the preceding sections, there is a continuum among these strategies. A company may first choose to reduce volumes, then limit varieties, then change channels, and finally institute substitutions. The result may be an entirely different strategy for fulfilling either independent or dependent demand. For example, suppose an auto manufacturer originally made ten types of cars that were stocked at 100 units at ten locations. It might incrementally move to replace them with three types of helicopters that take only 20 units for each type and are sold at three locations. Such an example would include a simultaneous downshift in volume, variety, and location and is also a full product substitution. However, in the end the firm's decisions have allowed it to meet customer utility (demand for transportation). The firm does so by matching the customer with

---

[23] Bell, J.E., D.A. Mollenkopf, and H.J. Stolze. (2013). "Natural Resource Scarcity and the Closed-Loop Supply Chain." *International Journal of Physical Distribution & Logistics Management*. Forthcoming.

available supply and potentially using fewer resources. Such decisions are not only strategic in nature, but may prove to be critical in the transforming world. Unlike Circuit City, firms that can adapt and flexibly change on both the demand and supply side of the supply chain will have the best chance of profitably surviving in an uncertain future.

Applying the Demand-Imbalance Mitigation Strategies

The eight demand-side imbalance types present unique challenges for future supply chain managers to consider. Using the mitigation strategies we offer, firms of the future and their supply chain managers should have a leg up when assessing demand-driven imbalances. In conclusion, let's consider what might have happened had Circuit City availed itself of our strategies during its struggles with customer demand. In all fairness, the company got many aspects of supply management right. But its demand management function suffered because its supply chain planners and managers paid inadequate attention to rapidly changing customer behavioral trends. In its heyday, Circuit City had built a vast retail network of stores and distribution facilities that could have been considered state of the art by mid-1990s standards. Its products were popular and sold vigorously through over 700 physical outlets. By many accounts, customers were happy with its service and selection. And then—things changed. Some early macrotrend-related effects began to influence Circuit City's customers.

The most prominent of these was the advent of electronic commerce. In the early '90s consumer electronics industry competitors relied exclusively on brick-and-mortar locations as their ubiquitous channels of distribution. Some adopted electronic channels more quickly and with greater depth than others. Stores such as Best Buy, realizing the technological savvy of their customers, quickly adapted, but Circuit City didn't. The company made no *channel/location* adjustment, sticking with bricks-and-mortar stores to the bitter end. In so doing, it missed the boat on website sales. Its persistence with using the web as almost purely a marketing tool, rather than a demand-generation vehicle, caused its inventory to grow stale and its brand to suffer.

At the same time, the company was insensitive to the different physical product formats that customers were beginning to demand. It failed to notice market trends toward smaller and more portable products. In essence, the company made no *form* adjustment. The marketing group failed to eliminate older desktops and laptops and lagged or missed out on new technology trends such as handhelds and touch-screen technology. This was especially damaging in light of competitors such as Apple's innovative products. Relatedly and perhaps more importantly, the company failed to shape demand for the stagnating products it was holding in inventory.

Additionally, its inability to understand the demand it was receiving caused Circuit City to suffer from overbearing inventory costs, which stifled liquidity and led to a rigid rather than innovative market presence. With over 700 physical store locations and several regional and national distribution hubs, the Circuit City inventory pipeline was wide, deep, and filled with expensive assets. The company held massive amounts of inventory at both stores and distribution centers and didn't adjust *volume and variety* to meet demand in innovative ways. Rather than minimizing inventory and selling to availability, the company stacked expensive units high and deep to cover up long lead times and poor forecasting and absorbed massive inventory costs. It ended up with too much dead or dying stock when trends shifted.

Recognizing the problem, the company tried to go lean, but in its exuberance for cost efficiency it fired over 3,400 of its most experienced sales reps. This action made Circuit City even less effective at generating and meeting demand. The result, which we've already shared, was calamity. The company flailed, seeking new ways to sell old products, when what it needed to do was adapt and actively manage the demand and supply imbalances in its supply chain system. A strategy of lean and postponed inventory, shorter lead times, demand shaping to blow out dying stock, and aggressive customer sensing would have led to a radically different result, we believe.

As more time passes, the continuing changes to our business environment are expected to be dramatic. Firms need to consider both the supply-imbalance and demand-imbalance mitigation strategies

we offer in this book to build an adaptive enterprise that will be prepared and ready to proactively handle the changes ahead. Using a
DSI strategy to manage the supply chain is an option for many companies. Doing so will facilitate the development of the innovative and
adaptive enterprise that will thrive in a transforming world.

Index

FT Press
FINANCIAL TIMES

In an increasingly competitive world, it is quality
of thinking that gives an edge—an idea that opens new
doors, a technique that solves a problem, or an insight
that simply helps make sense of it all.

We work with leading authors in the various arenas
of business and finance to bring cutting-edge thinking
and best-learning practices to a global market.

It is our goal to create world-class print publications
and electronic products that give readers
knowledge and understanding that can then be
applied, whether studying or at work.

To find out more about our business
products, you can visit us at www.ftpress.com.